BROKEN EAGLES

Broken Eagles

Luftwaffe losses over Yorkshire 1939 - 1945

Bill Norman

Leo Cooper

Other books by the author

Wartime Teesside
Luftwaffe Over the North
Failed to Return
No. 640 (Halifax) Squadron

500 648322

First published in Great Britain in 2001 by Leo Cooper
an imprint of Pen & Sword Books Limited
47 Church Street, Barnsley, South Yorkshire S70 2AS

*For up-to date information on other titles produced under the Pen & Sword imprint,
please telephone or write to:*
Pen & Sword Books Limited
FREEPOST
47 Church Street
Barnsley
South Yorkshire
S70 2BR

Telephone (24 hours): 01226 734555

ISBN 0-85052-796-1

British Library Cataloguing in Publication Data

Printed by CPI UK

CONTENTS

Acknowledgements

A lot of people have given me unselfish help in the preparation of this book and I wish to acknowledge my debt to all of them. However, there are some who have been especially kind. My greatest thanks must go to my wife, Judy, who has patiently put up with almost enforced isolation while I have busied myself with this task and who has developed an uncanny knack of knowing when tea or coffee is required by users of word processors. My friend Heinz Möllenbrok, an ex-3./KG2 pilot, has given me the benefits of his friendship and provided invaluable help with introductions to former KG2 crews. My friend Willi Schludecker, who once flew Dornier 217s with KG2, was unstinting in his help with information about Luftwaffe operations over England and readily demonstrated his willingness to help by visiting me in England with his friend Richard Flohr-Swann to ensure that he was more readily at my disposal. Melvin Brown and Steven Hall have been enormously generous with the loan of photographs, as will be seen from the number of times they are credited throughout this book, and I thank them for that. Luftwaffe historian Ulf Balke, whose book *Der Luftkrieg in Europa* proved to be a comprehensive and interesting account of KG2 operations over northern England, kindly provided invaluable help with first-hand accounts from former Luftwaffe crews who operated over northern England. The three volumes of the monumental *Blitz, then and now,* edited by W. G. Ramsey, have also proved extremely helpful. Stuart McMillan, of Skelton, also deserves special mention for producing the line drawings.

The help given by the following in the preparation of this book is also gratefully acknowledged: Michael Allen DFC, ex-141 Squadron; Hans Altrogge, ex-1./KG66; Don Aris, 141 Squadron historian; Günter Bartnik, ex-8./KG2; Rudolf Behnisch, ex-StabII./KG26; Reg Bell, Marske-by-Sea; Squadron Leader George Bennions DFC RAF (Ret'd); Karl Beuting, Germany; Günther Bischoff, Germany; Kevin Brady, Peterlee; Squadron Leader Lewis Brandon DSO DFC RAF (Ret'd); Bridlington Public Library; The Editor, *Brighton Evening Argus*; Giles Browne, Cheltenham; Heinrich Buhr, ex-KG2; John Cavanagh, Seaham; Peter Clark, Wooperton; Dennis Crosby, Fylingthorpe; Rudolf Dawson, Hartlepool; David Evans, Norton-on-Tees; Tony Fairhurst, *East Riding Advertiser*; Ernst-Karl Fara, ex-2./KG66; Werner Feige, Germany; Ernie Hardy, for research at the Public Record Office; Mr & Mrs N. Hegemann, Germany; Mrs M. Henderson, Thornaby; Peter Hepplewhite, Tyne & Wear Archives; Hans Hilpert, ex-Stab./KG26; Hartmut Holzapfel, ex-6./KG2; David Kirkwood, Holderness; Tim Kitching, Normanton; Friedrich-Wilhelm Koch, ex-KG4; Gotthard

Liebich, St Albans; Kurt Matern, Germany; George Mather, Whitley Bay; Group Captain E.L. McMillan, CBE, AFC, RAF(Ret'd), ex-409 Squadron, RCAF; Reinhold Metzger, ex-Ku.Fl.Gr.2./106; Jeff Moore, ex-604 Squadron; Karl-Heinz Mühlen, ex-6./KG2; Walter Myers, Sedgefield; Michael Page, Middlesbrough, for help with language translations; The Editor, *The Northern Echo*; Simon Parry; Dr Alfred Price; Wilf Priestnall, Marske-by-Sea; Ron Rawling, Scorton; Alex Revell; Vera Robinson, Redcar; Group Captain. N. Ryder CBE DFC RAF(Ret'd); No.604 Squadron Association; Ernst-Adolf Schneider, *Gemeinschaft Deutscher Seenotrettungsdienst*; Wing Commander E.A. Shipman, AFC RAF (Ret'd), ex-41 Squadron; Steve Simpson, Shap; Trevor Smith, Kelloe; Norman Sudron, Faceby-in-Cleveland; George Thomas jnr, Whitby; David E. Thompson, Eaglescliffe; Ken Wakefield; Squadron Leader R.W.Wallens, DFC RAF(Ret'd), ex-41 Squadron; Derek Walton, Seahouses; Stephen Walton, Imperial War Museum; Ken Ward, Bilsdale; Ken Watkins, Dorking; Peter Watkinson, Filey; Bill Wedgewood, Robin Hood's Bay; Geoff White, Ravenscar; John Wilson, Slingsby; Frances Wood, *Bradford Telegraph & Argus*; The Editor, *The Whitby Gazette*; William Woods, Laskill; The Editor, *Yorkshire Evening Post;* Matt Young, Stockton-on-Tees; Rolf Zöphel, ex-KG2.

The many people who kindly loaned photographs are acknowledged in the following pages; ownership of copyright has been credited in all cases where it is known.

German Air Force terms
used in the text

Luftwaffe organisation

Staffel: The Luftwaffe Staffel consisted of nine aircraft and was roughly equivalent to an RAF squadron. Staffeln (the plural) were numbered from 1 to 9.

Gruppe: Three Staffeln made a Gruppe, the basic flying unit of the Luftwaffe. Gruppen (the plural) were numbered in Roman numerals from I to III. The full complement of a Gruppe, including the Stab flight (see below), was thirty aircraft.

Stab: Each Gruppe had a Stab (a headquarters flight) of three aircraft..

Geschwader: Three Gruppen made a Geschwader, which had its own Stab flight of four aircraft. Thus a Geschwader at full strength had ninety-four aircraft and was roughly equivalent to an RAF Wing. The role of a Geschwader was indicated by a prefix. The prefixes used in this book are given below.

(F)	*Aufklärungsgruppe* (long range reconnaissance)
JG	*Jagdgeschwader* (fighter wing)
KG	*Kampfgeschwader* (bomber wing)
KGr	*Kampfgruppe* (bomber group)
Ku.Fl.Gr.	*Küstenfliegergruppe* (maritime cooperation group)
LG	*Lehrgeschwader* (training wing)
NJG	*Nachtjagdgeschwader* (nightfighter wing)
ZG	*Zerstörergeschwader* (fighter-bomber wing)

Unit notation: In view of the foregoing, the notation II./KG2, for example, refers to the second *Gruppe of Kampfgeschwader 2*. The more specific 4.II/KG2 refers to the fourth Staffel of KG2. Because Staffeln 4-6 made up Gruppe II, the notation 4.II/KG2 was usually abbreviated to 4./KG2

Luftwaffe ranks[1]
(with RAF equivalents)

Flieger (Flgr.)	Aircraftsman 2nd Class (AC2)
Gefreiter (Gefr)	Aircraftsman 1st Class (AC1)
Obergefreiter (Obgfr.)	Leading Aircraftsman (LAC)
Unteroffizier (Uffz.)	Corporal

Feldwebel (Fw.)	Sergeant (Sgt)
Oberfeldwebel (Obfw.)	Flight Sergeant
Stabsfeldwebel (Stfw.)	Warrant Officer
Leutnant (Lt.)	Pilot Officer
Oberleutnant (Oblt.)	Flying Officer
Hauptmann (Hptm.)	Flight Lieutenant
Major (Maj.)	Squadron Leader
Oberstleutnant (Oberstlt.)	Wing Commander

Other Luftwaffe terms used in text

Luftflotte:	Air fleet
Oberbefehlshaber:	Supreme Commander/Commander in Chief
Gruppenkommanduer:	Group commander
Seenotflugkommando:	Air-sea rescue unit
Seenotrettungsdienst:	Air-sea rescue service
Staffelkapitän:	Staffel commander
Werk nummer (w/nr):	Manufacturer's aircraft serial number (e.g 2086). Different from an aircraft's Geschwader and Staffel code (e.g 7A+KH), which was prominently displayed on the fuselage

RAF terms used in text

A.I.:	Airborne interceptor radar (on-board radar)
Bogey:	Unidentified aircraft
Deflection:	Firing guns ahead of target so that aircraft flies into cone of bullets.
Freelancing:	Operating independently; not under ground control
G.C.I.	Ground Control Interception (airborne interception controlled by a ground station).
Serial number:	Number allocated to the aircraft by the manufacturer. (e.g. K8889). Different from an aircraft's, squadron code (e.g. HU-T), which was prominently displayed on the fuselage.
Vector:	Direct or guide an aircraft by transmitted directions.

[1] From Alfred Price: *The Luftwaffe Data Book*. Greenhill Books. 1997

Introduction

In November 1997, a group of building workers clearing land for redevelopment at South Bank, Cleveland, unearthed the remains of a Second World War Dornier Do217 bomber of the German Luftwaffe unit *Kampfgeschwader 2* (KG2). The aircraft had crashed there in January 1942, minutes after being hit by gunfire from a merchant ship anchored off Hartlepool and seconds after colliding with the cable of a barrage balloon flying high over the River Tees. The blazing bomber plummeted on to the railway sidings of a local steelworks, where it made a crater some twelve feet deep. At that time, the sidings were being used for essential war work and so, after the charred bodies of three of the four-man crew had been recovered, most of the wreckage was bulldozed into the crater and the track was re-laid. The body of the fourth member of the crew was not found.

Following the discovery in 1997, a full excavation of the site was undertaken by a team of Royal Engineers working with specialists from an RAF Bomb Disposal Squadron. They found no ordnance other than small arms ammunition – but they did recover the mortal remains of Oberfeldwebel Heinrich Richter, the missing member of the Dornier's crew. Following an extended coroner's inquest, Richter's mortal remains were buried alongside those of his comrades at the Acklam Road cemetery, Thornaby-on-Tees, on 14 October 1998

I had investigated this particular incident in 1990, while researching material for my book *Luftwaffe over the North* (1993), and I had come to the conclusion then that there was a very good chance that the body of the fourth man was still in the wreckage. Thus the 'rediscovery' of the Dornier with its tragic secret was not a surprise to me but the extent of public interest in the case did take me back a little. It most certainly made a deep impression upon an ex-Luftwaffe pilot friend of mine who had travelled from Germany to act as the KG2 Association representative at Richter's funeral.

The media interest, both locally and nationally, was comprehensive but it was the more personal manifestations of public interest which made the biggest impression: the funeral service in a church filled almost to capacity by local people, a number of whom had witnessed the crash in 1942; and the interment witnessed by some two hundred persons in a Thornaby graveyard. The striking thing for me was that all of those people participated spontaneously, without pressure. One can only speculate why they should have felt the need or the desire to attend the funeral of a former enemy; a complete stranger from a foreign land. No doubt the nature of the discovery, as well as the association of the wreckage with more dramatic times, had some effect - but one hopes that common humanity also played its part.

Among those present, no doubt, were the merely curious but there were also others who felt a closer affinity. It did not escape the notice of my German friend that there were many ex-Service personnel paying their respects on the day: men and women who had done what they perceived to be *their* duty some sixty years earlier, who had themselves 'looked over the edge' but who – unlike Richter – had lived to tell the tale. The poignancy of the moment was not lost on them. Afterwards, an acquaintance of mine who had flown Beaufighters with the RAF in North Africa described the occasion as having been 'spiritually uplifting', while a friend who had flown Halifax bombers over Germany claimed that the burial of Richter had been 'a most emotional experience'. Strange comments, perhaps, when one considers that they were used in the context of a person totally unknown to all of those who were present - unless, of course, the circumstances of Richter's death reminded them of days long gone and, perhaps, of friends once known.

The public's response to the whole Richter incident re-focused my attention on Luftwaffe casualties over northern England. In *Luftwaffe over the North* I had merely listed the losses in an appendix, with very little consideration as to cause and effect. However, as a consequence of a number of enquiries from people who had attended the burial of the German airman – questions relating to the circumstances of other Luftwaffe losses over the North of England during the last war – I decided to research all of the German aircraft believed to have been shot down over the three north-eastern counties (from the Humber to the Tweed) during that time. This volume is a result of that process. It does, however, deal only with Yorkshire: the findings in respect of the more northerly counties of Northumberland and Durham are covered in a separate volume.

At least seventy-two German aircraft crashed in Yorkshire or off its coastline during the 1939-1945 conflict and 282 German aircrew became casualties of war: twenty-five per cent of those were captured; the rest were either killed or listed as 'missing in action'. This book records the losses of both aircraft and personnel and also gives details of the circumstances under which such losses occurred. Like *Luftwaffe over the North*, this book is not a history: it does not attempt to tell the story of the air war over the north of England during 1939-1945. Its purpose is to record incidents of aerial conflict and to offer a work of reference to all who might be curious about past events. Hopefully, readers will then be sufficiently motivated to embark upon their own researches and discover for themselves how the Second World War touched their own geographical area.

During Richter's funeral service, Hans Mondorf, the German Consul-General, said that he had been quite moved and surprised by the sympathy that the case had attracted and he attributed that response to, what he described as, '...the sense of fair play that the British soul enshrines...'. When I began researching material for this book I found a number of examples to illustrate that Mondorf's 'sense of fair play' was not merely a post-war phenomenon cultivated by the passage of time. As the reader will see, humanity towards an enemy in need also seems to have had its place in wartime, when one might have reasonably expected feelings towards a foreign foe to have been running high.

The men who fought each other in the skies over England some sixty years ago faced death and destruction on an almost daily basis. They were all brave men, irrespective of their nationality. In the post-war years, the humanity to which Hans Mondorf referred and which manifested itself on occasions in more dangerous days has developed further and one-time adversaries have extended the hand of friendship towards each other, as the following pages will show.

Bill Norman
Guisborough, 2001

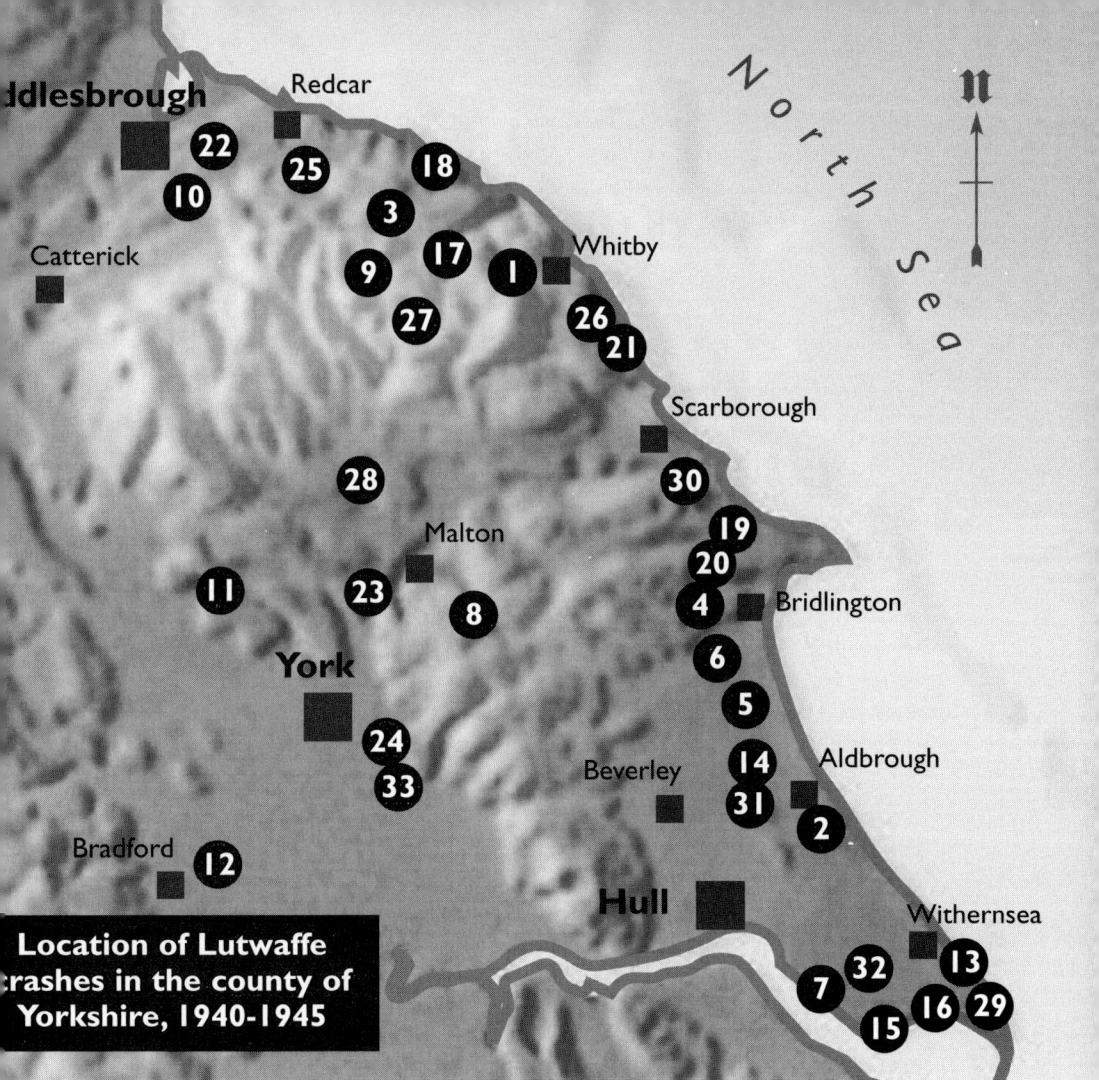

Location of Luftwaffe crashes in the county of Yorkshire, 1940-1945

KEY

1.	He 111	03.02.40	Whitby
2.	Ju 88	08.02.40	Aldbrough
3.	Ju 88	11.08.40	Scaling
4.	Ju 88	15.08.40	Nr Bridlington
5.	Ju 88	15.08.40	Barmston
6.	Ju 88	15.08.40	Fraisthorpe
7.	Ju 88	20.08.40	Ottringham
8.	Ju 88	27.10.40	Duggleby
9.	Ju 88	01.11.40	Glaisdale Head
10.	Ju 88	30.03.41	Barnaby Moor
11.	He 111	16.04.41	Huby
12.	Ju 88	05.05.41	Idle, Bradford
13.	He111	08.05.41	Withernsea
14.	He 111	09.05.41	Long Riston
15.	He 111	09.05.41	Sunk Island
16.	He 111	09.05.41	Patrington
17.	He111	03.06.41	Skelder Moor
18.	Ju 88	10.07.41	Staithes
19.	Ju 88	09.07.41	Speeton
20.	Ju 88	09.07.41	Speeton
21.	Ju 88	10.11.41	Ravenscar
22.	Do 217	15.01.42	South Bank
23.	Do 217	29.04.42	Coneysthorpe
24.	Ju 88	29.04.42	Crockey Hill
25.	Me 210	06.09.42	New Marske
26.	Me 210	06.09.42	Fylingthorpe
27.	Do 217	17.12.42	Wheeldale Moor
28.	Do 217	17.12.42	Hawnby
29.	Do 217	03.01.43	Skeffling
30.	Do 217	03.02.43	Muston
31.	Do 217	26.07.43	Long Riston
32.	Do 217	22.09.43	Newton
33.	Ju 88	04.03.45	Dunnington

1

DAYS OF CONFIDENCE
(1939-1940)

At the outbreak of the war between Germany and England in September 1939, the Luftwaffe was the strongest air force in Europe but it was armed only for wars of short duration and limited objectives. It had no special aircraft for long range strategic operations; its perceived function was to serve in a tactical role, principally as an adjunct to the German Army. The application of maximum force at the decisive point of a battle (the concept of *Blitzkrieg*) took precedence and thus the Luftwaffe's operational plans were based on the rapid destruction of enemy forces on the ground and the paralysing of the remnants of those forces long enough for the Germany Army to occupy the invaded country. For the German Air Force, this blitzkrieg tactic was made up of two phases. The first of these, in which surprise was of the essence, was an assault on the enemy's air force, aircraft-producing plants and ground installations. Success in this first phase then allowed the Luftwaffe to concentrate all of its available striking power in direct support of the German ground forces. The effectiveness of the strategy rested on the premise that campaigns would be short and sharp. That was the case with regard to invasions of Poland, Norway, the Low Countries and France – but the Battle of Britain changed the pattern and the war became prolonged.

On the eve of the Second World War there were four Air Fleets (*Luftflotten*) in Germany, each of which had responsibility for air operations in its own designated quarter of the country.[1] *Luftflotte 1* and *Luftflotte 4* – which had control over the northern and the southern quarters of eastern Germany respectively – were the strongest, having been reinforced for the impending invasion of Poland. The other two Air Fleets were responsible for the western half of Germany, *Luftflotte 3* in the south and *Luftflotte 2* in the north. The western edge of the operational area of *Luftflotte 3* bordered on Belgium and France and thus its operational functions westwards were restricted until those countries were invaded in May 1940 and the 'Phoney War' ended. *Luftflotte 2* bordered on Holland to the west but the German coastline (and its access to the North Sea) marked its northern boundary. Thus, during the first year of the war, operations against the east coast of Britain in general, and the north-east coast in particular, were usually carried out by aircraft of *Luftflotte 2*.

Although Britain declared war on Germany on 3 September 1939, the Luftwaffe initially abstained from attacking this country on a large scale. After Poland, the aircrews were rested and squadrons re-equipped in preparation for campaigns against Norway, France and the Low Countries in April/May of 1940. Perhaps the delay was partly political, with German leaders hoping that the speedy demise of earlier opponents of Nazi expansion would persuade an isolated Britain to agree terms without a fight, but there were military considerations too. The German High Command, who viewed their combat forces as being relatively small in number, believed that attacks on Britain would be better postponed until stronger forces were available. They also knew that a bomber offensive without fighter cover was doomed to failure for unless their, mainly short-range, fighter escorts could be located within operational distance of England, the attacking bombers would be highly vulnerable to assaults from British fighters. In addition, German fighters would need to be deployed near enough to England to allow sufficient operational time there to engage British fighters and destroy them. Until that was possible, relative quiet prevailed during the period which became known as the 'Phoney War'.

Unlike the continental nations that fell to German aggression, England had the advantage of being an island and was thus not readily susceptible to attack by land forces. The concomitant disadvantage was that it had to import the bulk of its strategic materials and foodstuffs by sea. Any intended invasion of England required the Luftwaffe to gain mastery of the air over the Channel in order to prevent any interference by the Royal Navy. Therefore, until the Luftwaffe was ready to test itself against the Royal Air Force, much of its time was spent on anti-shipping activities. For the first six months or so following the declaration of war on 3 September 1939, Luftwaffe activity in the north-east of England was restricted almost entirely to armed coastal reconnaissance, attacks on shipping and the mining of sea lanes and important river estuaries – which in the case of Yorkshire meant those of the Humber and the Tees. In spite of the comparative lull that characterized the opening months of the conflict, the air war came early to northern England. The sea lanes off the north-east coast offered favourable opportunities for anti-shipping activities and the Heinkel 111 bombers of *Kampfgeschwader 26* (KG26) and floatplanes of the *Küstenfliegergruppen* (naval co-operation units) were quick to seize the chance. However, such operations were carried out at a price and Yorkshire was credited with a number of 'firsts' in the opening months of hostilities. On 19 October 1939, the first German prisoners to be captured on English soil came ashore at Sandsend, having been shot down by Catterick-based Spitfires; on 3 February 1940, the first German aircraft to crash on English soil came down just north of

Whitby following an engagement with three Hurricanes from Acklington; on 3 April 1940, the first Spitfire (again Catterick-based) to be lost in the defence of this country shared a victory with a Heinkel 111 when each shot down the other off Redcar; and on the night of 19-20 June 1940, an air raid on ICI's chemical works at Billingham, Teesside, resulted in the first reported destruction of an enemy aircraft by a barrage balloon. On a less triumphal note, bombs dropped on steelworks at South Bank and Grangetown, Teesside, on 25 May 1940 produced the first civilian casualties to arise from a bombing raid over England during the 1939-45 period.

The coastal activities which characterized the months of the 'Phoney War' in the north continued for the rest of the year but, as will be seen in the following pages, bombing attacks against mainland targets did occur prior to the summer of 1940. It was then that Luftwaffe activity over this country quickened, following Germany's successful invasions of Denmark and Norway (9 April) and France and the Low Countries (10 May). By June, the Luftwaffe's operational bases in the west had moved much closer to Britain: *Luftflotte 2* had advanced its operational area into Holland, Belgium and a small part to northern France at the Channel coast; and *Luftflotte 3* had extended its area to include occupied France. In addition, a new Air Fleet, *Luftflotte 5*, had been established in Denmark and Norway. The month of June brought an increasing number of incursions over Yorkshire's coastal strip, particularly at night, with bombs occasionally being dropped over disparate parts of the North and East Ridings. Small-scale and widely scattered, such attacks were usually carried out by single aircraft apparently intent on testing defences rather than inflicting large-scale destruction – although the chemical works at ICI's plant at Billingham, on the north bank of the Tees, seems to have been singled out for particular attention on the night of 19-20 June 1940, when it was raided by an estimated twenty aircraft, believed to have been Heinkel 111s of *Kampfgeschwader 4* (KG4). Generally speaking, however, the damage from such early raids was inconsequential but such operations proved to be a highly disruptive nuisance to civilian and industrial populations alike.

Following the British Government's rejection of Hitler's offer of terms in mid-July 1940, the Luftwaffe was ordered to eliminate the RAF as a fighting force and to attack shipping and ports to prevent supplies reaching these shores. Although, as mentioned earlier, there had been anti-shipping activities as well as scattered attacks on mainland Britain prior to this date, from mid-July aggressive air activity was increased. Large-scale attacks aimed at shipping and RAF Fighter Command were launched in August 1940, when the Luftwaffe embarked upon a series of heavy daylight raids, mainly in the south of England. In the north, things remained relatively quiet, although the threats to coastal shipping continued and the sounding of air raid 'alerts' remained a regular feature of daily life when the enemy aircraft passing off shore threatened the possibility of turning towards land. In fact, there was no bombing of Yorkshire in any strength until 15 August 1940, when Junkers 88 bombers of the Aalborg-based unit *Kampfgeschwader 30* (KG30) launched a successful strike against Driffield aerodrome, although they lost several of their number to defending fighter aircraft. The story of the Battle of Britain in the summer of 1940 is well known and need not detain us here, except to say that northern-based fighter squadrons made their own contribution to the success of that campaign when they took on *Luftflotte 5's* combined forces of Heinkel 111s of KG26 and the Messerschmitt Bf 110s of *Zerstörergeschwader 76* (ZG76), over Northumberland and Durham, as well as the Junkers 88s of KG30, and inflicted heavy losses.

During August 1940, raiders ventured further inland, usually at night in order to evade day fighters. Bombs fell in all three Yorkshire Ridings, including coastal locations around Hull, Whitby and Middlesbrough, as well as around Harrogate, Leeds, Bradford and Huddersfield. However, as on previous occasions, such incursions were on a small scale and usually carried out by single raiders. In the months that followed, raids against land targets in the region remained small in scale and in impact until mid-December, when a total of 541 aircraft were sent to blitz Sheffield over two nights. During the second half of the year, RAF aerodromes appear to have been specifically targeted for bombing and strafing attacks, with those at Catfoss, Catterick, Dishforth, Driffield, Leeming, Lindholme, Linton-on-Ouse, Pocklington and Thornaby all receiving visits at one time or another.

While the Luftwaffe's anti-shipping sorties were carried out both by day and by night, those over the mainland usually took place at night – unless cloudy conditions in daytime offered a measure of protection – for daytime operations over Britain were not without danger. The Luftwaffe's lack of long-range fighter aircraft meant that northern targets were too far from continental bases to allow raiding bombers to be accompanied by effective fighter escorts. On the only occasion that such was tried, on 15 August 1940, the Luftwaffe's only long-range fighter, the twin-engined Messerschmitt Bf110, proved to be no match for the single-engined Spitfires and Hurricanes and such a tactic was never tried again.[2]

Britain's daytime fighter defences were highly effective, particularly when used in conjunction with radar plotting and Fighter Control. The former robbed the Luftwaffe of the elements of surprise which had served it so well in its continental campaigns; the latter enabled fighters to be directed to within sight of their targets without having to waste time and fuel on fruitless patrols. The effectiveness of Britain's air defences, and the losses inflicted by them, ultimately forced the German Air Force to abandon its large-scale daylight assault on RAF Fighter Command and its ground installations (principally in the south) in favour of large-scale attacks against industrial targets at night. Werner Baumbach points out that:

> '...*The daylight raids were abandoned due to losses. Existing aircraft, bombsights and armament were not up to the task... and night bombing of industrial centres, military installations, airfields, shipping and the mining of the English east coast was adopted as a method of weakening resistance and disrupting supplies.*' [3]

However, daytime operations in strength continued over the southern counties until October 1940 but by then the war of attrition against Fighter Command had failed to produce the expected result and the main thrust of attacks shifted to comparative safety of night raids, which allowed broader-based operations against industrial cities, supply networks and public morale with a view to bombing Britain into submission. The protection provided by the night, coupled with the general ineffectiveness of Britain's night time defences, allowed large-scale raids to be launched against urban targets further afield, both in the Midlands and along the western coast as far north as Liverpool.

Such was the poor state of Britain's defences against night raids at that time that night bombers came and went virtually as they pleased, although the lack of training in night bombing coupled with difficulties of navigation over sea and at night presented the Germans with potential difficulties. The Luftwaffe attempted to resolve those problems by using directional navigation beams (*Knickebein*) to guide night bombers to their destinations and enable them to bomb targets at night with some accuracy. Suitably equipped aircraft were able to follow a radio beam transmitted from a continental station and projected over the intended target. A second station in a different location transmitted a further beam and this intersected with the first over the designated objective to indicate the point where bombs were to be dropped. In the summer of 1940, when Britain realized that the Germans had this technology, it was viewed with some concern because Britain's lack of effective nightfighters gave little defence against night bombers which, it seemed, would always get through to their targets. The presence of *Knickebein* over England was first detected in June 1940 but by the following September British countermeasures had been developed to render detected beams unworkable. Such countermeasures included 'jamming' but it was soon realized that it was far better to mask the enemy transmissions. This was done by picking up the signals at British ground stations and re-broadcasting similar signals to create false intersections and to widen or distort beams to induce raiders to bomb in areas where they would inflict less damage. This masking of the beams was known as meaconing. A similar system was used to confuse Luftwaffe crews returning home after bombing raids and using direction-finding beacons located on the continent. Meacon stations in Britain intercepted the signals and re-radiated them, thus confusing crews seeking an accurate bearing for the homeward flight. There was a meacon station at Horse Close Farm, Marske, some six miles south of the river Tees, and it was one of seventeen such installations dotted around the country (see page 102).

By the late summer of 1940, the Germans were aware that *Knickebein* was being interfered with and towards the end of the year they introduced more sophisticated alternatives: *X-Gerät*, which used three secondary intersecting beams; and *Y-Gerät,* which used only the single navigational beam and which allowed the progress of the bomber to be monitored by its ground station at all times. *X-Gerät* was assigned only to the Heinkel 111s of *Kampfgruppe100* (KGr100), while *Y-Gerät* was taken by Heinkel 111s of III./KG26 – both of these units (with *II./Kampfgeschwader 55* (KG55), which relied purely on accurate navigation) comprising the Luftwaffe's emerging 'Pathfinder' force.[4] British countermeasures for both systems had been developed by early 1941 but revised versions of the beam systems were reintroduced by the Luftwaffe in 1942.

In the early years of the bomber war, Britain's nightfighter defences were in their experimental infancy and generally ineffective. A rudimentary nightfighter force of twin-engined Blenheim aircraft equipped with early airborne-interception radar devices was in the process of being established by 1940. However, until developmental problems could be solved and operational equipment refined, Spitfires and Hurricanes, the single-engined fighters which exacted such a heavy toll on raiders during the daylight hours, were pressed into service as nightfighters '...using the methods of daylight interception with searchlights substituting for the sun...'[5] to guide them to their quarry. The Spitfires and Hurricanes were subsequently joined by the Defiant but the use of ill-equipped day fighters for such a difficult and specialized task was a stopgap measure at best in which aircraft were often sent off into the night to seek raiders without knowing where to look, and with their crews often being more preoccupied with not getting lost.

The Chain Home radar stations dotted around the country gave long-range warning irrespective of the time on the clock and Fighter Control could guide fighters to within five miles of the attacking forces. In daylight that was usually near enough to allow fighters to see their targets, but at night the dark robbed them of their vision or, at least, severely impaired it, and interception was a game of chance. There were other difficulties too. Lewis Brandon has pointed out in his book *Night Flyer* that in the early days of the war few people had experience of night flying and that even fewer had experience of night fighting. In addition, air to ground communications were short-range and indistinct; cockpit instruments were poor for blind flying; not many airfields had runways and all landing grounds had poor lighting for take-off and landing; there were few aids to interception in the air and there was an absence of homing devices to bring fighters safely back to base.[6] Returning safely to base and landing in the dark was a major task and the accident rate was high. However, in spite of all these obstacles, the anti-aircraft guns, barrage balloons and single-engine day fighters miscast in a nightfighter role did enjoy occasional success but, generally speaking, the night bombers came and went virtually as they pleased. However, the weather and navigation difficulties meant that in the winter of 1940-41 large-scale destructive bombing attacks against England could only be effective against big inland targets – namely large cities, such as London and Birmingham – which could be found quite easily.

Notes

1. Alfred Price. *The Luftwaffe Data Book*. Greenhill Books (1997) fully explains the movements of *Luftflotten*, as well as offering much other useful information relating to Luftwaffe organisation and operational units, 1939-45.
2. See *Broken Eagles.2:Northumberland and Durham.* (to be published 2002).
3. Werner Baumbach: *Broken Swastika: the defeat of the Luftwaffe*. Dorset Press USA (1992) p81.
4. R.V. Jones: *Most Secret War.* Hamish Hamilton (1978) tells the fascinating story of the detection of the beams; Ken Wakefield: *Pfadfinder, Luftwaffe Pathfinder Operations over Britain 1940-1944*. Tempus (1999) fully explains the operations of III./KG26 and KGr.100.
5. Norman MacMillan: *The Royal Air Force in the World War, Vol.iv 1940-1945*, Harrap (1950) Chapt.1.
6. Lewis Brandon: *Night Flyer* William Kimber (1969) Chapt.1.

Losses
October 1939 - November 1940

1939

17 October 1939 (off Whitby)

Aircraft:	Heinkel 111H-1	F6+PK	w/nr ?	2.(F)/122
Crew:	Obfw. Eugen Lange	pilot	pow	
	Lt. Joachim Kretschmer	observer	+	
	Uffz. Bernhard Hochstuhl	wireless op	pow	
	Uffz. Hugo Sauer	mechanic	+	

Heinkel 111H-1 (coded F6+PK), of the reconnaissance unit 2.(F)/122, ditched in the North Sea some twenty-five miles east of Whitby at 17.00 hours on 17 October 1939 after being shot down by Flight Sergeant E.A. 'Ted' Shipman, Flying Officer Peter 'Cowboy' Blatchford and Sergeant Albert Harris in Spitfires of Green Section, 41 Squadron, Catterick.

The Heinkel had taken off from Münster and was on a photographic reconnaissance sortie in search of the battlecruiser HMS *Hood*, which was believed to be moored in the Firth of Forth. The flight on which they were intercepted was the second attempt they had made to reach the Firth of Forth that afternoon. On the first attempt they had got close to their destination and were at an altitude of 19,000 ft when they saw Spitfires emerging from the cloud layer 13,000 ft below. The Germans decided to leave and return later.

They were some eight miles off Whitby and flying northwards for the second time when they were spotted by Shipman but the Heinkel was pursued twelve miles further eastwards before the engagement took place. Kretschmer and Sauer were both killed early in the attack. Hochstuhl was wounded in the leg and barely escaped death when bullets scarred the top of his helmet. Lange enjoyed similar good fortune when the goggles he wore on his forehead were pierced by the bullet that grazed his earphones but he was unscathed. However, both engines were damaged in the attack and Lange was forced to ditch his aircraft in the sea. He and Hochstuhl took to their dinghy but they had no chance to transfer food and drink from the Heinkel before their plane sank. They were adrift for forty-three hours before they eventually made landfall in a rocky cove close to the Lythedale Sands at the base of the 150-feet cliffs just north of Sandsend, near Whitby, on 19 October 1939. By then, both were weak and Lange, in particular, was suffering from exposure.

Hochstuhl managed to climb a goat track to the LNER

Middlesbrough-Whitby railway line above the shore. He was captured near the entrance to Sandsend tunnel by LNER Special Constable George Thomas and taken to Sandsend railway station. When Thomas returned for Lange he was accompanied by Jack Barker, the Lythe duty police constable, and Frank Dring, a Sandsend painter. They found the pilot lying unconscious, perhaps dying, in his water-filled dinghy.

The route from the shore to the railway track was treacherous, and, given the steepness of the climb and the narrowness of the track that had to be negotiated, the group decided to deflate the dinghy and use it as a stretcher. With Barker at the front, Thomas at the back and Frank Dring underneath to prevent the dinghy from swaying so much that it would unbalance them and send them all crashing below, they pulled, clawed and occasionally crawled their way to the top. The prisoners were subsequently taken to the Whitby and District War Memorial Cottage Hospital, where they spent a couple of days recovering from their ordeal, before their removal to a POW camp.

Sauer's body was washed ashore near Whitby on 30 October 1939, and now lies in the German Military Cemetery at Cannock Chase. Lange and Hochstuhl – the first German fliers to be captured on English soil during the Second World War – were destined to spend the war years as POWs, mainly in Canada, and to live into old age. But at least they made it.

Of the three Spitfire pilots, two were destined not to survive the war. Albert Harris was killed the following day when the Whitley bomber in which he was a passenger crashed shortly after taking off from Catterick. The Whitley, K8996 of 102(Ceylon) Squadron, stalled at one hundred feet, crashed and caught fire; seven of the occupants were killed and two injured. 'Cowboy' Blatchford survived until May 1943, when, following an engagement with enemy fighter aircraft, he was forced to ditch in the North Sea, some forty miles from the English coast. Although searches of the area were made, he was never seen again.

Eugen Lange and Bernhard Hochstuhl did see most of their helpers

Bernhard Hochstuhl(left) and Eugen Lange(right) arrive in London [Authors' collection]

again - when they revisited Sandsend and Whitby in 1979, on the fortieth anniversary of their rescue. The only person not present at the reunion was George Thomas: he had died six months earlier. His son took his place[1].

21 October 1939 (east of Spurn Head)

Aircraft:	Heinkel 115B	S4+EH	w/nr ?	Ku.Fl.Gr.1/406[2]
Crew:	Oblt z. See Heinz Schlict		+	
	Lt. F. Meyer		+	
	Uffz. B. Wessels		+	

This aircraft was one of four Heinkel 115 floatplanes of Ku.Fl.Gr. 1./406 which were allegedly shot down off the East Yorkshire coast by Hurricanes of 46 Squadron, Digby (Lincs) on the afternoon of 21 October 1939. The Luftwaffe Loss Returns for this date record that four Heinkel 115 aircraft were lost off Flamborough Head[3] and that they were shot down over the sea or had to force-land there. However, the Loss Returns in the writer's possession give few details of the four aircraft and their crews and they show aircraft serial numbers which are largely indecipherable.

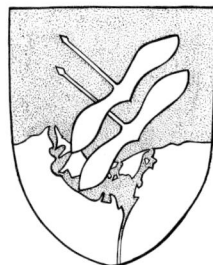

Küstenfliegerstaffel 1./406.

21 October 1939 was a misty and cloudy day, with visibility limited to approximately two miles. During the period 10.05 hours to 11.21 hours the ships of convoy FS24 were being shadowed by a Heinkel.115 as they sailed south off the Yorkshire coast. During the period of its surveillance, the Heinkel kept to the port quarter and remained some two to four miles astern of the convoy. Each time the enemy machine emerged from cloud it was engaged by guns of the convoy escort, but the aircraft was not deflected from its purpose. Shortly after noon, the southbound convoy FS24 met the northbound convoy FN24 and they began passing each other at a point between Flamborough Head and Spurn Head. Between 12.46 hours and 13.56 hours ten warship escorts and sixty to seventy merchant vessels were concentrated in an area twelve miles long and three miles broad. They presented an inviting target for any German aircraft willing to chance an attack and so it was hardly surprising when, at 14.40 hours, the minesweeper HMS *Halcyon*, steaming ten miles east of the convoy, reported that twelve enemy aircraft were approaching from the east.

In fact, the incoming raid had been detected by land-based radar long before that. 72 Squadron at Leconfield had already despatched six Spitfires of 'A' Flight at 14.15 hours to patrol Spurn Head; a further two Spitfires, from 'B' Flight, had taken off fifteen minutes later with instructions to patrol ten miles east of the Humber. 'A' Flight failed to locate the enemy and at 14.50 hours was ordered to land. Five minutes

later, 'B' Flight's Flying Officers D.F.B Sheen(in Spitfire K9959) and
T.A.F. Elsdon (K9940) reported fourteen Heinkel 115 floatplanes in
loose formation at 5,000 ft some fifteen miles southeast of Spurn Head.
Sheen and Elsdon dispersed the formation and engaged four of the
floatplanes before running out of ammunition. An entry in 72
Squadron's Operations' Record Book for 21 October credits Sheen and
Elsdon with two raiders 'destroyed'. However, both fighter pilots claimed
only 'possibles' because their victims were not seen to crash, although
Sheen and Elsdon were convinced that two of the Heinkels engaged were
so badly damaged that they would not have made it home. As the two
fighters turned towards land, two sections of Hurricanes appeared.

The two sections of Hurricanes of 'A' Flight, 46 Squadron, were
operating convoy patrols from their forward base at North Coates that
day. Red Section consisted of Squadron Leader P.R. Barwell (in
Hurricane L1802), Pilot Officer P.J. Frost (L1801) and Flight Sergeant
E. Shackley (L1817); Yellow Section consisted of Pilot Officer R.M.J.
Cowles (L1815), Pilot Officer R.P. Plummer (L1805), and Pilot Officer
P.W. Lefevre (L1892). At about 14.50 hours, 'A' Flight was in position
over Spurn Head at 10,000 ft. Five minutes later, Barwell was warned
that '...12 enemy floatplanes (were) approaching convoy from South East
at 1,000 feet'. At that time a convoy was some five miles east of Spurn
Head and in sight of 'A' Flight.

Barwell, anticipating a possible anti-shipping strike from the seaward
side of the convoy, led his fighters out beyond the ships, decreasing height
to 2,000 feet as he did so, and then ordered his Hurricanes to open out
into search formation. One of his pilots subsequently warned of a
suspicious aircraft on the port beam. Shortly after that, at 15.02 hours
and some twenty-five miles east of Spurn Head, Barwell saw a formation
of nine Heinkel 115 twin-engine floatplanes approaching from the
direction east-south-east. He estimated their height to be 4,000 feet and
their distance to be four miles. Just after being seen, the enemy formation
was fired upon by ships in the area. That defensive fire might well have
coincided with the Germans' sighting of 'A' Flight because the enemy
formation turned to starboard and proceeded to fly away from the
Hurricanes, which were now in pursuit and climbing towards them. With
a maximum speed of only 220mph, the enemy floatplanes were 100mph
slower than the fighters and thus had no hope of escaping. The
Hurricanes experienced no difficulty at all in overhauling the raiders and,
before closing for battle, had enough time to position themselves slightly
above their quarry with the sun almost dead behind them to mask their
approach.

The main engagement took place between 15.06 hours and 15.09
hours, thirty to thirty-five miles east of Withernsea. At the moment of

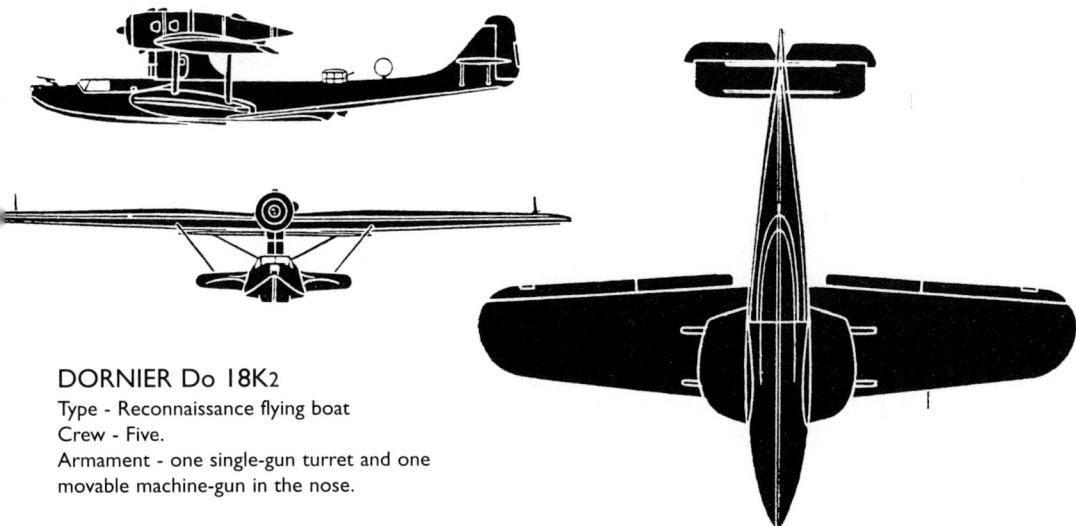

DORNIER Do 18K2
Type - Reconnaissance flying boat
Crew - Five.
Armament - one single-gun turret and one
movable machine-gun in the nose.

interception, the enemy formation was ragged and unevenly spaced and the Hurricanes approached it in line astern. As they got near, Barwell gave instructions for a No.5 Attack before choosing the left-hand aircraft of the formation and telling other pilots to pick their targets in order and from the left.

Barwell opened fire on his target at 400 yards. Although he later admitted that his rate of approach was rather high, he did not throttle back on his speed because another German aircraft – which was quite far behind the rest and almost abreast of Barwell as he attacked – was a potential danger. Thus he maintained speed and broke away under the tail of his target at thirty yards, leaving flames issuing from the Heinkel's starboard engine as he did so. When he turned his aircraft round and back towards his victim he saw the Heinkel diving towards the sea. Seemingly, the pilot tried to land on the water but his luck ran out shortly after touchdown, when the Heinkel's starboard wing folded back and the aircraft toppled over.

The Hurricanes then shot down three other Heinkel 115s in quick succession. Red 2, Pilot Officer Frost, attacked the aircraft that had been abreast of Barwell and there is the possibility that Red 3, Flight Sergeant Shackley, engaged the same aircraft after it had changed position in formation following Frost's attack. Whoever was responsible for the Heinkel's ultimate demise might be open to conjecture, but Frost saw flames flickering from the port engine before the plane crashed into the sea. The enemy formation broke up after the first assault and just after seeing his own target smack into the water, Barwell noticed one enemy aircraft diving away in a southerly direction. He followed and fired the remainder of his ammunition at it from a range of 300 yards. However, his attack was apparently without effect for the luckless Heinkel had to be engaged by three other Hurricanes – Cowles, Shackley, and Plummer – before it struck the water and turned upside down. Meanwhile, Pilot Officer Frost and Pilot Officer Lefevre followed and waded into a fourth enemy aircraft which tried to evade by flying in and out of cloud. After a long chase and repeated attacks, the Heinkel ran out of cloud. Following a final foray by the two Hurricanes, the enemy plane landed on water, apparently intact but with both engines stopped.

46 Squadron subsequently submitted claims for four enemy aircraft shot down. During the engagement, very little return fire was experienced by the Hurricane crews, although when the fighters landed back at Digby at 15.35 hours it was found the one aircraft had been hit four times. Two bullets had glanced off the leading edge of the port main plane, another had slightly damaged the engine cowling and a fourth had dented the fairing on the fuselage.

Complete crews were rescued from two of the German aircraft, though precisely from which ones is not known to the writer. They were subsequently landed and interrogated by Air Ministry Intelligence (A.I1(k)). As a result of the interrogation, it was believed that 72 Squadron had shot down one of the aircraft at 14.50 hours and that 46 Squadron had shot down the other at 15.10 hours. The writer does not know which fighter pilot was responsible for the demise of S4+EH. *The Blitz, then and now* (1987) claims that this aircraft crashed into the sea some five miles off Spurn Head, that is, in the area of the convoy, while the Luftwaffe Loss Returns give the area of all losses as being twelve miles from Flamborough Head. Squadron records available to the writer give no details of the crash site but the interception of the raiders by 46 Squadron twenty-thirty miles to the east of the Humber suggests that S4+EH fell to the guns of Sheen or Elsdon. The Air Ministry subsequently claimed that of the twelve Heinkels which had started out from Germany, not more than five got back to base. If that is so, perhaps Sheen and Elsdon were more successful than they had originally thought.

10 November 1939 (north-east of Scarborough)

Aircraft:	Dornier 18D		K6+DL	w/nr 804	Ku.Fl.Gr.3/406
Crew:	Oblt zur See Willhelm Lutjens	observer	missing		
	3 crew (unknown)				

While on patrol off the north-east coast on the morning of 10 November 1939, two Hudsons of 220 Squadron, Thornaby-on-Tees, were ordered to destroy a patrol of enemy aircraft operating seventy-five miles east of Spurn Head. At 11.25 hours Hudson H/220, piloted by Flight Lieutenant Sheahan, sighted a Dornier 18 (coded

Küstenfliegerstaffel 3./406

26

K6+DL) of Ku.Fl.Gr.3/406 and launched several attacks aided by Hudson A/220, piloted by Sergeant Scotney.

The first burst of gunfire from H/220 silenced the Dornier's rear gunner, while in the second assault bullets fired by A/220 during a diving head-on attack are believed to have struck the enemy machine's starboard wing. H/220s second effort scored hits on the Dornier's engines and fuselage while return fire from the German machine smacked into the starboard side of the Hudson and severed connections to the petrol gauge.

During subsequent forays, a sustained burst of gunfire from Sheahan's machine was held to within thirty yards of the enemy aircraft while the Dornier made a very steep turn to starboard. Some 250 rounds, fired at point-blank range, raked the seaplane from nose to tail. A/220 followed with an attack from 1,000 ft above and abeam of the enemy aircraft and directly from out of the sun. The Hudson fired some 300 rounds in this assault, the

HUDSON
(2 Wright Cyclone)
Reconnaissance Bomber
Span 65' 6" - Length 42' 2" - Height 11' 10½"

tracer strikes all around the cockpit and engine of the enemy machine bearing witness to the fact that bullets had found their mark. Seconds later, Scotney pressed home an attack from the enemy's rear starboard quarter and scored hits on the Dornier's engine and cockpit. As A/220 broke away in a climbing turn to port, H/220 carried out a diving manoeuvre amidships on the enemy's port side. The fusillade launched by Sheahan's Hudson appeared to strike the Dornier's stern as the enemy seaplane veered off to starboard. Sheahan then followed this assault with a diving starboard turn before lining up his guns and firing the last of his ammunition into the engines of the enemy from starboard amidships. The Hudson then passed directly over the enemy aircraft, bullets from

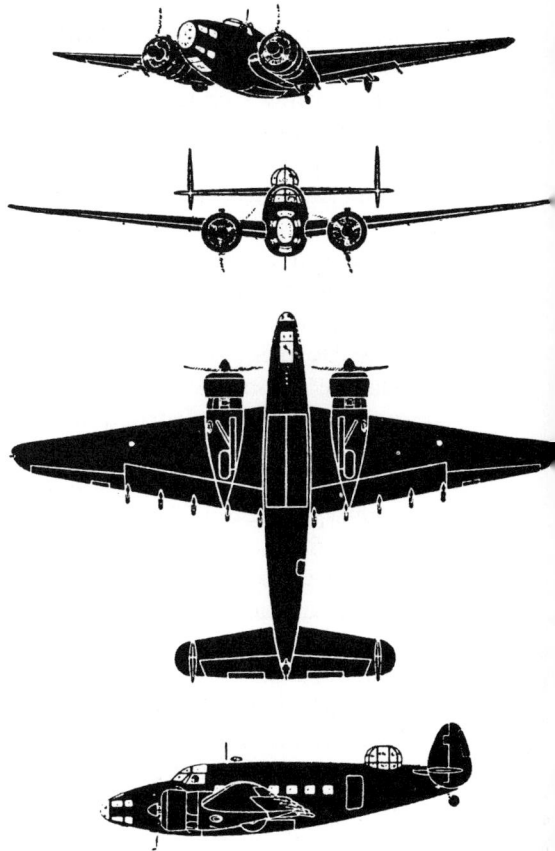

the Dornier's front gun striking the rear part of H/220s fuselage as Sheahan swept low over his victim at not more than fifty feet. By then, the Dornier's engines were beginning to throw out blue smoke, which steadily increased in volume. The enemy machine was east-north-east of Scarborough when it landed heavily on the sea.[4] H/220, short of fuel and with its petrol gauge connections severed by the first bullets, then returned to Thornaby, leaving A/220 to shadow their victim. A/220 remained on station, circling the downed seaplane from 11.50 hours until 1350 hours. An hour after its forced-landing, the Dornier was seen to heel over and capsize, just after three of its crew climbed into a dinghy. The Dornier's observer, Oberleutnant zur See Wilhelm Lütjens, did not survive the incident. The rest of the crew were rescued by Dutch vessels and presumably returned home.

At about 13.50 hours, A/220 (with Sergeant Culver at the controls and Sergeant Scotney in the Second Pilot's seat) sighted another Dornier 18, astern and about 300 feet below. A/220 attacked immediately, a burst of about fifty to seventy-five rounds from the Hudson's front gun seeming to score amidships, and Culver's rear gunner also managed sharp bursts which appeared to land on the enemy's engines and fuselage. While the seaplane flew figure-of-eight turns as an evasive manoeuvre, Culver then delivered an attack on the Dornier's starboard quarter, the Hudson's front and rear gunners both squeezing off short bursts of fire. In the third and final assault, delivered from out of the sun, Culver managed a long burst from the front gun. The result of this attack was a little doubtful but as A/220 pulled into a steep climbing turn with a view to another attack, the rear gunner of A/220 got in a good burst to port at the engines and bow of the enemy machine. Thus Culver kept station 300-400 ft above and to port of the enemy aircraft. He continued to maintain this position until both aircraft entered cloud and the enemy was lost. Although the enemy aircraft returned fire throughout the engagement, the Hudson crew felt that the level of response was very much inferior to that from the first Dornier.

17 December 1939 (off Whitby)
Flying Officer Terry Webster and Pilot Officer Tony Lovell, 41 Squadron, Catterick, had their first taste of action when they were scrambled in mid-afternoon to intercept a Heinkel 115 which was attacking a coastal convoy off Whitby. Webster managed to hit the Heinkel with some of the 500 rounds fired before it escaped to the safety of cloud and was not seen again.

EYEWITNESS
Night Patrol (1)

Some of the difficulties, and dangers, faced by day fighter pilots whose aircraft were assigned to nightfighter duties before the introduction of appropriate equipment are clearly illustrated by the following: (see also p.38)

'*During the bitter winter of 1939-1940, our Spitfire Squadron (No.41) was on day and night readiness at Catterick. There were many day scrambles and occasional night ones. Detailed for a night patrol one night over the Middlesbrough-Hartlepool area, I climbed to 15,000 feet through broken cloud in moonless visibility and settled on patrol without too much difficulty, occasional pin-points of light on the ground betraying the strict blackout. Radio silence was imperative, the wind forecast at patrol height was westerly, and I settled down to maintain position, with instrument panel lights giving only the faintest glimmer and the Merlin engine, as usual, humming gently to itself in throttled-back economical cruise condition. A peaceful scene, with no radio messages to tell me that German aircraft were on reconnaissance in the area. I was in no hurry to get home: the bar had closed long ago. A cigarette would have been a pleasure but it must be postponed.*

'*Within half an hour, the cloud below had increased to 10/10ths and I was having some difficulty maintaining position, using my watch to calculate the patrol legs and turns. Coming to the end of an hour's patrol, I broke radio silence and called base for a 'homing' to get back to Catterick. Silence. I tried again – and again. To my relief, Control came up on the line, weakly, to tell me that my transmission was faint but that I was to steer 090 degrees. I could not believe my ears: 090 degrees would take me out into the North Sea, not home. They must have given me a reciprocal: I needed a 270 course, not 090 to get back. A check, and again I was told to steer 090. Very reluctantly, I steered 090 and, after a few minutes, Control came up much stronger and I was able to let down and get back to the airfield.*

'*Little did I know that during my patrol the top wind direction had changed completely – through 180 degrees. Above cloud, I had turned – as I thought – at the end of each leg into the wind in order to keep station. Actually, I had, unknowingly, turned down wind and had consequently drifted from, or had been blown right off, my patrol line and back over the Pennines. I was crestfallen that I had very nearly made a mess of the incident, but I consoled myself with the thought that the elements make no concessions to the frailty of man. I had been lucky, as others in similar circumstances had not... .*'

Squadron Leader R.W. 'Wally' Wallens DFC RAF (Ret'd) Spitfire pilot, 41 Squadron, 1939-40

1940

3 February 1940 (Whitby)

Aircraft:	Heinkel 111H-3	1H+FM	w/nr. 2323	4./KG26
Crew:	Fw Hermann Wilms	pilot	pow	
	Uffz Rudolf Leushake	observer	+	
	Uffz Karl Missy	wireless op	pow	
	Uffz Johann Meyer	mechanic	+	

In the early morning of 3 February 1940, Heinkel 111s of KG26 attacked shipping off the Farne Islands and along more southerly stretches of the north-east coast. The Admiralty War Diary for the day claims that as many as twenty-three enemy aircraft might have taken part in these operations. Details of the results of the raids off the Northumberland coast will appear in volume 2 of this book but shipping was also attacked off the Yorkshire coast. Among those vessels affected in the latter area were the Swedish steamer *Mertainer*, bombed and gunned off Flamborough; the London-based steamer *Harley*, also attacked off Flamborough; the Whitby vessel *Kildale*, which lost six of her crew when she was bombed, gunned and set on fire off the Humber; the trawler *Nairana*, damaged while fishing in Bridlington Bay; and the collier

veſtigium leonis

KG 26 (Löwen)

Hermann Wilms and his crew, whose He111 crashed near Whitby on 3 February 1940. L-R: unknown; Hermann Wilms (pilot); Karl Missy (wireless operator); Johann Meyer (mechanic); Rudolf Leushake (observer) [via C & N. Hegemann]

Yewdale and Grimsby trawler *Rose of England*, both of which were attacked and damaged by two Heinkels within sight of Scarborough.

However, the damage inflicted was not all one-sided. Berlin Radio subsequently acknowledged the loss of three Heinkel 111s. Two of those were shot down off the Northumberland coast; the third, Heinkel 111 (coded 1H+FM) crash-landed just north of Whitby. The Admiralty was of the opinion that two other enemy aircaft might also have been lost, one off the Farne Islands and one whose radio distress signals were intercepted from far out in the North Sea. However, examination of the Luftwaffe Loss Returns for the day reveal the Royal Navy to have been too optimistic: no other loss is registered but the Returns do show that a fourth Heinkel suffered forty per cent damage and was forced to crash-land on its return to base.

Heinkel 111 1H+FM was intercepted five miles east of Whitby at 09.40hours by Flight Lieutenant Peter Townsend, Sergeant Jim Hallowes and Flying Officer 'Tiger' Folkes in Hurricanes of 43 Squadron, Acklington - the only fighter station in the three north-eastern counties not snow-bound that day.

While Hallowes positioned himself to head off any escape attempt, Townsend launched the first assault. When he broke away, the Heinkel's starboard engine was trailing black smoke and Rudolf Leushake was lying dead in the nose of the enemy machine. Folkes launched the second attack from dead astern, his bullets raking the fuselage of the enemy machine and mortally wounding the ventral gunner, Johann Meyer, in the stomach. The defence of the raider then rested solely on the

Uffz Rudolf Leushake. [Via C&N. Hegemann].

Heinkel 111 (1H+FM) of 4./KG26 that crashed near Bannial Flatt Farm, 3 February, 1940. [Author's collection].

shoulders of dorsal gunner Karl Missy, who did not stop firing, even when his attackers' bullets almost severed his right leg. After an abortive attempt to escape in cloud and with one engine stopped and the other damaged, the bomber crash-landed at Bannial Flatt Farm, at the Sleights cross roads some four miles north of Whitby. It was the first German aircraft to crash on English soil during the Second World War.

Catterick, 6 February 1940. The burial of Johann Meyer and Rudolf Leushake. [via Mrs V. Robinson]

Flying Officer John Simpson, of 43 Squadron, noted that when Townsend landed back at Acklington he (Townsend) was obviously very excited but still had thoughts for his foes. He just said: 'The poor devils, I don't think they were all killed'[5]. The next day, Townsend, who was to become romantically involved with Princess Margaret in the post-war years, visited Missy in Whitby hospital and gave him gifts of oranges and cigarettes. In 1969, he and Karl Missy met in less hostile circumstances and remained friends until Missy's death in 1981.

The original intention was to bury Rudolf Leushake and Johann Meyer in Whitby, but such was the intensity of local feeling against 'German fliers who attacked defenceless fishing vessels' that it was necessary to seek an alternative. Thus they were removed to Catterick, where they were buried with full military honours on 6 February 1940. On each coffin there was a wreath and a card: 'From 43 Squadron, with sympathy.' The bodies have since been exhumed and now lie in the German Military Cemetery at Cannock Chase, Staffordshire.

In June 1945, North Riding County Council erected a plaque to commemorate the incident. It can be seen on a stone pillar at Sleights Lane End, four miles north of Whitby, at the junction of the A171 and A169.[6]

3 April 1940 (off Redcar)

Aircraft:	Heinkel 111H-3	1H+AC	w/nr. ?	Stab II/KG26
Crew:	Lt Rudolf Behnisch	pilot	pow	
	Lt Georg Kempe	observer	pow	
	Uffz Albert Weber	wireless op	pow	
	Uffz Alfred Bächle	mechanic	pow	
	Obstlt Hans Hefele		pow	

This aircraft was based at Lübeck-Blankansee and was on an armed reconnaissance sortie against British shipping when it was shot down fifteen miles off Redcar by Flight Lieutenant Norman Ryder in a Spitfire of 41 Squadron, Catterick.

Flying conditions over the North Sea were poor that day, the cloud base was down to 600 feet and visibility, reduced by a combination of mist and rain, was down to three or four miles. At Catterick there were those who openly speculated on the wisdom of mounting a coastal patrol at all that morning but the matter was taken out of their hands when it was reported that a German bomber was attacking shipping four miles north of Whitby. Flight Lieutenant Norman Ryder was 'scrambled' at 12.21 hours. He launched his attack seventeen minutes later.

Shortly before his brush with Ryder, Behnisch had raided a small convoy and his port engine had been damaged by naval gunfire but he was unable to feather the propeller. Thus he was flying at near stalling speed and he could not climb into the protective clouds. Additionally, a shell hole in the port wing was so wide and caused such high wind resistance that he could not steer a straight course.

When Ryder made his interception, north-east of Whitby and four miles off the coast, it was immediately apparent to him that the raider was already in trouble for it was flying at reduced speed and at 400 feet, just below the cloud base. Ryder had to throttle back and circle in order to slow down before attacking from astern. The raider's vulnerability was emphasised as Ryder began his own slowing manoeuvres for the Heinkel slanted, as if to climb, but it could make little headway. There was no other form of evasive action after that.

As he prepared for his one and only attack, Ryder heard two bangs below his engine as enemy bullets struck their mark, but he chose to ignore them. Moments later his own six-second reply stopped the Heinkel's starboard engine and Behnisch was forced to ditch in the sea. He chose to land close by the Scarborough fishing boat *Silver Line*, the Lewis gunner of which also fired a burst at the bomber before it struck the water. Seemingly the gunner, Tom Watkinson, registered

January 1940. Lt. Rudolf Behnisch of Stab II/KG26, whose Heinkel 111 (1H+AC) was shot down off Redcar by F/Lt Norman Ryder, 41 Squadron, Catterick, 3 April 1940. [Rudolf Behnisch]

a number of hits and wounded the Heinkel's observer, Georg Kempe, in the head. Minutes later, engine damage forced Ryder to opt for ditching alongside the Hartlepool trawler *Alaskan*. However, when he was fifty feet above the waves, and with *Alaskan* still half a mile away, Ryder's engine gave up just as he slid back the hood. The Spitfire fell sharply into the heavy swell and ploughed into a seven-foot wall of water.

The sudden deceleration catapulted Ryder forward and he was knocked unconscious. He regained his senses when his aircraft started to sink beneath the waves. It was only with the greatest difficulty that Ryder managed to evacuate his aircraft as it settled towards the seabed. When

Trawler Lewis gunner battles it out with a He111. [*The War* March 1940]

January 1940. Rudolf Behnisch (centre) with members of another crew alongside his He111 (1H+AC). Uffz Albert Bächle is second from the right. [Rudolf Behnisch]

Spitfire pilots of No. 41 Squadron, c. December 1940. Norman Ryder is second from the right. [G/Capt N. Ryder]

Some time after Norman Ryder's rescue by the Hartlepool trawler *Alaskan*, the pilots of No. 41 Squadron presented the boat's skipper, Bill Caske, with an engraved tankard (above). This momento of the rescue is now held by Bill Caske's daughter, Mrs Mavis Wright, of Hartlepool. [Author]

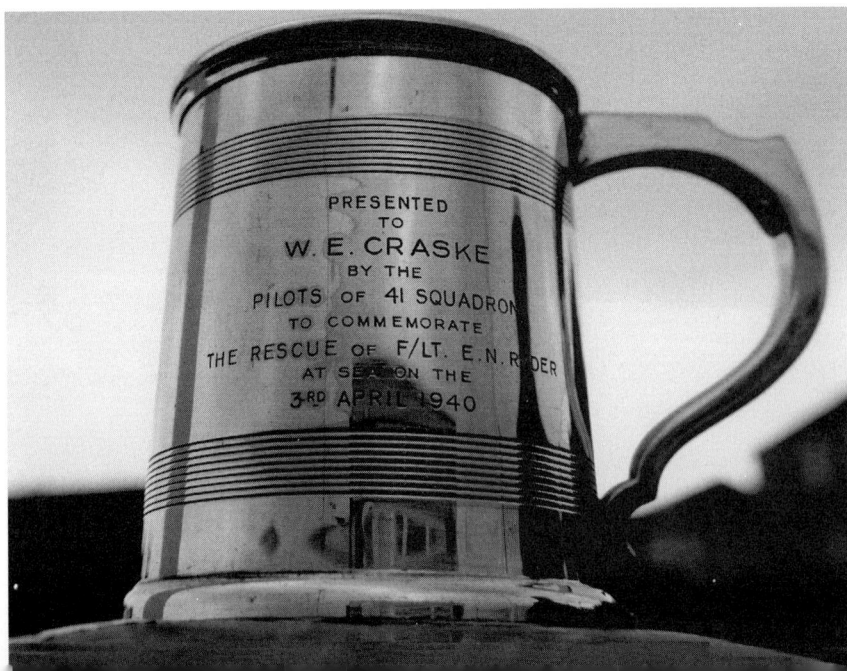

PRESENTED
TO
W. E. CRASKE
BY THE
PILOTS OF 41 SQUADRON
TO COMMEMORATE
THE RESCUE OF F/LT. E. N. RYDER
AT SEA ON THE
3RD APRIL 1940

he reached the surface, he was able to remain afloat only with the aid of his parachute pack – a point he discovered when he initially discarded it and started to sink!

Both crews were rescued by fishing boats, Ryder being landed at Hartlepool by *Alaskan* and Behnisch and his comrades at Scarborough by *Silver Line*. Hans Hefele, *Gruppenkommadeur* of II/KG26, had wanted to see for himself how such armed reconnaissance patrols operated and had gone along as an additional gunner. Ryder's aircraft (N3114) was the first Spitfire to fall to the guns of the Luftwaffe and the first British fighter to be shot down while protecting the shores of England during the Second World War.

On 6 April, 1940, the men of *Silver Line* were received at Scarborough Town Hall by the Mayor, when their part in the bringing down of the Heinkel and rescuing its crew were officially recognized with the presentation of a silver statuette of a lifeboatman to each of them. (The crew of *Silver Line* always believed that they had put paid to the raider and they quoted one of the Germans as confirming this. However, they refused to contest the RAFs claim to the victory). After leaving the Mayor's office they kept a promise made to a foreign foe three days earlier: they visited the injured Kempe in hospital and presented him with gifts of oranges and cigarettes[7].

19-20 June 1940 (Teesmouth)

An unknown German aircraft struck the balloon cable on No.2 site (in the south-west corner of the Ironmasters' District, Middlesbrough.) of 938 Barrage Balloon Squadron at 00.21 hours, 20 June 1940, during an air raid which had ICI Billingham as its target, although some bombs also fell on the Ironmasters' District. Contemporary reports state that the aircraft flew on for four minutes before No.33 balloon site (at North Tees Works gate, Seal Sands) reported it crashing into the sea off the mouth of the Tees. The Air Ministry later confirmed the aircraft as having been destroyed. On 23 June 1940, the Squadron received congratulatory telegrams from Air Vice Marshal Boyd and from the Air Officer Commanding 33 (Barrage Balloon) Group for snaring the first German aircraft to be brought down by barrage balloons in England. However, the credit for this success is challenged by the War Diary of 43rd Anti-Aircraft Brigade, which attributes equal credit to a Spitfire, a barrage balloon and the Tees guns.

Assuming that the balloon was the prime cause, it resulted in the first reported destruction of an enemy aircraft by a balloon squadron in this country during the Second World War, but not the first whose destruction was confirmed by wreckage. Neither aircraft nor crew were recovered and thus little is known about them. However, KG4 carried out the attack on Billingham and it is likely that the victim belonged to that unit. The Luftwaffe Loss Returns for this period do record that a Heinkel 111H-4 with four crew of 2./KG4 failed to return from an operation to Middlesbrough but the Returns give no other information.

25-26 June 1940 (off the Humber)

Aircraft:	Heinkel 111P-2	5J+BL	w/nr. ?	3./KG4
Crew:	Lt Helmet Furcht	pilot	missing	
	Hptm Heinz Schröder	observer	missing	
	Obfw Martin Hartel	wireless op	missing	
	Fw Eugen Seitz	mechanic	missing	

This aircraft was en route to Birmingham when it was intercepted over Withernsea by Pilot Officer D.S. Smith in Spitfire of 616 Squadron, Leconfield, who had been scrambled at 00.25 hours on 26 June 1940. He shot down the Heinkel 111 (coded 5J+BL) shortly after midnight and it crashed into the sea off the Yorkshire coast. The crew of Oberleutnant Schwarz, also of KG4, probably witnessed the loss when they saw an aircraft falling in flames about twenty miles east of the Humber.

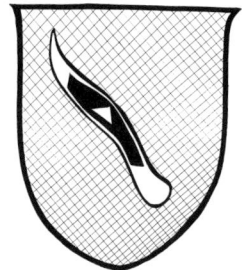

Kampfgeschwader 4 (General Wever)

Hauptmann Schröder was the Staffelkapitän of 3./KG4. The bodies of Helmut Furcht and one other were recovered from the sea (at position 53°33'N/00°27E) some days later by HMS *Brazen* and are believed to have been given a seaman's burial. On the same night that 5J+BL was shot down, another Heinkel 111 (coded 5J+DH) lost its gunner-mechanic, Unteroffizier Hoffman, who was shot through the head when the raider was attacked over the Humber by a nightfighter.

EYEWITNESS
Night Patrol (2)

Some of the difficulties, and dangers, faced by day fighter pilots whose aircraft were assigned to nightfighter duties before the introduction of appropriate equipment are clearly illustrated by the following (see also p.29)

'They were doing some works to the grass runway at Catterick so it was unfit for night flying. As there were no night-fighter aircraft (Blenheims – 219 Squadron) available for use, we maintained a section of two Spits at

Leeming for night 'readiness'. At dusk on 27 June 1940, I landed at Leeming for a night of 'readiness'. At about 02.00 hours on 28 June, a dark night, I was 'scrambled' to 9,000 feet over Middlesbrough for a target attacking the town. The flare path was two glim lamps and a 'totem pole' at the far end.

'I saw nothing (of the raider) but was vectored 045° on a plot going out to sea. Nothing was seen (Can you imagine this possibility in a Spitfire belching (exhaust) *flames several feet in front of you?). When I ran out of R/T contact (TR9 was a very poor and doubtful performer), I turned back on reciprocal and when back in contact was vectored 090°. No joy – and when contact on R/T was lost once more I turned back once more. Finally, I was vectored 140°. Again, no sighting, though the Controller, a WAAF, continually reported the target as being out there.*

'In the end, I was told to 'pancake' so I asked for a course for Leeming (a QDM). The reply was, would you believe it, 'What is your position?' I could not believe it! I had been under control on several different vectors for about forty-five minutes, in a day fighter on a dark night and without any navigation facilities. I am afraid that I lost my cool and said: 'How the bloody hell do I know?'. That ended any hope of help from the ground and nothing more was heard of them. So I had to find my own way back to Leeming. Mental Dead Reckoning did the trick and by mentally plotting the directions flown I reckoned 270° would help me find the coast at Whitby. I was lucky: flying low, I could see the breakers against the land almost at Whitby. Then, continuing 270°, I homed on the beacon and landed on a glim lamp flare path.

'outcome of the episode was a 'ticking off' by the Station Commander for swearing at a WAAF. He said, of course, that he would have done the same!'

Wing Commander Ted Shipman, AFC RAF(Ret'd)
Spitfire pilot, 41 Squadron, 1940

Three days after Pilot Officer Smith's success on the night of 25-26 June, 616 Squadron, Leconfield, probably added to its score sheet when Spitfire pilot Pilot Officer Roy Marples caught a Heinkel 111 in the Withernsea area. He had been scrambled at 23.55 hours to patrol Pickering-Driffield at 10,000 feet At about 00.15 hours he spotted the bomber when it was illuminated by searchlights in a position approximately between Catfoss and Withernsea, when the raider was flying east at a height of 15,000 feet. Marples attacked from dead astern and below, opening fire from 250 yards. The Spitfire's first burst of machine-gun fire was returned by the raider's ventral gunner, but there was no reaction from that source after Marples had fired a second time. Then a thick plume of white smoke began issuing from the enemy aircraft and Marples thought he saw flames coming from both engines. As Marples broke away preparatory to making a new attack, the searchlights went out and when he last saw the bomber it was going towards the sea in a gentle dive. The Spitfire pilot then lost his quarry when it entered clouds at 9,000 feet. Later that night, the crew of a Heinkel 111 were picked up off the coast. They claimed they had been shot down by a twin-engined fighter – so Marples was awarded a 'probable'. However, examination of the Luftwaffe Loss Returns reveals no relevant loss for this date.

1 July 1940 (east of the Humber)

Aircraft:	Heinkel 111H-4	5J+EL	w/nr. ?	3./KG4
Crew:	Obfw Hermann Raisbach	pilot	pow	
	Obltz See Friedrich-Wilhelm Koch	observer	pow	
	Fw Alfred Weber	wireless op	pow	
	Obfw Rudolf Ernst	mechanic	pow	

On 1 July 1940, Heinkel 111 (5J+EL) was detailed to attack the chemical works at Middlesbrough but the town was spared the possibility of some destruction when the bomber's crew spotted Spitfires in the area. Although they had not been seen by the fighters, the Germans thought it prudent to fly to Hull, their secondary target. They subsequently dropped sixteen 50kg high explosive bombs near the Saltend oil depot, where they

HEINKEL 111
Type - Bomber
Span 74' 3" - Lenght 54' 6" - Height 13' 9"

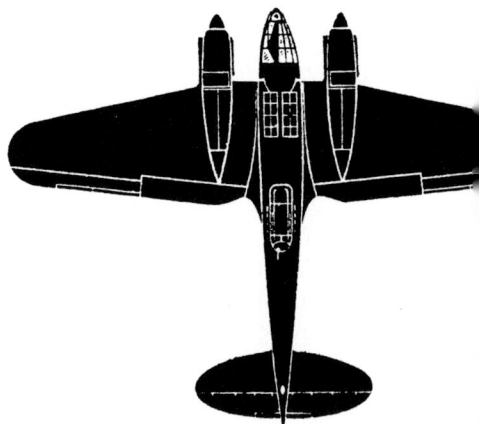

April 1940. Oblt zur See Friedrich Koch and his crew of 3./KG4 practising dinghy drill. The experience proved quite useful on 1 July 1940. [F-W Koch]

punctured (and set fire to) a petrol tank containing 2,500 tons of petrol. The Heinkel suffered minor damage from anti-aircraft fire over Hull and was making good its escape when it was shot down by three Spitfires of Yellow Section, 616 Squadron, Leconfield. The raider crashed into the sea twenty-five miles east of Spurn Head at 17.00 hours and its crew was rescued by HMS *Black Swan*.

The three Spitfires had taken off at 16.31 hours with instructions to patrol six miles north-west of Bridlington at 15,000 feet. They were then vectored to Withernsea at 10,000 feet but because they were then below cloud and could see no raiders they climbed 3,000 feet higher and found a Heinkel on the cloud top. Yellow 1, Flying Officer Miller, opened fire and saw tracer bullets enter the bomber's fuselage. Return fire was experienced from the bomber's ventral and dorsal gun positions before the Heinkel took cover in the cloud and Miller had to break off his attack.. The Section was then vectored to Scarborough at 15,000 feet in thick cloud – and discovered nothing – before proceeding to Hornsea to investigate another 'bandit' at 8,000 feet: it turned out to be an RAF Whitley. Yellow Section was then ordered to land. They were returning to Leconfield when they saw anti-aircraft fire over Hull, decided to investigate – and found a Heinkel 111 proceeding out to sea, having bombed oil tanks on the Humber.

After a two-minute chase, the bomber's gunners began firing at Yellow 1 (Miller) as he closed to 200 yards before pressing the gun button. He reduced the range to point-blank and fired all of his ammunition before breaking away, but by then the return fire from the Heinkel had ceased. As Miller broke downwards and to the left, Yellow 2, Flying Officer J.S. Bell, was closing up behind him. Bell opened fire at 250 yards and broke away when no more than seventy feet separated him from his quarry. In the time it took to close the gap he exhausted virtually all of his ammunition in three sustained bursts, without encountering return fire. He saw his incendiary shells strike home and bits fly off the enemy machine before smoke spewed from both engines and the port motor burst into flames. Then it was the turn of Yellow 3, Pilot Officer J. Brewster.

Brewster commenced firing at about 220 yards and saw his tracer bullets rip into the fuselage and wings of the Heinkel, transforming the metal skin on the top port side of the fuselage into cascading debris, some of which damaged his own aircraft. When the range was reduced to 100 yards, oil spattered his windscreen and his own aircraft was enveloped in a circular cloud of black smoke. Both impeded his vision and he broke away to the right. By the time he was ready to launch another attack, he was at 4,000 feet of altitude and the Heinkel was below him, on fire and diving towards the sea. He manoeuvred to attack again, his diving turn bringing him dead astern of the crippled raider, but then the oil on his windscreen masked his view: he lost sight of the bomber and did not see it again.

Karl Gunderlach[8] points out that both Weber and Ernst were wounded in the engagement. Francis K. Mason[9] states that the bomber (which he mistakenly claims belonged to KG26) was badly damaged and struggled south, only to ditch off the Suffolk coast, where the crew were picked up and landed at Harwich. However, the combat reports of the fighter pilots clearly show that the encounter occurred off the Humber, although Koch's account of the incident[10] states that after being picked up by HMS *Black Swan* he and his crew were transferred to another anti-submarine escort and taken to Harwich, where they were put ashore at noon the next day.

1 July 1940 (east of Whitby)

Aircraft: Heinkel 115		M2+CL	w/nr. ?	Ku.Fl.Gr.3/106
Crew:	Obfw Rudolph Worms	pilot	pow	
	Lt zur See Gottfried Schröder	observer	pow	
	Uffz Siegfried Soest	wireless op	pow	

M2+CL was on a mine-laying sortie when engine failure caused the aircraft to force-land on the sea thirty miles off Whitby at 04.00 hours on 1 July 1940. The crew, one of whom was injured, were adrift in the dinghy for thirty hours before being rescued by a naval vessel, which landed them at Grimsby. It was probably this particular aircraft that an air-sea rescue Heinkel 59 (D-ASAM) was searching for when it was shot down off Hartlepool later the same day.[11]

Küstenfliegerstaffel 3./106

2 July 1940 (off Withernsea)

Flight Lieutenant W.J. Leather (in Spitfire K9970), Pilot Officer J.R.G. Sutton(K9981) and Pilot Officer J.W. Lund(K9918), all of Red Section, 611 Squadron, Digby (Lincs.) were airborne during the period 08.35-10.00 hours and were patrolling seaward of Withernsea when they sighted an enemy aircraft fifteen miles from the coast and at 23,000 feet of altitude They gave chase as it turned eastwards. The enemy aircraft, which was identified as a Dornier 17, was overhauled sixty-five miles later.

As the fighters closed in, all three pilots noted that their quarry was, unusually, coloured silver on top, and Leather also noted that it fired off a recognition cartridge just before it was engaged in combat – but that was to no avail. At 09.15 hours Red 1, Flight Lieutenant Leather, ordered a No.1 attack and all three pilots got successive bursts into the enemy machine from 200 yards. Leather attacked first, the Dornier's rear

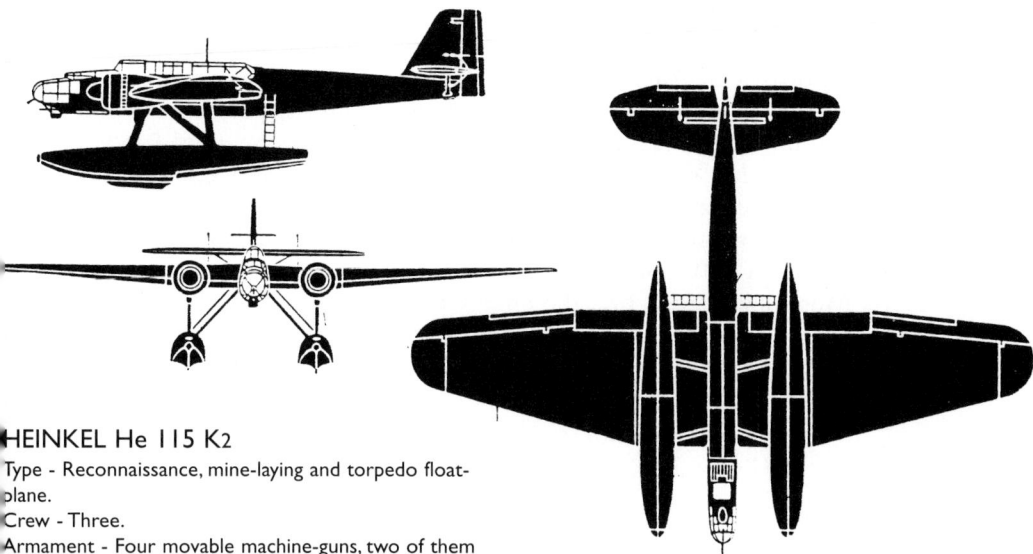

HEINKEL He 115 K2
Type - Reconnaissance, mine-laying and torpedo float-plane.
Crew - Three.
Armament - Four movable machine-guns, two of them remotely controlled from the rear of the motor nascelles.

gunner attempting to defend with bursts of tracer which went high over the Spitfire's port wing. The rear gunner ceased firing after Leather's second burst and as the Spitfire broke away there was a flash from the enemy's port engine, followed by thick black and white smoke from both motors. Pilot Officer Sutton, Red 2, followed and was also greeted by tracer, but it was without effect and ended after Sutton's first burst of fire. After the three pilots had attacked in succession, Flight Lieutenant Leather went in for a second assault. Pilot Officer Sutton followed him and emptied his guns into the enemy aircraft, which was last seen losing speed and gliding sharply towards the sea, with black smoke still streaming from both engines. Owing to the distance from home and the consequent risk of petrol shortage, Red Section did not remain in the area to confirm the demise of the Dornier, but Sutton did linger long enough to watch the crippled plane disappear from sight below him. The Spitfires returned to base unharmed. Back at Digby it was considered very unlikely that the enemy aircraft could have survived the attack so far from land and the trio were awarded one 'unconfirmed'.

Further details of this aircraft and its crew are currently not known to the writer but Francis K. Mason claims that the German aircraft was a Do215 of *Aufklärungsgruppe Oberbefehlshaber der Luftwaffe*.[12] The Luftwaffe Loss Returns for this date do show that such an aircraft failed to return from operations over England but no details are provided in respect of crew or the area of operations.

3 July 1940 (off Withernsea)

On the morning of 3 July, three Spitfires of Green Section, 616 Squadron, Leconfield, intercepted a Dornier 17 which was stalking a convoy off the Yorkshire coast. Flying Officer George Moberley, Pilot Officer Hugh Dundas and Flight Sergeant Burnard each made two attacks and the enemy aircraft crashed into the sea. During the engagement, Pilot Officer Dundas's aircraft was hit three times in the wing but no major damage was caused.

Green Section had been ordered off from Leconfield at 08.48 hours to patrol Hornsea at 7,000 feet. On arriving over the town, Green 2, Dundas, saw an enemy aircraft in the distance at an altitude of 4,500 feet and just in cloud. Having informed Moberley, his Section Leader, Dundas then led the Section in the chase. They caught up with the raider, identified as a Dornier 17z displaying a yellow 'G' outside the crosses on the mainplane, ten miles east of Withernsea and Moberley led the Spitfires in a Section attack.

As Moberley opened fire, the enemy aircraft did a very steep turn to port but its attacker managed a five-second burst before overshooting and breaking away hard right. Dundas then took up the assault on the enemy's right-hand side and got into range immediately. By that time, the Dornier's starboard engine was emitting little puffs of black smoke. Dundas opened fire at 250 yards range and got so close to the raider that it was completely masked by smoke before the fighter broke away in a climbing turn to starboard that took the Spitfire up through the cloud. Green 3, Burnard, then joined the fray, launching a fusillade from 300 yards and closing right in before being joined once again by Dundas, who managed one short burst in a beam attack before swinging away to create space for Moberley. Seconds later, when Green 1 returned and waded in with a beam attack on the Dornier's port side, considerable smoke began pouring out of every quarter of the enemy machine. Executing a steep turn which brought him back on to the Dornier's tail, Moberley exhausted what remained of his ammunition in a third and final assault, by which time the Dornier was done for. Hugh Dundas recalled the incident nearly fifty years later, although he mistakenly gave the date as 7 July 1940:

'...the German pilot tried frantically to elude us. But nowhere was the cloud solid: he was bound to come out into the gaps and by good fortune we maintained contact with him, worrying at his heels like spaniels hunting in cover. He fought back gallantly – desperately would perhaps be a more appropriate word – and for a time his rear gunner returned our fire, though it was an unequal exchange which must have been utterly terrifying for him. His tracer bullets streamed past and I received a hit in the outer part of my port wing, but the advantages were all in our favour. The rear gunner was silenced and the dying Dornier descended in its shroud of black smoke, to crash into the sea a few miles east of the convoy'. [13]

Withernsea coastguards reported seeing an enemy machine crash into the sea twenty miles east of the town. Moberley circled for a while as two destroyers (one of them marked F12) in the area made a search for survivors, but the results of their quest are not known at the time of writing.

Another Do 17 was intercepted and damaged by Dundas and Burnard during the same sortie. Dundas had noticed it – undamaged and flying in and out of cloud at 2,500 feet – as he broke away from his beam attack on the first machine. The two Spitfires pursued it for nearly fifty miles out to sea, firing short bursts whenever the German emerged from a break in the clouds. At first, they encountered considerable return fire from the top rear turret, but there was none at the finish. When they left for home, the Dornier was still flying '...but it appeared to be in distress, climbing slowly and disappearing into the cloud, which was 10/10 at 2,500 feet...' Its ultimate fate is not known. Examination of the Luftwaffe Loss

Returns for 3 July 1940 reveals that I./KG3 lost one Do 17z (pilot – Oberleutnant-Scharpkowski) on war operations but the location and the cause of the loss are not given. Thus there is the possibility that Scharpkowski was 616 Squadron's victim but currently there is no evidence to link this aircraft with 616 Squadron's claim.

8 July 1940 (Aldborough, East Yorks)

Aircraft:	Junkers 88A-1	5J+AT	w/nr. 3094
9./KG4			
Crew:	Hptm Kurt Rohloff	pilot	+
	Uffz George Abel	gunner	pow
	Uffz Artur Kühnapfel	wireless op	pow
	Uffz Heinz Oechler	mechanic	pow

There is a measure of doubt about who was responsible for the shooting down of this aircraft, for it was claimed by Hurricanes of Green Section, 'B' Flight, 249 Squadron, Church Fenton (Flying Officer D.G. Parnall, Pilot Officer H.J. Beazley and Sergeant A.D.W. Main) and by Flying Officer A.D.J. Lovell and Sergeant J.W. Allison, 41 Squadron, Catterick. Both Squadrons credited their pilots with the victory, but each section of Hurricane and Spitfire participants felt that the victory was theirs.

Lovell and Allison sighted the Junkers 88 at 11.30 hours, when it was flying at an altitude of 18,000 feet seven miles north-east of Scarborough. The German crew later explained during interrogation that they had just located a north-bound convoy when they were attacked by two Spitfires.

Tony Lovell ordered a No.1 attack, and carried out the first assault with Allison following close behind. Lovell began his approach from slightly below his quarry but found the enemy's slipstream so upsetting that he lifted his Spitfire slightly and attacked from slightly above. In so doing, the fighters emerged from the blind spot of the German dorsal gunner and he was able to get sight of them long enough to take aim.

As the Spitfires closed in, they were met by cannon fire but, seemingly, suffered no hits. Lovell managed four bursts at his target and exhausted his ammunition in his one and only pass. His gunfire produced two observable effects: the second burst prompted the Junkers' pilot to jettison all of his bombs at once and the fourth burst chipped large fragments off the raider's fuselage and tail and also stopped the cannon fire from the dorsal turret.

The German crew later explained that their dorsal gunner was wounded during that first engagement and that the Junkers' starboard engine was stopped. Rohloff, who was the Staffelkapitän, then jettisoned

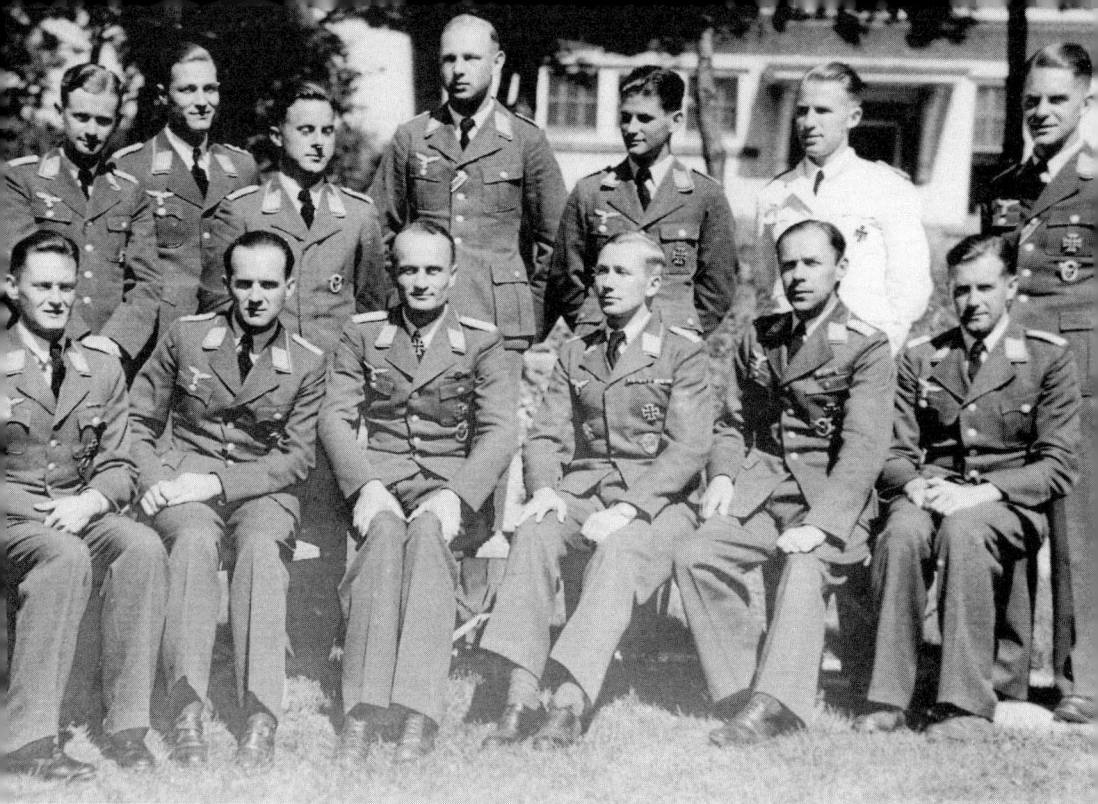

1942. *KG4 personnel in POW Camp 30, Bowmanville,Ontario(Canada).*
Front L-R: *1. Hptmn Eugen Eichler(1./KG4), whose He111(5J+IH) crashed near Westerhope, Newcastle/Tyne, 6 May 1941; 2. Oblt.U. Jordan (StabII./KG4) whose He111(5J+DM) ditched off Cley next the Sea(Norfolk) 19 June 1940; 3. Oblt. H. Kell(3./KG4) whose He111(5J+BL) was shot down over London, 14 September 1940; 4. Maj. D.Frhr. von Massenbach(StabII./KG4) who, with Jordan, was in He111(5J+DM) when it ditched off Cley next the Sea(Norfolk) 19 June 1940; 5. Oblt.z.See F-W Koch(3./KG4), whose He111(5J+EL) was shot down off the Humber on 1 July 1940. 6. unknown; 7. Oblt. Pollitz.*
Back L-R: *1. Lt H-J Backhaus(6./KG4) whose He111(5J+FP) crashed into the sea off Margate on 19 June 1940; 2. unknown; 3. Oblt J. von Arnim(4./KG4) whose He111(5J+AM) crashed in Cambridgeshire on 19 June 1940; 4. Hptmn. Ganzert; 5. Oblt. Simon; 6. Lt Hölscher; 7. Oblt. Heier; 8. Oblt.z.See Paul Tholen-(Stab I./KG4) whose He111(5J+ZB) ditched off Withernsea(East Yorks)-on 8 May 1941. 9. Oblt. Paas.* [F-W Koch]

[*NB Captions showing cause of captivity give ranks at time of capture; other ranks as at 1942]

his bomb load in the hope of climbing to the protection of substantial cloud. However, this plan was ultimately discarded because the port engine was also failing and so, as Lovell broke away to the right, the Junkers stall turned and started gliding towards land. As the Junkers moved among clouds, Jack Allison proceeded with his own attack and managed to squeeze off two bursts of gunfire, to which there was no reply from the German gunners. Interestingly, Allison noted in his combat report that '...three Hurricanes were circling about at the time...'

The Hurricane pilots attacked at 11.31 hours, but the combat report of No.249 Squadron's section leader, Flying Officer Parnall, clearly shows that Lovell and Allison got there first. Parnall states that the Hurricanes were at 19,000 feet and patrolling fifteen miles north-east of Flamborough Head when he noticed a Junkers 88 proceeding south at the same height. He formed his section into line astern and was about to commence a No.1 attack '...when a Spitfire started attacking(the Junkers)...'. According to Parnall, the Spitfire fired for about three seconds (which suggests that Parnall saw Allison's aircraft in attack) and then broke away. Parnall mentions that at that point there was '...slight smoke issuing from port engine (of the Ju88)...' but that the bomber was taking no evasive action... The three Hurricanes then attacked in turn, with the Junkers attempting to evade with stall turns and slow flying while dodging in and out of broken cloud. Parnall managed a nine-second burst, which commenced at 350 yards and ended when he broke away ninety yards from his target. At no time did he notice any return fire – until later on, when he experienced concentrated fire from the bomber's front turret at 9,000 feet as the Junkers 88 suddenly came out of cloud about 700 yards off Parnall's starboard beam. Green 2, Beasley, and Green 3, Mains, followed Parnall's foray with attacks of their own. Beasley managed three bursts and Mains followed with two more. By then, the Junkers was down to 10,000 feet and entering cloud with both engines apparently on fire.

Tony Lovell's version of the encounter is somewhat different. He saw the Hurricanes '...carry out one quick attack each without any further ill effect to the bomber...'. Perhaps anticipating a disputed claim,

> *'I followed the bomber down and did a quick dive past him to get the lettering on the fuselage. All I could see was a large yellow 'A' on the cockpit side of the black crosses.'*

Recognising the hopelessness of his situation, Rohloff ordered his crew to abandon the aircraft. They managed to bale out successfully but the pilot crashed with his aircraft and was killed. Aldbrough police gave the crash site as a wheat field between Aldbrough and Crossmere Hill, six miles south of Hornsea. (i.e. in the area of OS 240385 – 250376). Later reports submitted by Air Intelligence AI1(g) revealed that the aircraft was riddled by bullets and that the vital shots appeared to have been in the port engine, which caught fire. When the aircraft crashed, the accompanying explosion resulted in the distribution of the wreckage over a large area, but there were sufficient clues to identify it as being 5J+AT. Of the three crew members who baled out, one was captured at Aldbrough and another at Burton Constable. The third was taken in circumstances which captured the public imagination, as the following newspaper report illustrates:

'*When the crew of a German bomber landed by parachute on the North East coast, the wife of a farmer arrested one of the airmen, taking his revolver and handing him over to some motor-cyclists. Three of the crew jumped with parachutes, landed safely and were captured. The pilot, who was unable to get clear of the machine - which crashed into a wheatfield - was killed. One of the crew was arrested by Mrs N. Cardwell, a centre leader of the WVS and wife of an LDV Section Leader. She is believed to be the first woman in this country to perform such a feat. Modestly claiming that she had not done anything more than anyone else in similar circumstances would have done, Mrs Cardwell said on Monday:*

"*One of my foremen came to the door of my sitting-room this afternoon and said some German parachutists were coming down. I went straight to the telephone but found it was out of order so I rushed to the door and saw a huge airman parachuting slowly to the ground. He looked as if he was coming right into my garden.*

"*I did not know what he was going to do, and I told my groom's boy to go on his bicycle for the police. But in the meantime I had to do something. We had been told that we had to deal with parachutists very quickly before they had chance to do any damage. I went into the garden and saw the airman limping across the paddock towards the house. There were two or three people about, but they didn't do anything so I walked up to the man and told him to put his hands up. He did not understand, until I made signs and he raised his hands in the air. I pointed to the automatic pistol in his belt and he nodded and, smiling wryly, handed it to me.*

"*He was very quiet and seemed very distressed by the sight of his burning plane about half a mile away. He was about 6ft 3ins and a typical blonde German. He seemed pale and shaken. I walked with him in front of me to the road. We waited for about half an hour before the police and soldiers arrived and took the airman away.*"

Mrs Cardwell was not armed, "not even with a broom-stick".'[14]

The three Germans were first taken to the Infantry Training Centre, Beverley, before their removal to POW camp. On 12 July 1940, the *Whitby Gazette* reported that Mrs Cardwell had been awarded the OBE for her part in the incident.

The various reports relating to this incident are both confused and confusing. For example, Aldbrough police reported that the Junkers had been brought down by three Spitfires (the same number as the Hurricanes) and that the fight appeared to have taken place over Skipsea.

However, during interrogation, the German crew referred to two Spitfires and apparently made no mention at all of Hurricanes being involved. According to Humphrey Wynn, 249 Squadron shot down the bomber fifteen miles north-east of Flamborough Head, but the combat reports show that that was the place where the Junkers 88 was first sighted by the Hurricanes.[15] Additionally, an Air Ministry Intelligence report in the writer's possession states that Lovell and Allison engaged their Junkers 88 at 11.42 hours, while the local police reported that the 'Aldbrough' raider crashed at 1155 hours – which seems to point to two enemy aircraft being involved. Further evidence of two German aircraft being involved is suggested by the claim by Francis K. Mason that a Junkers 88 of *Lehrgeschwader* 1 piloted by Oberleutnant Meyer was shot down by 249 Squadron and crashed in the sea off Hornsea at 11.25 hours. Meyer was killed; the three other crew members were posted missing.[16]

9 August 1940 (off North-East coast?)

Aircraft:	Heinkel 111H-4	5J+?K	w/nr. ?	2./KG4
Crew:	Fw. Richard Schmidt	pilot	missing	
	Gefr. Herbert Ebald		missing	
	Fw. Hans Geisdorf		missing	
	Uffz. Wilhelm Soffel		missing	

Karl Gunderlach lists this crew has having failed to return from operations against industrial targets in Hartlepool on 9 August 1940.[17] No other details of the fate of this aircraft are known at the time of writing, except that it was based at Soesterberg, Holland. The Luftwaffe Loss Reports for 9 August 1940 shows that an Heinkel 111H-4 of 2./KG4 was shot down by flak near Flamborough Head and that two of the crew were killed and two were missing. In view of the fact that aircraft from Soesterberg that were destined for Hartlepool would probably have passed Flamborough, it is thought that 5J+?K was the aircraft caught by the flak.

EYEWITNESS
Mining operation to Middlesbrough: KG26

In the months before the outbreak of war, a number of enthusiasts in the German Fleet Air Arm had been developing anti-shipping techniques with regard to bombing and for mine-laying by parachute. A branch of that Service operating under *Führer der Seeluftstreitkräfte* was subsequently granted permission to operate independently of the navy with regard to mine-laying, including operations in shallow ports out of reach of naval vessels. Mining sorties began in November 1939, when the

50

first mines were sown in British coastal waters. The task was initially undertaken by Heinkel 115 floatplanes, which dropped their weapons from heights of 900 feet or less, but these were later superceded by Heinkel 111 bombers. In February 1940 a special Command (*Fliegerdivision IX*) was created for mine-laying operations and was to operate outside of the direct influence of the navy.

In July-August 1940 I./KG26 was based at Aalborg-West and it was from there that the unit launched its day and night bombing attacks against shipping and port targets along the east coast of Britain. Around the middle of the year, the unit extended its range of anti-shipping activities when it was called upon to take part in 'special operations' – the mining of British ports on the east coast.

At the time, the chosen crews had not been trained for such duties but they were very competent in over-sea navigation, which was considered to be the most important factor for their intended new tasks. To lay mines they needed to acquire exact knowledge of the shipping lanes as well as the shipping channels in and out of ports but their subsequent training also included the reading of sea charts, the study of the signals and beacons of wartime waterways and also low water marks. Crews also needed to have precise information about dropping heights and the required speed of the aircraft at the point of releasing the mine. All of these aspects were important – but the most important was the ability to navigate precisely. When they were considered ready, they were sent to lay mines at port entrances, including those of the Tyne and Tees.

Two types of parachute mines were in use at that time: 500kg and 1,000kg. These were suspended from the underside of the aircraft fuselage. A parachute was packed into a sealed chamber in the tail of each mine and the rip-cord for each parachute was shackled to a loop on the underside of the plane. The rip-cord required a pull equal to 300kg to operate it: that was provided when the mine was released from the aircraft. The mine, supported by the parachute, would then descend to the sea. The parachute was secured to the weapon by a soluble plug which dissolved upon immersion in water. This allowed the parachute to detach itself from the mine and drift away so that the mine's location would not be betrayed. The exact locations of all mines were recorded on charts by the operational unit so that when hostilities were finally over and international trade was eventually resumed, all mines could be found and cleared.

One evening in the summer of 1940 I./KG26 sent almost the entire Gruppe on a mining operation to north-east England. Half the Gruppe went to the Tyne; the rest to the Tees. The aircraft took off individually at five-minute intervals so that each crew would not by hindered by other aircraft during its mine-laying operation. The diagonal flight across the

North Sea took almost two hours. One of the crews taking part was that of Lt. Kühn, a Heinkel 111 pilot with 2./KG26, who found that such operations were not without danger.

'We flew at 500m altitude. Below us was broken cloud, otherwise it was a clear night with good visibility. We were carrying two 1,000kg mines, suspended under the fuselage where the large bombs usually hung. The mines were somewhat fatter and they had no fin because they were to be floated down to the sea by parachute.

'We were flying with mines for the first time. Until then, we had been specialists in the war against shipping while other units - KG4 and the maritime groups – had been responsible for mining. But we were a sea war unit – so why shouldn't we also lay mines? Our mission was to mine the shipping channel into the port of Middlesbrough. We had precise sea charts showing water depths and navigation buoys and we knew it all exactly because it had been talked through back home.

Over the sea we checked the wind by estimates based on the crests of waves: apparently our weatherman was right! [After crossing the sea]… *we steered for the coast to the north of the port entrance* [river mouth]. *From there we wanted to run south to the northerly cape* [Hartlepool headland?] *of the port channel and from there make a timed run using stopwatch and compass. It was better still to be able to fly by sight and compass.*

'We saw the coast ahead of us – a darker line on the already dark horizon. We got closer until we were under the steep coastline. We then flew south along it: our position was correct. Then the coast ran almost north-south. No searchlights; no flak. All was quiet. Almost too quiet. Then a bay came into view [Tees Bay] *to the right of us. That must have been the port entrance; the port installations were visible behind it.*

'Then it went all wrong. First a searchlight, then a lighthouse, then powerful flak was dancing all round us. We stayed out to sea, off the port, and were down to zero altitude. Meanwhile, before us to our left we saw a buoy marking the channel. We flew along it and dropped our mines… one… two… about one hundred metres apart.

'The first fell OK then the second was released. There was a jolt in the aircraft, as if the brakes had been applied in the air. The airspeed indicator went back with a jerk. The gunner, who was in the ventral turret on the underside of the aircraft and was observing the launch, screamed: 'The parachute has opened but it's caught on the plane!' The 'chute was open behind us and could be clearly seen. The wireless operator also saw it. We pulled the emergency release line – but nothing happened. Then, once again, another powerful jerk and the nightmare was over. It all lasted only a few seconds but we were already considerably lower in altitude. The opened parachute had reduced both our height and our speed – and had

given us a powerful fright besides. Nevertheless, the mines were laid: the first in the target area; the second on the edge of the channel but in deeper water to seawards.

'What had gone wrong? How could the 'chute have opened itself? Could it have been that the ripcord had been wrongly fixed on – perhaps to the first mine? Before the drop, everything was in order. The parachute had not opened itself before. Perhaps the cap retaining the parachute had blown away – perhaps when the first mine was dropped?

'While we were in the air we could not discover anything further. We were glad that all had still gone well and that the second mine had been dropped with the parachute. If the thing had hung on a second longer it would have certainly have caused us to crash; we certainly could not have managed to stay airborne while dragging an open parachute behind us.

'After landing, our engines had not properly stopped before our mechanic was out of the aircraft and looking to find what was wrong. 'Nothing', he said. 'All gone'. What was all gone? He meant the mine suspension unit for the second mine. The suspension unit for the first mine was still there intact. But the second was gone…. We could only speculate as to how the mistake had been made – but we hoped that it was a technical error.

'The next day we went on another mining operation. The southern entrance to Scapa Flow was our target.'

Leutnant Kühn, pilot, 2./KG26

11 August 1940 (Scaling, near Whitby)

Aircraft:	Junkers 88A-1	7A+KH	w/nr. 2086	1.(F)/121
Crew:	Fw Otto Höfft	pilot	pow	
	Oblt Hans Marzusch	observer	pow	
	Fw Karl-Heinz Hacker	wireless op	pow	
	Lt Heinrich Meier		+	

This aircraft was on a photo-reconnaissance sortie to North Yorkshire when it was intercepted over Helmsley by three Spitfires of 41 Squadron, Catterick. It was shot down and crashed at 19.08 hours on Newton

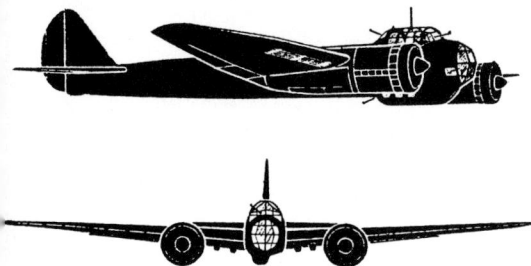

JUNKERS Ju. 88 A-1 (Jumo 211A)
Type - Long-Range Bomber
Span 59' 0" - Length 46' 6" Height 15' 0"

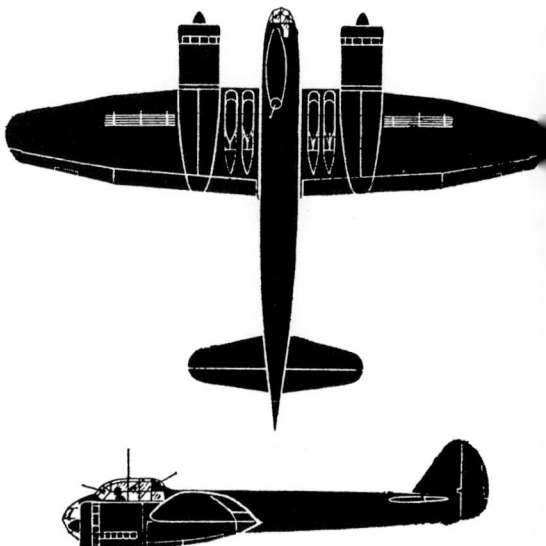

Three of the crew of Ju88 (7A+KH) that crashed on Newton Moor on 11 August 1940. L-R; Fw Höfft, Oblt Hans Marzusch and Fw Karl-Heinz Hacker. [Melvin Brown and Stephen Hall].

Moor, near to Calais House Farm, Scaling.

7A+KH was based at Stavanger, Norway, and had been ordered to carry out a high altitude photo-reconnaissance of the Bomber Command aerodromes of Disforth and Linton-on-Ouse, perhaps in preparation for the large-scale daylight raid on the north of England which occurred on the 15 August. Heinrich Meier was a communications' specialist whose job, presumably, was to gather radio intelligence. At 18.53 hours the Ju88 crossed in at 15,000 feet over Whitby, where it was immediately identified by the town's Abbey Plain observation post as it passed over '...at great speed in nearly a direct line for Dishforth.'

Lt Heinrich Meier, the wireless communications specialist who was killed when his Ju88 (7A+KH) was shot down near Scaling, 11 August 1940. [Mrs M. Henderson]

The Junkers was 18,000 feet over Helmsley and on its way home when it was intercepted by Flying Officer 'Wally' Wallens, Flying Officer John Boyle and Sergeant Edward 'Mitzi' Darling at the start of an aerial battle which would continue to the coast and which would prompt almost the entire congregation at Ugthorpe church to leave the evening service and go outside to witness the dog-fight as it progressed over Skelder Moor and towards the sea.

The Junkers was attacked three times by the Spitfires. The starboard engine was knocked out in the first attack, Meier was killed in the second attack, and the port engine was hit in the third attack. Whether Höfft considered the possibilty of an escape to seaward is a matter for

54

Ju88 (7A+KH) on Newton Moor, August 1940. [Author's collection]

conjecture. But the prospect of a 400-mile trip across the North Sea (assuming his – unlikely – escape from the Spitfires) on one damaged engine would not be attractive. He did fly out over the water, however, but only for a short distance – just far enough to prompt the local Observer Corps post to wonder whether the Germans had dumped their camera offshore – before swinging back low over Hinderwell. At 19.08 hours and with the fighters still in attendance, Höfft made a wheels up landing on the North Yorkshire Moors, (it is believed) some 500 yards east of the junction of the A.171 and B.1266, about a mile from where Scaling dam is now sited.

When the first sightseers arrived on the scene, Höfft, Hacker and Marzusch were standing near their aircraft: the body of twenty-one year-old Heinrich Meier lay close by. By then the aircraft and its crew were being guarded by men from a nearby searchlight site.[19] When they had seen the aircraft making its approach, they had taken a machine-gun with them in anticipation of trouble, but, fortunately, it had not been needed. They took it upon themselves to keep the curious – and the souvenir hunters – at a respectable distance, pending the arrival of a more permanent guard.

The three survivors were soon taken from the site. Aided by Hinderwell police sergeant Wellburn, Aaron Hart, an Ugthorpe butcher and special constable, used his butcher's van to transport them to Whitby police station, while Meier's body was removed to Thornaby. The plane remained on the moor for some days, a focus of interest until its removal.

Meier's body was subsequently buried in the RAF plot at Acklam Road cemetery, Thornaby-on-Tees, and remained there until 1954, when his parents requested its transfer to Germany.[20]

15 August 1940 (Flamborough Head area)

The Battle of Britain was at its height in August 1940. Shortly after noon on Thursday, 15 August, the Luftwaffe – believing that available RAF fighter squadrons were heavily committed in the south of England – launched a two-pronged, daylight attack from bases in Denmark and Norway against aerodromes and industrial targets in north-east England. Fifty Ju88s of KG30 were briefed to attack Driffield aerodrome, East Yorkshire, shortly after sixty-three Heinkel 111s of KG26 (based at Stavanger, Norway) had raided the aerodromes at Dishforth and Linton-on-Ouse, with Newcastle, Sunderland and Middlesbrough as secondary targets. However, the Heinkels, which were escorted by twenty-one Messerschmitt Bf110D twin-engined fighters of I./ZG76, were intercepted by northern-based fighter squadrons before they could reach their objectives and their attack failed. The Ju88s of KG30 were more successful.

At the time that the Luftwaffe's attack on the far north was fading, the other one was opening up over East Yorkskshire. Shortly before 13.30 hours an estimated fifty Ju88s of KG30, based at Aalborg, crossed the east coast in the area of Filey-Flamborough Head. The main body went on to attack Driffield aerodrome; others raided coastal targets, including Scarborough and Bridlington, but damage in those places appears to have been on a small scale.

According to the Operations Record Book of RAF Station Driffield, thirty enemy aircraft bombed and machine-gunned the aerodrome. They dropped over one hundred bombs of various calibres, destroyed ten Whitley bomber aircraft, damaged four hangars and destroyed the west wing of the Officers' Mess. Thirteen people (including one civilian) were killed; sixteen(including two civilians) were hospitalised and five suffered slight injuries. The attackers were intercepted over the East Yorkshire coast by twelve Spitfires of 616 Squadron, Leconfield, six Hurricanes of 73 Squadron, Church Fenton, and thirteen Blenheim Mk.1s of 219 Squadron, Catterick. All of these took their toll on the attacking force – but not quite to the extent that they thought.

In the heat of the battle many of the defenders damaged raiders, which then broke away streaming smoke, seemingly having sustained critical damage. The defending fighters were not always able to follow to witness the eventual outcome because of the battle that was raging, and thus a damaged enemy might sometimes have been claimed as 'destroyed'. The subsequent report of *Enemy Air Force Operations* – 15 August 1940, compiled by Air Intelligence after the attack and based on the claims finally allowed, attributed the following victories to the participating squadrons:

73(Hurricane) Squadron: 7 destroyed; 3 probably destroyed; 3 damaged.
616(Spitfire) Squadron: 8 destroyed; 4 probably destroyed; 1 damaged.
219(Blenheim) Squadron: 1 probably destroyed; 4 damaged.

This proved to be an exaggeration. The Luftwaffe Loss Returns record that nine aircraft failed to return from Driffield and that a further three crash-landed on their return (see below). On the basis of claims made by fighter pilots who saw their victims *crash*, the following does, perhaps, offer a more realistic picture – but it still provides a tally which exceeds the Luftwaffe's loss figures.

616 Squadron, Leconfield: Pilot Officer D.S. Smith and Flight Lieutenant R.O. Hellyer shared a Ju88 that crashed in the sea off Flamborough; Flight Lieutenant D. Gillam sent one crashing into the sea some five miles east of Flamborough; Pilot Officer H.S. Dundas and Pilot Officer R. Marples shared one that crashed into the sea ten miles east of Flamborough; Flying Officer G. Moberly shot one down into the sea some thirty miles east of Flamborough and Sergeant James Hopewell shot down one that crashed just north of Bridlington.

73 Squadron, Church Fenton: Flight Lieutenant R.E. Lovett sent one Ju88 crashing into the sea four miles off Flamborough Head; Sergeant J.J. Griffin put one into the sea east of Bridlington; Sergeant A.L. McNey shot down one into the sea ten miles east of Hornsea and was credited with another that crashed on land; Pilot Officer D.S. Scott watched 'his' Ju88 crash and explode on land some four miles south of Bridlington; and P/O P.E.G. Carter was responsible for the Ju88 that crashed four miles off the coast six miles south of Flamborough.

The reader will have noticed that even this 'sightings' approach produces eleven enemy aircraft 'destroyed', which exceeds the Luftwaffe losses by two aircraft. Clearly, there must have been duplication somewhere but the 'who' and the 'where' are difficult to identify. However, it is possible to give details of some of the lost crews.

Many of the records of the Luftwaffe were, on Goering's orders, destroyed towards the end of the war. Those that survived are incomplete. Thus it is possible to give details of only five KG30 crews who were lost on the Driffield raid and these appear below.

Perhaps it is worth pointing out that in recent years a number of monographs have been written about the Driffield operation and it would seem that the writers of such have relied heavily upon the loss details given by Francis K. Mason[21] and have repeated them in their own accounts. Mason's *Battle over Britain* is a monumental work but there are occasional errors in it. Some of these relate to bomber losses and fighter claims for 15 August 1940 and are addressed below.

Aircraft:	Junkers 88C	4D+DR	w/nr. ?	7./KG30
Crew:	Oblt Werner Bachmann	pilot	pow	
	Uffz Werner Evers	observer	pow	
	Fw Georg Henneske	wireless op	+	
	Flgr Robert Wakther	gunner	pow	

This aircraft was shot down by Sergeant James Hopewell of 616 Squadron, Leconfield, and crash-landed alongside the Bridlington waterworks reservoir, Scarborough Road, at about 13.30 hours. Hopewell had taken off with Green Section at 13.00 hours but subsequently became separated from his colleagues. He was patrolling by himself off Flamborough Head at 9,000 feet when he sighted a Ju88 flying east 500 feet below him. He immediately moved in to attack and managed a short burst from 400 yards before the enemy aircraft turned on to a northerly course and started to climb. Hopewell's second assault was a quarter attack from the starboard side: two three-second bursts from 300 yards with one and half rings' deflection. His

Kampfgeschwader 30 (Adler)

ammunition appeared to penetrate the cockpit and wings of the raider, which then started to bank to the west. As Hopewell followed, he continued to pump bullets into the engines and tail unit of his victim and noticed that parts of the enemy machine were disintegrating. At that point the German then pushed his nose down and made for the coast. Hopewell managed five more bursts of machine-gun fire before the Junkers finally landed, in Hopewell's words, '...in estimated position 3 mls NNW of Bridlington...'

Various publications in the past have claimed that this aircraft crashed at Sledmere, at Hornby, at Hunmanby – and even as far away as Lancashire! The fact that it came down alongside the waterworks reservoir at Bridlington is confirmed not only by Hopewell's combat report but also by Grindale resident and eye-witness Harold Beecroft, whose brother was subsequently photographed alongside the aircraft (see below). *The Blitz, then and now vol.1*(1987) shows a photograph of this aircraft on page 200 of the book but is in error when claiming that it is Ju88 4D+KL (see below). Other writers have also wrongly attributed Hopewell's victory to other fighter pilots and have erroneously identified the deceased wireless operator of 4D+DR as the pilot of the Junkers. However, in all of the above respects, the *official* records tell a different story. The body of the German wireless operator, Georg Henneske, was buried in Bridlington cemetery on 19 August 1940; it has since been removed to the German Military Cemetery at Cannock Chase.

Aircraft:	Junkers 88A-5	4D+KL	w/nr. ?	3./KG30
Crew:	Uffz Ludwig von Lorentz	pilot	pow	
	Uffz Heinrich Kenski	observer	pow	
	Uffz Heinrich Prumann	wireless op	pow	
	Gefr Johann Göbel	gunner	pow	

Francis K. Mason maintains that this aircraft was shot down by Pilot Officer Carter, in a Hurricane of 73 Squadron,[22] but there is evidence to suggest that this particular Junkers was shot down by Sergeant A.L. McNey, of the same unit. McNey's combat report relates that after attacking a low-flying Ju88 that eventually went into the sea ten miles east of Hornsea, he exhausted his remaining ammunition on another low-flying Junkers. He did not see it crash but when he last saw it, it was doing a gentle side-slip about one mile from a bombing range. Wreckage was later found near the position indicated by McNey and he was credited with the victory. Skipsea, just to the south of Barmston, had a bombing range close by in 1940 and might well have been the site to which McNey referred.

Further evidence is, perhaps, also provided by a report from Officers of 'A' Company, 1st. Battalion, Royal Welch Fusiliers,[23] whose mess caravan was on the south side of Barmston village. Men of the Durham Light Infantry were manning the coast just to the north of Barmston's single street. The report relates that the bomber from which four prisoners were subsequently taken was seen to '...bank low round the church tower with its port engine on fire, circling north and disappearing

This Ju88A-5 of 3./KG30 is believed to be 4D+KL, which is thought to have crashed at Fraisthorpe, 15 August 1940. [via Ken Watkins]

Ju88C (4D+DR) of 7./KG30 alongside the waterworks reservoir at Bridlington. Harold Beecroft's brother is leaning on the fuselage. [Bridlington Public Library].

as it landed in the Durham Light Infantry sector...' (i.e. to the north of the Welch Fusiliers – so we can assume that the Junkers approached from the south and, perhaps, from the direction of the bombing range?). When the Fusiliers reached the site, the port engine and wing were on fire. No.31 Anti-Aircraft Brigade Intelligence Report for 15 August 1940[24] gives the crash site as Fraisthorpe (although the Fusiliers' report suggests Barmston), just to the north of where the following aircraft came to earth.

Aircraft:	Junkers 88	4D+?M	w/nr. ?	4./KG30
Crew:	Fw Rudolf Bihr	pilot	+	
	Fw Robert Pohl	observer	+	
	Uffx Severin Kürsch	wireless op	+	
	Uffz Arnalf Neumeyer	gunner	missing	

The combat report of Pilot Officer D.S. Scott of 73 Squadron, briefly describes how he attacked an aircraft which he subsequently watched crash and explode in a cornfield four miles south of Bridlington. No.31 Anti-Aircraft Brigade Intelligence Report for 15 August 1940 gives the crash site as Hamilton Hill Farm, Barmston, although the Fusiliers' report suggests Fraisthorpe, The writer believes that Scott's victim was 4D+?M because only three German aircraft are known to have crashed on land - and two of those have already been accounted for. The fact that two identifiable members of the crew of this aircraft, Kürsch and Pohl, were buried at Bridlington Cemetery on 19 August 1940 alongside the communal grave of two 'unknown' German fliers (Bihr and Neumeyer?) who were also buried on 19 August, perhaps adds further supporting evidence.

Aircraft:	Junkers 88C	4D+?R	w/nr. ?	7./KG30
Crew:	Lt Wolf-Dietrich Riede	pilot	missing	
	Uffz Fritz Hartwich	observer	+	
	Flgr Richard Ulbrich	wireless op	missing	
	Uffz Peter Panhuysen	gunner	missing	

The writer knows little about this particular aircraft, except that it was targeted on Driffield and that it failed to return to its base. The fact that only one member of the crew was found might well link 4D+?R with the claim of Sergeant T.E. Westmoreland, of 616 Spitfire Squadron, who caught a Ju88 at 6,000 feet when it was heading out to sea near Bridlington. During the course of the engagement, Westmoreland saw white smoke coming from the bomber's port engine and then saw one of the German crew bale out. On his final assault, Westmoreland dived through the slipstream of the Junkers but when he turned to pick up the target once again, it was no longer in sight. If Hartwich was the parachutist this aircraft must have ultimately crashed in the sea – but whether it did or not must remain in the realms of conjecture.

Aircraft:	Junkers 88	4D+?S	w/nr. ?	8.KG30
Crew:	?	pilot	?	
	Uffz Joachim Resin	observer	missing	
	Fw Alfred Schumann	wireless/op	missing	
	Uffz Werner Jünnemann	gunner	missing	

The writer knows little about this aircraft, other than it failed to return from operations against Driffield. The name of the pilot is missing from the Luftwaffe Loss Return because only part of the original document survived Goering's fire.

Others: The Luftwaffe Loss Returns show the above losses resulting from the attack on RAF Station, Driffield, on 15 August 1940, as well as the following less-detailed losses:

Two Ju88C aircraft of I./KG30 failed to return.

One Ju88C of III./KG30 which had Driffield as its target failed to return.

One Ju88 of 8./KG30 believed lost over the English east coast. Four injured.

One Ju88C aircraft of III./KG30 crash landed in Holland.

One Ju88C aircraft of III./KG30 crash landed at Aalborg West.

One Ju88A-5 of II./KG30 crash-landed at Oldenburg.

16 August 1940 (in the Humber?)

The Luftwaffe Loss Returns show that Heinkel 111H-4 (IT+ ?L) of *3/Kampfgruppe126* (3./KGr.126) was shot down by flak while on a sortie to Hull. The Returns show Oberleutnant Volkmar and four crew as 'missing'. Francis K. Mason agrees with the cause and the crew loss and claims that the Heinkel crashed in the Humber.[25] However, the claims of a Dutch researcher[26] that the body of Oberleutnant *Folkmar* of KGr.126 was washed ashore at a north Holland beach on the 15 August 1940, suggests that the Heinkel might have crashed much farther from the Humber than Mason claims. Mason also explains that KGr.126 was previously a coastal reconnaissance unit but was absorbed into the Luftwafffe's strategic bombing force in mid-1940.

20 August 1940 (Ottringham, near Hull)

Aircraft:	Junkers 88A-1	4D+IS	w/nr. ?	8./KG30
Crew:	Uffz Franz Georg Wolff	pilot	pow	
	Fw Gugo Keller	observer	pow	
	Uffz Wilhelm Rautenberg	rear gunner	+	
	Uffz Werner Hans Kruczinski	wireless op	+	

Junkers 88 (4D+IS) of 8./KG30 was caught over East Yorkshire by Hurricanes of Green Section, 'B' Flight, 302 (Polish) Squadron, Leconfield. The Squadron had been declared operational just two days earlier and the Junkers 88 became the unit's first 'kill' when it was shot down by Squadron Leader Bill Satchell, No.302s commanding officer. It crashed near Ottringham, five miles south-west of Withernsea, shortly after 19.00 hours. Seemingly, 358 Anti-Aircraft Battery at Halsham (two miles north of Ottringham) also laid claim to this aircraft (see the final paragraph of this entry).

Interrogation of the surviving crew members of the German bomber by Flying Officer J.R. Robinson, of RAF Station Leconfield, revealed that the Ju88 had left Aalborg, Denmark, in the company of two other machines. Each was carrying four 250kg bombs with the intention of bombing British harbours and aerodromes.[27] 4D+IS lost contact with the other two Junkers as they flew across the North Sea and was alone when it made landfall slightly north of Hull, in cloud and at 6,000 feet. It was attacked at an altitude of 3,000 feet by three Hurricanes shortly after 19.00 hours at a point between Hull and Spurn Head.

The fighters were led by their squadron commander, Squadron Leader Bill Satchell(Green 1), who had been ordered to patrol Hull at 5,000 feet. When he saw a twin-engined aircraft below his starboard bow he dived at once to a position above and slightly behind the 'bogey' and identified it as a Ju88.

Anticipating the first assault, Wolff dived into cloud while his own rear gunner, Willi Rautenberg, pumped tracer bullets at the pursuing Hurricanes. Satchell managed just one short burst of gunfire with full deflection before the Junkers found more dense cloud cover and managed to evade for some three minutes. When the raider re-emerged into clear air the Hurricanes were immediately on his tail.

Satchell continued his assault with a fusillade which began at 300 yards range and ended at 50 yards, when the Hurricane had to break away quickly to avoid collision. It was soon after Satchell opened with that second burst of fire that the German rear gunner ceased to reply and Satchell saw no more tracer speeding in his direction. Generally, the defensive fire from the Ju88 had been ineffectual during the engagement, but when Satchell landed back at Leconfield he found that German bullets had been nearer than he had thought: his own propeller had been holed, but only once. His own gunfire, however, was more directed and more closely concentrated: in the second assault he saw his own tracers smacking home all around the centre of the fuselage of his quarry.

In each case, Satchell delivered his attacks from above and slightly behind the bomber, and in each instance Wolff attempted to meet the threat with steep left-hand turns which occasionally brought the momentary protection of cloud – but it was an uneven contest. It was in the second attack that Kruczinski and Rautenberg were wounded, the starboard engine was put out of action, the port engine was hit and the cockpit was set on fire. When Satchell was forced to break away to avoid collision, he observed his wing-man (Green 2) on the enemy's tail, '... but only for a very short period before the enemy aircraft went into clouds...' It was not seen again and was presumed to have crashed. This was confirmed later by telephone

When Wolff recognized the extent of his difficulties, it was too late to bale out and so he decided to jettison his bombs and find a place to set down his aircraft in order to save the wounded. The machine was on fire when it crash landed, but Wolff, Keller and Kruczinski managed to get clear. Local ARP reports state that the Junkers came down at 19.04 hours and crashed in flames in the third field to the south of Otteringham Baulk railway crossing, on the main road alongside Westlands plantation. It was still burning fiercely at 20.03 hours. The three Germans were captured and were placed in the charge of locally billeted men of the Cameron Highlanders but it was some time before Rautenberg was found: he had fallen out of the machine before it came to rest and was subsequently discovered, wounded and badly injured, in the opposite corner of the field.

Franz Wolff and Hugo Keller were slightly wounded as a result of the crash and spent some days in York Military Hospital. Wilhelm Rautenberg and Werner Kruczinski were taken initially to an army medical post at Patrington before being transferred to Hull Infirmary. However, both were so badly wounded they died there within two days of the crash, Rautenberg on the 21 August and Kruczinski the day after. They now lie in the German Military Cemetery at Cannock Chase, Staffordshire.

Claims made in a number of post-war accounts of this incident are at odds with claims made in contemporary documents. Francis K. Mason[28] claims that six Hurricanes (i.e. a whole Flight) took part in the interception, but the Operations Record Book of 302 (Polish) Squadron, as well as Satchell's combat report, refers only to Green Section(usually only three aircraft). *The Blitz, then and now. Vol. 1*[29] gives Patrington as the location of the crash but local ARP records in the Beverley Records Office give, what the writer has assumed to be, a precise location at Otteringham (two miles north-west of Patrington), a location confirmed by John Peskett,[30] the Air Ministry's AI1(g) investigator of the site in 1940. Peskett points out that 358 Anti-Aircraft Battery at Halsham(two miles north of Ottringham) also laid claim to this aircraft and he was asked by a Second Lieutenant Martin of the Battery to procure a tail swastika from the plane for the AA unit. *The Blitz, then and now*(1987) also wrongly gives Kruczinski the rank of Oberfeldwebel but the Luftwaffe Loss Lists (*Verlustliste*) at Deutsche-Dienststelle, Berlin, shows him to have been an Unteroffizier. Flying Officer Robinson's intelligence report shows that Rautenberg died on 21 August, although the entry in *The Blitz, then and now* (1987) suggests otherwise. It is of interest to note that, according to Robinson, Wolff also flew against Driffield on 15 August 1940.

21 August 1940 (east of Scarborough)

Aircraft:	Heinkel 111H-2	A1+?T	w/nr. ?	9./KG53
Crew:	Fw Otto Henkel	pilot	+	
	Hptm Georg Pfeiffer	observer	+	
	Gefr Fritz Nussbaum	gunner	+	
	Uffz Hans Kiauk	wireless op	+	
	Gefr Kurt Christ	gunner	+	

This aircraft of KG53 (*Condor Legion*), based at Lille-Nord, was shot down fifteen miles east of Scarborough at 16.25 hours by Pilot Officer E.A. Shipman in a Spitfire of Green Section, 41 Squadron, Catterick. All of the Heinkel crew were lost, including Hauptmann Georg Pfeiffer, who was the Staffelkapitän of 9./KG53

Ted Shipman was leading Green Section, which included Pilot Officer G.A. Langley and Sergeant Frank Usmar. The three Spitfires had taken off from

LEGION CONDOR

*Kampfgeschwader 53
(Legion Condor)*

the Squadron's forward base at Greatham(Hartlepool) at 16.08 hours with orders to patrol Scarborough at 20,000 feet. On arriving on his patrol line, Shipman was ordered to vector 110° at 9,000 feet. When the Spitfires were fifteen miles out to sea and flying through broken cloud Shipman was informed that one enemy aircraft was two miles ahead and on the same course. He saw it almost immediately and ordered 'Line Astern' before leading the fighters into the attack.

Shipman opened fire from dead astern at a range of 350 yards, closing to 200 yards and firing 1,444 rounds in one burst. There was some return fire from the raider's upper turret, but it was without any noticeable effect. The enemy aircraft, a Heinkel 111, did not attempt to evade during the attack, but immediately afterwards it began to dive and use the bottom fuselage gun, again without effect. The Heinkel's starboard fuel tank then caught fire, and the starboard engine began to emit white smoke. The bomber then commenced a turn to starboard, as if to return to land, but the turn developed into a steep spiral dive to starboard and the aircraft fell vertically into the sea. The starboard wing broke off just before the machine hit the water. Shortly afterwards, the Heinkel disappeared completely, leaving a patch of blazing fuel on the water. There was no trace of survivors.

Fifty years later, Ted Shipman recalled his encounter with the Heinkel:

'Over Scarborough I got behind a Heinkel. Gave it a real good dose. People write about the rattle of the guns, but with eight firing together it's never a rattle, more a great, sustained roar. His wing caught fire and down he went, spiralling. The thing I remember is that his rear gunner kept potting at me right to the last moment that he went in. I didn't jump for joy at it... I was never elated at a success... I knew that I had ended four or five men over Scarborough, but I didn't feel guilt. I knew it was them or us.'

It may well be that this particular raider dropped bombs in the area prior to being intercepted. *The Beverley Guardian* (24 August 1940) reported that on the 21st August an enemy plane suddenly appeared from the clouds and dropped a number of high explosive bombs on 'a coastal town'. A hotel, a shop and some residential property were damaged, and two fatal casualties occurred, both in the hotel. One of them, a soldier, was in his bath, and the other, a maid was working at the top of the building. It was reported that the raider was brought down, having been intercepted by British fighters as it attempted to get away over the sea. Apparently, it was the fourth raid that particular *'north-east coastal town...'* had suffered.

26-27 August 1940 (over Teesside?)

During an 'alert' which lasted for the period 22.25-03.45 hours there were a number of reports from searchlight units and anti-aircraft batteries that parachute troops were dropping in the Billingham area and also on the south side of the river Tees. Billingham Parish Church bells rang out the alarm and one gun site actually sent out a patrol to round up parachutists allegedly seen dropping near the battery – but they found none. During the air raid, the Tees anti-aircraft batteries fired a total of 503 rounds and were praised for their harassing and accurate fire, which was maintained during continuous raiding and which resulted in the absence of bombing. The Tees batteries claimed a direct hit on one aircraft and claimed the destruction of two others. An unidentified air raid summary in the writer's possession refers to the bombing of West Hartlepool that night, when the town was lit up by flares and an '...enemy plane was seen falling into the sea on fire...' It was believed that one or two parachutists may have baled out of wrecked enemy aircraft and thereafter shell puffs in searchlight beams became additional 'parachute troops'. The alarm was false. To date, the writer has no other information relating to the enemy aircraft allegedly shot down.

26 September 1940 (off Yorkshire coast)?

On 27 September 1940 the Middlesbrough *North-Eastern Evening Gazette* reported that an enemy aircraft had been shot down after raiding Whitby and Skinningrove. A Spitfire was credited with the 'kill'. However, to date the writer has found no further details of this claim.

27 October 1940 (Duggleby, near Malton)

Aircraft:	Junkers 88A-5	5J+ER	w/nr. 6129	7./KG4
Crew:	Oblt Friedrich Franz Podbielski	pilot	pow	
	Uffz Hans Heier	observer	pow	
	Uffz Karl von Kidrowski	wireless/op	pow	
	Uffz Oskar Piontek	gunner	+	

In the late afternoon and early evening of Sunday, 27 October 1940, German aircraft launched a series of attacks on aerodromes in East Anglia, Lancashire and Yorkshire. A number of those were in the Malton area: Linton-on-Ouse, Catfoss, Leconfield and Driffield. The streets of Beverley were machine-gunned at 18.10 hours and three people suffered slight wounds in North Bar. RAF Leconfield was bombed eight minutes later but suffered minor damage, although a Polish airman is thought to have been seriously injured. Three Junkers 88s delivered a low-level attack on Driffield at 18.00 hours, when a number of small calibre bombs were dropped and the aerodrome buildings were machine-gunned. However, no casualties resulted and practically no damage was done. Seconds after the attack, two of the bombers flew northwards and passed

Ju88 (5J+ER) of 7./KG4 under guard at Duggleby, near Malton, October 1940.
[By courtesy of Northern Echo].

close to a searchlight site of 4 Troop, 411 Battery, 54 Searchlight Regt. RA(TA), which was located on the A.166 at Fimber Field Farm, between the East Yorkshire villages of Fridaythorpe and Wetwang,.

In October 1940, Stockton-born Matt Young was a Lewis Gunner with 'D' Section, 411 Battery. It was his job to defend the searchlight site in the event of air attack. On a clear day, the men at Fimber could see the aerodrome at Driffield from their raised position on the Wolds. But in the early evening of 27 October 1940, the airfield was masked by haze.

Fifty-two years later, Matt recalled that:

'Sergeant Fraser had just arrived with the ration wagon. He was on site when we heard the bombs dropping at Driffield aerodrome. We couldn't see anything because of the haze, but I immediately went to the gun position and we got orders from HQ at Huttons Ambo that we could engage the enemy - but at first we couldn't see anything.'

Then two Ju88s gradually emerged from the haze. They were in loose formation and not flying very high. The bombers 'flew in almost a straight line from Driffield; straight up the hillside...' towards the

Lewis Gun crew of No. 4 Troop, 411 Battery. 54 Searchlight Regt, RA (TA) at Weston Grange, near Malton. L-R: Lance Bombardier 'Teddy' Bear, Gunner Fred Bycroft, Gunner David Evans [via David Evans]

searchlight position. As they drew near, Matt felt the urge to shoot but Fraser refused permission on the grounds that 'they might fire back' and made Matt wait for a safer opportunity.

Matt Young, Lewis Gunner, 1940 [Matt Young]

> *'Just before they reached us, they started to bank to starboard, as if making for the coast. When they were about halfway round, he let me fire. I set the gun going, followed my tracers and fired the full pan of forty-seven rounds into the port engine of the one nearest me. They got round with their tails towards us and I put on another pan and fired again, but I don't know if it did any good.'*

Civilian eyewitnesses at Fridaythorpe later claimed that one of the bombers 'veered off' as a consequence of the gunfire. Shortly

The Officer Commanding,
No_4._Troop._411_Battery.

     I am to advise you that the A.A.Command have admitted the
following claim :-
    Category 1 27th Oct. 40. 1 Aircraft by 411 Bty shared by 38 Lt.A.A.
(Destroyed).   Regt., Driffield.

    Category 1 is that category in which all enemy aircraft known
to be destroyed are placed. The detachment concerned is, of course
No.4/5, Detachment Commander 4446794 L/Sgt Moody A.
    I wish to convey my congratulations to all concerned in this
excellent achievment and in particular to congratulate 4453740 Gnr
Young M who was No.1. on the gun.
    I am particularly impressed by the fact that your No.4/5
Detachment had thought out and selected in advance the man judged
most suitable to act as No.1. on the gun in the event of attack by
low flying enemy aircraft, and it is good to know that such forethought
has been rewarded.
    Sgt. Fraser's command of the situation was, as was well to be
expected, of the highest order and No.2. on the gun No 4453898 Gnr
Crowe A.H. also deserves special mention.
    I enclose sufficient copies of this letter for you to issue
personally to the men concerned.
    Copies of this letter have also been sent to O.C.s. All Troops
who should arrange to circulate such copies round their Detachments.

Hutton Hall,
Malton.
7.11.40.
                      Captain,
                Commanding 411 Bty.,
      54th Searchlight Regiment R.A.,T.A.

No.4.Troop 5 copies.
Nos.1,2&3 Troops 1 copy each.
File 1 copy.

Matt Young's commendation. [Matt Young]

afterwards, Junkers 88 5J+ER of 7./KG4 crash-landed at Manor Farm,
Duggleby, near Malton, and came to rest alongside the ancient barrow of
'Duggleby Howe'. The rear gunner, Oskar Piontek, was the only casualty.
It is not clear whether he was thrown out of the machine on impact or
whether he jumped out before the aircraft came to rest, but when he was
found under the tail it was clear that he was badly wounded. He was freed
by his Luftwaffe crew mates and members of the local Home Guard
working together to help a fellow human being. Piontek subsequently
died from his injuries and now lies in the German Military Cemetery at
Cannock Chase.

    The demise of the Junkers was subsequently attributed to 411 Battery
in general, and to Matt Young in particular, and both received
commendations from Command HQ. However, a detachment of 38
Light Anti-Aircraft Regt, employed in the defence of Driffield
aerodrome, also claimed the Junkers as theirs. In the enquiry that
followed, it was decided that both claimants should share the victory.

    However, there is a twist to this tale. This particular Ju88 had been
ordered to attack Linton-on-Ouse – not Driffield – and its navigator,

Hans Heier, firmly believes that Linton was the target they bombed. Certainly, three Ju88s struck at Linton that evening, at about the same time as the raid on Driffield. And when one of them made a low-level strafing run over Linton it was, according to the Station's Operations' Record Book , given '...*such a hot reception that it veered off to the north..and may have been the one that was brought down afterwards...* (at Duggleby)'

When the writer first researched this incident for publication in *Luftwaffe over the North* a number of eyewitnesses stated that they had seen the 'Duggleby' Junkers in difficulties over the villages of Wharram-le Street, North Grimston and Settrington shortly before it crashed. The flight across these villages by the crippled bomber fitted comfortably with Matt Young's account and his subsequent commendation. However, in August 1998, seventy-year old John Wilson, of Slingsby, offered an account that sheds more light on the likelihood of the Linton-on-Ouse scenario.

In October 1940, he was living at North Ings Farm, between Terrington and Sheriff Hutton, where there was a searchlight site. He recalls that in the late afternoon of 27 October 1940:

'*I saw three German aeroplanes going over and heading towards Easingwold. They weren't very high. Later, about five o'clock, one came back. I was standing near the gate to the searchlight site, near to some soldiers who were on guard duty. The plane was very low. If I'd had a stick long enough, I could've touched it. Its left engine was on fire and the plane had to rise to get over the trees. As I recall, the right-hand engine had stopped and the left one was still going – but it was on fire. I told the men it was a German, but they didn't believe me. It flew over Terrington and towards Malton. Then we heard that it crashed at Duggleby.*'

John Wilson's account puts the flight path of the crippled Ju88 further west – nearer to Linton but still in line with North Grimston and Settrington – and increases the likelihood that it was damaged over Linton-on-Ouse and passed nowhere near Fimber Field Farm. Matt Young's 'victim' seems to have got away. *The Blitz, then and now. Vol.2* [31] does attribute the 'kill' to anti-aircraft units at Linton-on-Ouse aerodrome, but in 1993 the available evidence pointed in Matt Young's favour.

The raid on Linton caused no casualties to personnel, but a limited amount of damage was done to the aerodrome itself. The gunners there were not given a 'share' of the Junkers.

27-28 October 1940 (off Redcar – or the Humber?)

Aircraft:	Junkers 88A-1	5J+HS	w/nr. 6048	8./KG4
Crew:	Oblt Dietrich Marwitz	pilot	missing	
	Obfw Werner Mehrbach	observer	missing	
	Gefr Karl Herold	wireless op	missing	
	Uffz Hubert Schmitz	gunner	missing	

During the night of 27-28th October 1940, twenty-nine hostile raids were plotted in the Tees area. Most of these enemy aircraft were operating out to sea, perhaps mine-laying or searching for a convoy, but there were also unconfirmed reports of bombs dropping near the mouth of the Tees and near Skinningrove Ironworks.

There was anti-aircraft fire from the Tees guns at 18.55 hours, 21.17 hours, 22.30 hours, 23.25 hours, 23.34 hours, 00.06 hours, 00.13 hours, and 00.20 hours – mostly from batteries nearest the mouth of the river, and it was aimed at raiders flying at heights ranging from 5,000 – 15,500 feet. It is claimed that one hostile aircraft was at 9,000 feet when it was hit by the Tees 'K' site AA battery (located at military map ref. 025428) and was seen to explode and crash into the sea off the Tees mouth at 00.25 hours on 28th October.

There seems to be little doubt that a hostile aircraft did crash in the area that night. 27 October was the twenty-first birthday of Violet Alexander (née Thorpe), of Gosforth Terrace, Redcar, and she remembers that a direct hit was scored on a raider that night, although she claims that it crashed somewhere off the town's pier. The incident was reported in the *North Eastern Evening Gazette* on 28 October 1940:

> *'One enemy machine believed to have been brought down off NE coast during several air raids last night and early today. AA batteries put up the heaviest barrage heard so far in the area. The machine was heard flying out to sea. Suddenly there was a brilliant red glow in the sky, followed by a terrific explosion which wrecked windows in the coast town... . Then there was silence.'*

It is not known for certain that the Ju88 (5J+HS) of 8./KG4 listed above is the aircraft which was shot down off Redcar but this aircraft failed to return from a mine-laying sortie over England that night and is believed to have been shot down by anti-aircraft fire. The Luftwaffe Loss Lists (*Verlustliste*) at the Deutsche-Dienststelle, Berlin, state that this crew was lost while on operations '...mine-laying in the Humber estuary. Aircraft sent wireless message – ditching in sea...'. Reference to the Humber puts 5J+HS in the general area of Teesside, while references to AA fire and to ditching provide additional similarities to the Redcar example. Marwitz was the Staffelkapitän of 8./KG4.

1 November 1940 (Glaisdale Head, near Whitby)

Aircraft:	Junkers 88A-1	4D+TS[32]	w/nr. 7089	8./KG30
Crew:	Fw Wilhelm Wowereit	pilot	+	
	Obfw Hans Schulte-Mäter	observer	+	
	Uffz Alfred Rodermond	wireless op	+	
	Uffz Gerhard Pohling	gunner	+	

On 14 December 1994, two officials of the Thornaby-on-Tees branch of the Royal British Legion laid a wreath on the grave of a Luftwaffe airman, Unteroffizier. Gerhard Pohling, in the town's Acklam Road Cemetery. The tribute, which has been carried out bi-annually since 1948, is one of only twenty similar tributes nationwide requested by the German War Graves Commission on behalf of relatives and is usually placed on the 20 December, the anniversary of Pohling's birthday in 1914.

Unteroffizier Gerhard Pohling was the air gunner of Junkers 88 4D+TS who was killed when his aircraft crashed into the hillside at Glaisdale Head, thirteen miles west of Whitby, in the early evening of Friday, 1 November 1940. The Junkers was one of five German bombers destroyed over this country during the night of 1-2 November 1940, the other four evidently having London as their target.

The bomber belonged to 8./KG30. It had set out from its base at Gilze-Rijen (Holland) and apparently was en-route to attack the RAF aerodrome at Linton-on-Ouse[33] when it struck high ground at the head of the dale and burst into flames. Pieces of the plane were strewn over a wide area.

Investigators from the Air Ministry Intelligence Branch [AI1(g)] who examined the site identified the engines as Jumo 211Bs and found traces of several MG.15 machine guns; two 250kg bombs and ten 50kg bombs were also found unexploded near wreckage. The investigators concluded that the cause of the crash was not certain – and this inconclusive verdict appears to have given rise to a measure of speculation in the local area.

Military personnel alongside the burnt out wreckage of the Ju88 (4D+TS) of 8/KG30, that crashed at Glaisdale Head, near Whitby, in the early evening of 1 November, 1940 [Author's collection]

The crew of Ju88 4D+TS (w/nr. 7089) were killed when their aircraft crashed at Glaisdale Head, near Whitby, on 1 November 1940. They were buried in Thornaby's Acklam Road cemetery, where they still lie. [Trevor Smith]

The *North-Eastern Evening Gazette* (2 November 1940) suggested an element of official secrecy regarding the cause when it stated that:

'...It would not be wise to give details of the manner in which the machine was destroyed, but there is reason to believe that our successes were the result of new methods of defence which were forecast last week'.

Precisely what those 'new methods' were have yet to be determined by this writer. The *Whitby Gazette* (2 November 1940) claimed that:

'Ground defences opened fire, and it is thought that the machine was hit, and the pilot killed or severely injured, which would account for the plane crashing...'

Some contemporary local reports claim that the aircraft was struck by ground fire shortly after it crossed the coast near Whitby. Others maintain that the raider flew low up the Glaisdale valley in misty conditions and had insufficient altitude to clear the high ground at the head of the dale. It is interesting to note that the War Diary of 43 AA Brigade[34] records that between 14.10-14.15 hours Skinningrove ironworks was bombed and gunned by a single raider and that two high-explosives fell on the railway line near the Talbot furnace, making craters 30ft across and 20ft deep. Six people suffered minor injuries in the raid, which also caused some damage to the track and slight damage to buildings. The War Diary also records that the raider was engaged by light machinegun defences at the works. If there is any connection between Ju88 (4D+TS) and the bombing, it might well be that the cause of the crash was a combination of gunfire and low flying.

The crew of four were killed. One man was found dead near the wreckage on Friday night but the onset of darkness meant that the bodies of the remaining crew members were not recovered until dawn the next day. One was wearing a partly opened parachute and appeared to have been dragged by the plane or had baled out and had hit the ground before his parachute had fully deployed. The other two had been thrown from the machine. Strangely, when the bodies of the crew were found it was noted that all were barefooted, which suggests that the fliers thought that they were over the sea and that they knew they were coming down. If that were the case then the possible causes of the crash which are given above may not be true at all. The average age of the crew was twenty-three. They were all buried with full military honours at Acklam Road Cemetery, where they still lie.

NOTES

1 For a full account of this incident see Bill Norman: *Luftwaffe over the North*, Leo Cooper/Pen & Sword. 1993. pp20-27.
2 1/406 was in the process of changing to 1/506. Hence the 1/506 coding S4+EH.
3 *The Blitz, then and now vol.1*(ed. W.G. Ramsay) Battle of Britain Prints International. 1987. p40 disputes this and shows S4+EH as having crashed into the sea five miles east of Spurn Head and S4+GH and S4+DH as having come down in the Wash.
4 The Luftwaffe Loss Returns give the location as being 12 miles off the English coast.
5 Hector Bolitho: *Combat Report, the story of a fighter pilot*. Batsford. 1942 p45.
6 For a full account of this incident see Bill Norman: op.cit. pp28-37.
7 A full account of this incident is given in Bill Norman op.cit. pp38-47.
8 Karl Gunderlach: *Kampfgeschwader' General Wever' 4*, Motorbuch Verlag Stuttgart . 1978. p86.
9 Francis K. Mason: *Battle over Britain*, Aston Publications. 1990. p101.
10 In Bill Norman op,cit pp52-55.
11 See *Broken Eagles.2 : Northumberland & Durham* (to be published 2002).
12 Francis K. Mason: op.cit. p103.
13 Hugh Dundas: *Flying Start*, Stanley Paul. 1988. pp30-31.
14 *Bridlington Chronicle*, 12 July 1940.
15 Humphrey Wynn(ed): *Fighter Pilot - a self portrait by George Barclay* (1976) pp36-37.
16 Francis K. Mason: op. cit. p113.
17 Karl Gunderlach op.cit. p90.
18 Based on Rudi Schmidt: *Actung-Torpedos Los!: der stratigische und operative Einsätze des Kampfgeschwader 26*. Bernard & Graefe Verlag. Koblenz 1991. pp66-68.
19 1 Troop, 414 Searchlight Battery (55 Regt. TA 2/5 DLI).
20 See Bill Norman: op.cit. pp57-59 for a full account of this incident.
21 Francis K. Mason.: op.cit p209.
22 ibid.
23 Held by Archives Dept. RAF Museum, Hendon.
24 WO166/2254 in Public Record Office.
25 Francis K. Mason: op.cit. p216.
26 Hans Nauta, contributor to the Internet Luftwaffe Discussion Group *12 O'Clock High* (2 May 2000)
27 *The Blitz,then and now. Vol.1* 1987. p221 claims that Wolff's target was the Coastal Command aerodrome at Thornaby(Teesside).
28 Francis K. Mason: op.cit. pp229-230.
29 *The Blitz,then and now. Vol.1*. ibid.
30 S. John Peskett: *Strange Intelligence*. Robert Hale. 1981. pp94-95.
31 *The Blitz,then and now. Vol.2* 1988.pp203.
32 AI1(k) Report No.847/1940 (File AIR40/2401) in Public Records Office gives the code as 5J+TS (i.e.8./KG4), which was deduced from papers found in the wreck. The discrepancy is, perhaps, explained by the fact that III./KG4 (of which 8./KG4 was part) was re-designated III./KG30 on 15 October 1940.
33 This according to the Luftwaffe Loss Returns and the Luftwaffe *Verlustliste. The Blitz, then and now vol.2*.1988. gives Church Fenton as the target.
34 WO166/2280 in Public Records Office.

2

CHANGE OF DIRECTION
(1941)

When the possibility of an early victory against Britain faded in the early months of 1941, the Luftwaffe Operations Staff placed the emphasis on blockade and devoted more attention to attacking Britain's maritime trade, though the night assaults on the mainland continued until May 1941. Major destructive raids were launched against Britain's principal ports in the south, west, and north-west of England, as well as south-west Scotland and these continued into May.

Things were somewhat quieter in the Yorkshire area where anti-shipping operations, particularly the mining of coastal shipping lanes, remained the principal activity. This was interspersed with scattered bombing raids throughout the county, with areas near to the coast tending to receive most attention. February saw a slight quickening of raid activity over the north, with accelerated mining operations off the coast and the bombing of Hull on three separate occasions in the last week of the month. However, the effects of the latter were minimized by the presence of cloud which impeded the raiders' visibility over the target area. March brought an increase in the scale of Luftwaffe operations over the north, with two damaging attacks on Hull and one on Sheffield (by 117 aircraft) in the last two weeks of the month, while scattered small-scale raid activity occurred over a wide area of the county. In April 1941, the nation's principal ports saw some of the heaviest bombing of the war to date but there was no activity in the north to match the ferocity of the assaults occurring elsewhere. However, attacks on coastal shipping were stepped up and bombs regularly exploded in the coastal strip some twenty miles wide from the Humber to the Tees. Hull experienced small-scale raids on six separate occasions in April, while other coastal centres, including Middlesbrough, East Cleveland, Whitby, and Bridlington, all received low-key attacks at various times. Further inland, bombs also fell on Masham, the York area, Market Rasen, Driffield and Sheffield but all were relatively inconsequential in their effects.

The highly destructive attacks on the nation's principal ports continued until mid-May. In Yorkshire, unfortunate Hull remained the Luftwaffe's principal target, the port being bombed on no less than seven separate occasions, including two major raids on consecutive nights in the second week of the month. Sheffield also felt the Luftwaffe's wrath with a sizeable raid at about the same time. After that, the frequency and severity of Luftwaffe operations over Britain fell away markedly, for Hitler was thinking of Russia and forces were withdrawn from the West for operations on the Eastern Front.

In June 1941, the war against this country was virtually put on hold when Germany embarked on a 'short' pre-emptive campaign against Russia to remove, what the German High Command perceived as, the potential threat to Germany's back door. The invasion of Russia had a marked effect on the Luftwaffe's ability to wage war against Britain because the majority of its frontline aircraft were transferred eastwards for the Russian campaign, leaving the remaining forces in the West seriously weakened. *Luftflotte 2* moved its main operations from the Low Countries to the east and *Luftflotte 3* – which had itself lost units to the invasion force – was left to fill the gap. Further north, *Luftflotte 5* was forced to extend its boundaries eastwards to include Finland, while much further to the south *Fliegerkorps X* was endeavouring to meet air requirements in the Mediterranean and North Africa. In addition to all of this, the RAF was increasing its bombing operations over Germany, thus making it necessary for the Luftwaffe to increasingly allocate limited resources to home defence.

The months that followed June saw scattered attacks continuing over the northern region. These were usually carried out by isolated raiders, although two raids on luckless Hull in July resulted in a total of fifty persons killed, with a further eleven persons suffering the same fate in a further attack four weeks later. By August 1941, nearly eighty per cent of the Luftwaffe's aircraft were operating against Russia and its strike capabilities in the West had been severely curtailed.

After the move eastwards, the units bearing the brunt of operations in the West were KG30 (by then relocated from Scandinavia to Holland and France) and KG2, both of *Luftflotte 3*. However, those limited forces ranged against Britain were reduced even further towards the end of 1941 when the anti-shipping focus shifted towards attacks on the Arctic convoys supplying Russia, and units of KG30 were assigned to that purpose and moved to Norway. In effect, this left KG2 as virtually the only operational bomber unit carrying the war to Britain – and with aircraft resources roughly equivalent to no more than two or three RAF squadrons.

In spite of these restrictions, *Luftflotte 3* was expected to continue the fight against Britain's industrial centres, as well as maintaining operations against shipping and ports. To this end, they were allocated the latest bombers, including the Do217 and the most recent versions of the up-dated Ju88, but neither had the attacking capacity or the numbers equal to the task. Increasingly, *Luftflotte 3* could mount attacks on Britain only by drawing on crews under training and by 'borrowing' crews from other theatres of operations.

As mentioned earlier, from its inception, the Luftwaffe air arm had been developed as a tactical tool of the German army. That strategy had worked well until the summer of 1940, when the Battle of Britain proved to be a major setback. By 1941, the strategic situation had changed further and the German Air Force, fighting on so many fronts, found that its additional commitments far outweighed its operational resources. It could no longer concentrate the bulk of its forces to support a single campaign and this had implications for the war against the British mainland. In 1944, while reviewing Luftwaffe operations against England in the preceding three years, Hauptmann Otto Bechtle pointed out that:

'The air war against England as conducted after the beginning of the campaign against Russia was a struggle against superior forces, i.e. against a superior, highly-developed, constantly strengthened and improved defence. Tasks that were formerly carried out by 600 bombers had to be achieved by 60, which was the average daily operational strength of all bomber units in the West in 1942-43.'[1]

NOTES

1 Hptmn Otto Bechtle (1944): *Luftwaffe operations against England, their tactics and deductions, 1940-43*, Document 2390 Tin 38 Imperial War Museum.

Losses
January 1941 - December 1941

2 January 1941 (Humber estuary)
The Luftwaffe Loss Reports record that He111P (w/nr.2690) of 1./KG4 suffered twenty per cent damage and Unteroffizier Alois Kolb (mechanic) was wounded in an engagement over the Humber. The cause of the damage is not stated.

9 February 1941 (Humber)

Aircraft:	Junkers 88A-5	4D+FM	w/nr 8102	4./KG30
Crew:	Uffz Hans Weber	pilot	missing	
	Uffz Erich Latzel	w/operator	missing	
	Uffz. Kurt Rosa-Maier	gunner	missing	
	Uffz. Willi Kruse	mechanic	missing	

The Luftwaffe Loss Reports record that this aircraft failed to return from an operation to the Humber and cites combat with fighter aircraft as being the cause of the loss. The location of the loss is not given.

10 February 1941 (off the Humber)
Two crews of the newly-formed 255 Squadron, Kirton-in-Lindsey (equipped with Boulton-Paul Defiant aircraft) were awarded 'probable' victories on the night of 10 February 1941. The Squadron Operations Record Book shows that Flight Lieutenant Richard Trousdale and his gunner (believed to have been Sergeant Chunn) had an encounter with a Heinkel 111 six miles east of Spurn Head at 22.58 hours and that Pilot Officer Roger Hall (with gunner, Sergeant H.D.F. Fitzsimmons) had combat with an He111 eight miles east of the Humber estuary at 23.14 hours. These were accepted as the Squadron's first victories but examination of the Luftwaffe Loss Returns reveal no details of aircraft that might fit the stated circumstances.

Pilot Officer Hall's combat report reveals that he had taken off at 22.28 hours and had initially been directed north of Spurn Head, where enemy aircraft were operating. He was at 8,000 feet and flying south towards the Humber when he saw an eastward-bound Heinkel 111 1,000 feet below him and silhouetted against the sea. Hall dived in a starboard turn that took him below and in front of the bomber. On that first pass, Fitzsimmons managed a short burst into the starboard beam of the enemy machine. On his second approach, Hall once again passed below and in front of the Heinkel, his gunner this time managing a longer burst of gun-fire that found the underside of the raider's forward fuselage.

When the Defiant went in for the third time, Fitzsimmons' bullets were seen to strike the port side of the front section of the target. The Heinkel was descending all the time during the engagement and was down to 3,500 feet when Hall made his third and final pass. At no time did he witness any response from the enemy gunners but Fitzsimmons did observe a blue flash, which he thought might have been tracer or an explosion, which momentarily blinded him. Whatever it was, it did not damage the Defiant. The enemy aircraft was last seen diving towards the sea at an estimated 300mph and was eventually lost from view in the sea haze. Hall and Fitzsimmons were awarded a 'probable', the combat report registering the fate of the Heinkel as 'inconclusive'.

Roger Hall subsequently told of his encounter with the Heinkel in his highly readable book *Clouds of Fear*[1]. The account, which appears below, provides an interesting comparison with Hall's first report of the combat.

'We had been orbitting for almost an hour without seeing anything, when quite suddenly, I caught sight, from the corner of my eye, of a Heinkel 111 gliding silently and apparently furtively towards the coast and out to sea beneath us... . The Heinkel was apparently unaware of our existence as we approached it from above, for it continued on its course out to sea. We came down behind it and on its port side, but we were going much too fast and overshot it. We wanted to get in front of it and sit in close formation with it so that our guns could fire backwards into the cockpit. Having overshot the Heinkel, I pulled out sharply to port into a steep turn trying to absorb some of our speed in doing so. We pulled round into a starboard turn after this and came into the bomber once more. I felt certain that we should have been seen by the bomber's crew by now but it still persisted on its original course, and as we came in underneath and in front of it, we got no fire from its guns. We were about eight miles out to sea when I gave Fitz the order to fire.

'Our aircraft shuddered slightly as Fritz opened up on the bomber with the four turret guns pointing directly backwards and firing up at the bomber's cockpit from a range of little more than twenty yards. I looked over my shoulder as he fired and saw the great Heinkel sitting gracefully like a bird of prey above us as though quite stationary. I could see our bullets hitting the bomber's centre section from underneath and the shots were like small dancing sparks creeping forwards up to the cockpit of the enemy machine. The flashes from our own guns were a luminous purple in the moonlight and their reflections cast their light back on to the perspex of the gun-turret.

'For what seemed an age Fitz continued to pour his shots into the front part of the Heinkel without anything seeming to happen. Then quite suddenly but quite slowly the huge aircraft started to roll on to its starboard wingtip, like a fighter in slow motion; very gracefully, and in a lazy but

79

dignified way. The roll persisted beyond the vertical and I pulled our own machine out of the way for fear that it might fall on to us. When the Heinkel had got just beyond the vertical it started to dive and pull away to starboard and away from us, but there was no sign of fire about it at all. I think we had managed to kill the pilot for our bullets had pierced the perspex of the cockpit. We followed the bomber into its dive and closed in for another attack as it went down. We came up on its port quarter and moved in on it from a distance of fifty yards or so but in a vertical attitude. We were both going down towards the sea now and at a considerable speed. Fitz opened fire again at the bomber and I told him to aim at the engines. He did so and shortly after he had opened fire , the port engine of the bomber caught fire.

'I was wondering what the crew of the bomber were doing or whether they were all dead. Perhaps they had thought themselves quite safe once they had crossed the English coast on their way home, and had been pulling cigarettes out and lighting up when we attacked them. I'm certain that their front gunner was not at his post when we came in at them. The port engine of the bomber was now beginning to burn fiercely and the flames from it were lighting up the remainder of the machine, making its black crosses conspicuous. Beneath us was the top of a low bank of cumulus and it looked as though the bomber was going into it. I told Fitz to give it another burst before it went into the cloud and we pulled in a bit closer. As we did so a small explosion occurred somewhere in the region of its port engine nacelle and flame and pieces of incandescent metal flew towards us and threatened to hit us. I kept the Defiant a fair distance from the bomber after this and Fritz opened fire from where we were. The bomber was now lower and nearer to the cumulus. Fire was streaming from almost the entire machine and the light from it illuminated the moonlit cloudbank beneath it, turning it a dull orange colour and giving a fantastic and cruel sort beauty to the whole scene. I was pondering this scene in a detached sort of way when, without warning, the whole vault of the night sky burst into light. There was a gargantuan explosion and the very firmament seemed to reverberate about us as the bomber disappeared and dissolved itself into a gigantic white-hot cloud of fire which turned night into day. The stars in their courses became a dull red in the heavens and the cumulus beneath became a vivid white – a ghostly white, superb in its awesome beauty. The Defiant was hurled by some enormous shock wave out of its course, like a leaf in the wind.

'For a few helpless seconds I was unable to unfasten my gaze from the scene. The cloud of fire spewed forth incandescent pieces of material trailing spirals of darkened smoke behind them. It descended slowly towards the top of the cumulus and as it approached the cloud top glowed a burning yellow. Then the blackened body of the aircraft's fuselage with oily smoke *coming from it, could be seen against the whiteness of the cloud as the remains of the machine disappeared into it.... When it had gone, the night about us seemed horribly dark, and for a moment I experienced a feeling of utter horror and loneliness and my hands were shaking and my knees trembling.... Ours had been the first machine shot down in the squadron's short history.'*

Given that Roger Hall's combat report makes no mention of the enemy machine being on fire or exploding – both of which are noteworthy occurrences which would have strengthened his claim – one is tempted to think that the account which appears in his book relates to a different incident altogether.

13 March 1941

The Luftwaffe Loss Reports show that on 13 March 1941 a Do17z2 (w/nr.4248 and coded U5+DA) of Stab/KG2 failed to return from operations against Hull. The crew, Feldwebel Rückner (pilot), Oberleutnant Hans von. Kieser(observer), Feldwebel Heinz Genehr (wireless/op) and Leutnant. Benno Meyer(mechanic), were lost. This aircraft was shot down by J.R.D. Braham(with Sergeant Ross) in a Beaufighter Mk.1 of 29 Squadron, Wellingore(Lincs) and crashed into the sea off Skegness. Brabham recounts the incident in his book *Scramble* (Kimber 1985).

30 March 1941 (Barnaby Moor, Teesside)

Aircraft:	Junkers 88A	4U+GH	w/nr 0115	1(F)/123
Crew:	Lt Wolfgang Schlott	pilot	+	
	Lt Otto Meingold	observer	+	
	Fw Willi Schmigale	wireless op	+	
	Uffz Hans Steigerwald	gunner	+	

This Ju88A of 1/*Aufklärungsgruppe 123*, [1(F)/123] was on an armed photo-reconnaissance sortie to Manchester when it was intercepted over south Durham by two Spitfires, flown by Flight Lieutenant Tony Lovell and Pilot Officer Archie Winskill, of 41 Squadron, Catterick. They had been scrambled at 14.50 hours with orders to patrol Seaham Harbour. An incoming raider had been plotted approaching the English coast north of Sunderland; if it swung south, Lovell and Winskill would be well placed to intercept it.

While daylight incursions over the British coast were always dangerous – and the raiders would have been well aware of the risks – perhaps Schlott and his crew felt reasonably safe at their altitude of 25,000 feet. With the 6/10 cloud layer 18,000 feet below providing an occasional back-cloth of brilliant white against which any interceptors might be

The wreckage of Junkers 88 (4U + GH) of 1. (F)/123, which crashed on Eston Hills, 30 March 1941, being inspected by personnel from 41 (Spitfire) Squadron, Catterick. [Author's collection].

spotted – and with their aircraft's light blue undersides blending in totally with the sky above – the combination of height and camouflage might well have given grounds for optimism.

When Lovell and Winskill emerged from cloud at 7,000 feet and into clear blue sky, they could not see the Junkers. Five minutes later, when they had climbed to 17,000 feet, they spotted a vapour trail some 7,000 feet above them, to the left of their position and moving south. The Spitfires changed course and, in Lovell's words, '...climbed flat out in a climbing turn and followed the trail, which hid us very effectively...'. So

A manufacturer's plate taken from Ju.88 (4U+GH) of 1 (F)/123. [Author's collection].

effective was that particular camouflage that the Spitfires were able to close to within 250 yards of their quarry. Then Lovell elected to execute an attack with a three-second burst of machine-gun fire which shot away pieces of the bomber before it dived away steeply towards cloud with the fighters in pursuit.

When the trio had weaved through the cloud they were over Redcar and observers in the town might well have expected the Ju88 to crash there, given that its pursuers were close behind and '...pumping terrific bursts of gunfire into him...'. Minutes later, eyewitnesses in Normanby saw the bomber '...flying over the hills from the direction of Middlesbrough - but then it suddenly dropped...' and the chase was over. The Junkers drove deep into the peat on Barnaby Moor, Eston Hills (at military ref. V0537), its explosive impact creating a huge crater, scattering wreckage over a 400-yard radius and obliterating the three occupants.

The fourth member of the crew, the ventral gunner, Hans Steigerwald, had taken to his parachute only moments before, and at about the same time as his plane struck the moor, the gunner broke through the cloud which hung over the woodlands flanking Flatts Lane, perhaps a mile to the west of the crash site. But his luck was out. The parachute on which he had pinned his hopes had not deployed properly: it was streaming above him like a long ribbon when he crashed to his death among the trees. He was buried in Acklam Road Cemetery, Thornaby-on-Tees, where he still lies.[2]

1 April 1941
The War Diary of 43 AA Brigade[3] records that at 15.15 hours on 1 April 1941 a lone He111 was engaged by 40mm anti-aircraft fire at RAF Leeming and was hit in the wing. The enemy machine was also engaged by the Tees heavy anti-aircraft guns and by unrotated projectiles ('Z' guns) as it made its way out to sea. It is not known whether the aircraft suffered critical damage.

8 April 1941 (off Humber?)

Aircraft:	Junkers 88A-5	4D+KK	w/nr 0541	2./KG30
Crew:	Uffz Helmut Öwich	pilot	missing	
	Gefr Hans Holaseck	observer	missing	
	Gefr Sebastian Daigele	wireless op	missing	
	Gefr Werner Lück	gunner	missing	

The Luftwaffe Loss Returns for 8 April 1941 show that this aircraft ditched east of the Humber (exact location not stated) due to engine problems.

15-16 April 1941 (Huby, near York)

Aircraft:	Heinkel 111H-5		A1+AL	w/nr 9370	3./KG53
Crew:	Fw Karl Menzel	pilot	pow		
	Hptm Werner Höring	–	pow		
	Obfw Rudolf Lackner	observer	pow		
	Uffz Oskar Seltmann	wireless op	pow		
	Fw Alfons Wächter	mechanic	pow		

This aircraft, loaded with one 1,000kg bomb and 700 incendiary bombs, was one of four belonging to 3./KG53 targeted on port installations at Belfast on the night of 15-16 April 1941. *The Blitz, then and now vol.2* (1988) claims that after crossing in over Flamborough Head, the aircraft developed engine trouble over Kirby Stephen, Cumbria, and the crew decided to abort the mission. The Heinkel was over Ripon on its return flight when its starboard engine burst into flames. All of the crew, including Werner Höring, the Staffelkapitän, baled out after jettisoning the 1,000kg bomb. A1+AL came to earth at Bull Lane Bridge, Huby, at 02.00hours on 16 April; its crew landing close by. (see *Eye Witness* below).

EYE WITNESS
Digging out a wartime memory

Strensall-resident Gerald Inns has been interested in historical aviation ever since he was a schoolboy during the last war. In 1941 he saw the He111 of 3./KG53 come down at Huby. According to Gerald, it was shot down by Bofors guns defending the aerodrome at Linton-on-Ouse and crashed at Bull Lane Bridge, Huby, at 02.00 hours on 16 April 1941, making a deep crater and scattering wreckage over a wide area. He recalls that:

'It was like a gigantic Catherine wheel. On fire. Looping round and round. Engines revving and out of control. The five members of the crew baled out and were arrested by our village policeman, Paddy Teasdale. The next day there was great excitement and the lane was full of ladies, gentlemen, children, push-bikes and prams all heading towards the scene of the crash. I was one of them: it was the highlight of the week.'

One summer's day in 1971, memories of that night flooded back when he helped members of the York Aircraft Preservation Society to excavate the crash site. They recovered the engines, propellers and other items of equipment, but Gerald believes that he missed a major prize:

'We used a JCB to dig down to twenty-five feet. By then we were waist-deep in water, glycol and oil. I put my hands down in the water and I could feel the two MG15 machine-guns in the nose. But by then it was five o'clock – and my wife wanted to go and see The Sound of Music. I never did get the MG15s.'

Gerald Inns (left) and Mr Newby, son of the original tenant of Low Bohemia Farm, with a propellor from the German bomber that crashed near Huby in 1941. (Trevor Smith).

The propellers were given to Mr Newby, tenant of Low Bohemia Farm, who had allowed the dig to take place on his land, while other artefacts excavated from the site evenutally found their way to the Yorkshire Air Museum at Elvington – but not all of them. In 1996, Gerald Inns and the writer re-visited Low Bohemia Farm and discovered that one of the propellers – a small part of Yorkshire's aviation past – was still lying in a barn close by the spot where it came to earth fifty-nine years earlier.

4-5 May 1941 (off Bridlington)

Aircraft: Junkers 88A-5		3Z+FP	w/nr 7117	6./KG77
Crew:	Oblt Martin Baumann	pilot	+	
	Obfw Karl Auernhammer	observer	+	
	Fw Wilhelm Hopfer	wireless op	+	
	Obfw Emmerich Schieting	gunner	pow	

The Luftwaffe Loss reports states that this aircraft failed to return from operations to Belfast. *The Blitz, then and now. Vol.2* (1988) states that it ditched in the sea off Bridlington at c.00.15 hours after its engines failed. Three of the crew were killed but Schieting was rescued by a passing ship.

4-5 May 1941 (Idle, Bradford)

Aircraft: Junkers 88A-5		M2+DK	w/nr 0656	Ku.Fl.Gr.2/106
Crew:	Oblt Ernst Jürgens	pilot	pow	
	Oblt z See Reinhold Metzger	observer	pow	
	Obfw Hans Beeck	wireless op	pow	
	Fw Heinrich Jänichen	gunner	pow	

This Ju88 (M2+DK) was on its way to lay mines in Belfast harbour when it was intercepted and shot down by a nightfighter shortly after crossing the Yorkshire coast. The bomber crashed on to John Barker's timber yard, close by a block of four cottages in High Street, Idle, at 00.45 hours on 5 May, shortly after the crew had baled out. On impact, the Junkers exploded in a ball of flame. Two of the cottages, Nos. 13 and 15, were completely demolished and two were badly damaged by fire. Two civilians were killed and four were injured. Two of those later died as a result of their wounds.

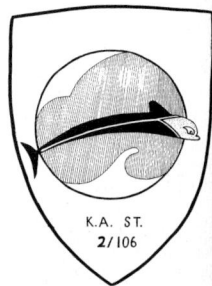

Küstenaufklärerstaffel 2/106

Barker's son, Fred, was on duty with the ARP when the crash occurred. In January 1977, the *Bradford Telegraph & Argus* recorded his memories of the incident:

'I heard this plane overhead. Its engines were racing and then dying away and it was obviously in trouble. All of a sudden there was a bump, and

then dead silence. This was followed by a whooping sound and the plane burst into flames. I then realized that the plane had crashed in our yard, which was about eighty yards from where I was standing. I ran up the High Street to get to it, but as soon as I opened the shop I was met by flames.'

In a letter to the writer in 1998, Reinhold Metzger, a veteran of Spain and Poland who had also carried out torpedo and mine-laying operations along Britain's coast before taking part in the Battle of Britain, explained what happened that night:

'Nine squadron aircraft were to attack Belfast harbour, where the Americans had landed war material. I had been there several times before and knew the area. When we started from Schipol (Amsterdam) some English bomber squadrons attacked as we were preparing to take off. Some thirty minutes afterwards, while circling over the airfield to assemble the squadron, another English bomber squadron came and we saw them beneath us so I don't know whether all of the planes took off.'

'When we came over English territory, there was no defence: no balloons, no searchlights, no fighters. That was very suspicious. I said to my crew

The crew of Ju. 88 M2+DK of Ku. Fl. Gr. 2/106 that crashed at Idle, Bradford, on the night of 4-5 May 1941. L-R: Obfw. Hans Beeck (wireless/op), Oblt.z. See Reinhard Metzger (observer), Oblt. Ernst Jürgens (pilot), Fw. Heinrich Jänichen (gunner). [Reinhold Metzger].

that this circumstance promised a hard operation. I had made my statement when we saw that the last plane of our squadron was attacked by fighters and went down on fire. Some short time afterwards, another plane went down on fire. ... . Though we had orders to remain at 3500 metres altitude, we flew higher so that we could dive faster if we were attacked. The maximum height we could go to without oxygen was 4,500-5,000 metres... .

'*As much as I remember, the plane that shot us down was a Beaufighter, a fighter plane with cannons, and* not *a Defiant. The fact that I could not reach it with my machine-guns, whilst the English pilots hit us, seems to me the only explanation. However, I don't know it exactly, because in the night it is impossible to recognize the type...The English planes – there were three or four – were out of reach..... .*

The wreck of Ju. 88 M2+DK in Barker's timber yeard, 5 May 1941. [Bradford Telegraph &Argus].

'*The right wing was hit and the sheet metal was gone. There was fire around the motor. In the last stage, Jänichen and Beeck went out by parachute to reduce the weight. I cut all things heavy in weight and threw it out of the plane, even the machine-guns and ammunition, because Jürgens and I tried to come back to France. The plane stopped spinning after equipment (and the bomb load) was jettisioned and Jürgens restored control... . Suddenly I saw a fighter coming beneath us and he attacked us with machineguns. Three other fighters were coming above but they did not hit us. The most dangerous was the one coming from below. The only thing I could do was to hide behind the armour plate to get not wounded or killed. All of the plexiglass was riddled. The plane turned in a circle and got afire.*

'*The only chance was to get out, which was very difficult. Because of the centrifugal force I was stuck to the right-hand side of the plane and I had to hold the steer on the left side so that Jürgens could get out of his seat. I wonder now that we did it without panic: at that time we had stronger nerves.*'

All of the crew got down safely. Jänichen landed near Farnley, Otley, and was captured by a policeman patrolling on a motorbike. He was taken on the pillion to Otley police station. Metzger landed near the Ings Hotel, Guiseley, and was also taken to Otley police station. Jürgens landed in a field off Town Lane, Idle, where he was found by a local youth, who took him to the Town Lane police box. It is not known where Beeck landed but all subsequently met up later at Bradford Town Hall, where they were placed in cells to await collection by the military authorities the next day.

It is believed that RAF personnel removed the wreckage the next day, except for an engine which was so deeply buried it was left where it landed – and, presumably, remains to this day.

The Luftwaffe Loss Returns for the night of 4-5 May 1941 show that Ju88 M2+DK was one of two Ju88A-5s lost by Ku.Fl.Gr 2./106 on the Belfast raid that night. The other was M2+EK (w/nr. 5201) but the location of the loss and its cause are currently unknown to the writer. However, Metzger's account suggests that a nightfighter might have been responsible. To date, the writer has been unable to identify the night fighter unit responsible.

7-8 May 1941 (Withernsea)

Aircraft:	Heinkel 111H-5	5J+ZB	w/nr 3987	Stab L/KG4
Crew:	Oblt z See Paul Tholen	observer	pow	
	Obfw Hans-Karl Schröder	pilot	pow	
	Fw Willi Schreiber	wireless op	+	
	Obfw Alfred Hoffman	mechanic	+	

This aircraft was on operations to Liverpool when, it is believed, it was shot down by Pilot Officer R.P. Stevens, (in Hurricane V7120) of 151 Squadron, Wittering, which was in process of changing from Hurricanes to Defiants.

Stevens was airborne 01.10-03.30 hours on 8 May and was engaged in patrols over Hull. During the course of his duty he intercepted three enemy aircraft and destroyed two, both of them He111s. Coastguards and Observer Corps personnel saw 5J+ZB ditch in the sea close in shore and some 600 yards off Withernsea at 02.28 hours. Part of the aircraft remained visible after ditching. At 03.45 hours, Withernsea Sub Control reported that two airmen had been taken prisoner and two others were being attended to by First Aid Services. Seemingly, they were being attended to in their aircraft for Withernsea reported at 04.30 hours that

> '...it has been found impossible to get the injured airmen out of the machine. Waves are breaking over it. The two prisoners have been taken in charge by the Hampshire Regiment and conveyed to the local HQ.'

It seems that the unfortunate airmen had to be left to their fate. Later in the day, the body of a German airman was washed ashore at Holmpton (three miles south of Withernsea) and was taken to Withernsea Mortuary at 12.30 hours.

8-9 May 1941 (Long Riston, near Beverley)

Aircraft:	Heinkel 111P-4	G1+FP	w/nr 3000	6./KG55
Crew:	Fw Gerhard Ender	pilot	+	
	Fw Heinrich Müller	observer	pow	
	Uffz Bruno Schakat	wireless op	+	
	Fw Georg Schopf	mechanic	pow	

G1+FP belly-landed at Long Riston at 01.30 hours on 9 May 1941 after being damaged by a nightfighter. It came down in a field on the boundary of the villages of Long Riston and Catwick and landed only yards from the farmhouse home of Walter Kirkwood and his family.

The Heinkel's observer, Heinrich Müller, subsequently told Ken Wakefield that G1+FP was part of a Pathfinder unit and was en route (from Chartres) to bomb a steel works in Sheffield when it was ordered to attack Hull instead.[4] As it turned for the new target, the Heinkel was caught by a Defiant nightfighter and in the attacks that followed, the night-fighter set fire to the bomber's port engine, stopped the starboard motor and killed the pilot, Gerhard Ender. Seemingly, there was no option for the crew but to bale out. Schopf went out at just over 900 feet, landed heavily and broke his neck. However, he did survive. Bruno Schakat was less fortunate: he also baled out but his parachute caught on the tail of the aircraft and he was unable to free it; he was dragged to his death as the aircraft crash-landed. Müller had also intended jumping but that option was discarded when his parachute opened before he could evacuate the bomber. Thus he wrestled with the controls in the hope of

Fw. Gerhard Ender (right) and Heinrich Müller (centre) were two of the crew of He. 111P-4 (G1+FP) of 6./KG55 that crash-landed at Long Riston on the night of 8-9 May 1941 after being shot down by a Defiant of 255 Squadron, Kirton in Lindsey. [Ken Wakefield].

He. 111P-4 (G1+FP) of 6./KG55 that crash-landed at Long Riston on the night of 8-9 May 1941. [Via David Thompson].

force-landing the machine.

Holderness farmer David Kirkwood, was 12 years old when he and his father stood watching German aircraft flying over Criftens Farm and heading out to sea on their home-ward journey. What he saw that night has been recorded by Joan Hersey, in her booklet *Riston Remembers, 1939-45,* (1995).

> 'Suddenly, one damaged Heinkel flew low and circled back over Farnton Wood, heading straight over the fields and just missing the ends of farm buildings, towards the house. Two (sic) airmen had been seen to bale out successfully, another had his parachute caught up on the tail-fin of the plane as the pilot desperately looked for a place to crash-land the aircraft.

He. 111P-4 (G1+FP) of 6./KG55 that crash-landed at Long Riston on the night of 8-9 May 1941 is removed from the site. [David Kirkwood via Tony Fairhurst].

'To this day, David can still remember the terror of seeing the plane flying straight for his home, knowing that his mother, younger brother and sister were inside. He felt the rushing draught of air as the Heinkel passed only yards from the house; he recalls vividly seeing the dead crewman being dragged behind the aircraft as it skimmed the hedges before crash-landing in the field just beyond his home.

By this time his father had dashed inside and, armed with a 12-bore shotgun, he ran across the road towards the plane, quickly finding the injured pilot crouching in the ditch beside Catwick Lane. In the meantime, David's mother had cycled to the village in order to telephone the police, who then alerted the Army. Very soon, members of the Catwick Home Guard were on the scene and the pilot was taken to Beverley Military Hospital to be treated for shot wounds to his knee...'

Seemingly, in his conversations with Ken Wakefield, Müller made no mention of having suffered shot wounds but Wakefield has speculated (in a letter to the current writer on 6 November 1999) that Müller's injuries might have been due to his not having had sufficient time to strap himself in to Ender's seat before touching down. Whatever the cause of the observer's injuries, they were serious enough to keep him in hospital for five months. It is believed that Ender and Schakat were initially buried in Long Riston churchyard; they now lie in the German Military Cemetery, Cannock Chase.

8-9 May 1941 (Sunk Island, Spurn Point)

Aircraft:	Heinkel 111H-5	A1+FM	w/nr 4006	4./KG53
Crew:	Uffz Günter Reinelt	pilot	+	
	Uffz Franz Magie	observer	pow	
	Uffz Jakob Kalle	wireless op	+	
	Obgfr Rudolf Lorenz	mechanic	+	
	Gefr Heinrich Wülf	gunner	missing	

This aircraft was also targeted on Sheffield but it was shot down by a Defiant of 255 Squadron, Kirton-in-Lindsey, and crashed at Sunk Island (military map ref. A7639). Air Intelligence investigators recorded the crash as having taken place at 02.00 hours on 9 May, but Civil Defence observers in the area noted that 'At 01.25 hour a fighter plane was seen to fire at an enemy plane over Keyingham. The plane crashed on the Stray at Sunk Island'[5].

Investigators from Air Intelligence reported that the Heinkel had been destroyed by fighter action and had sustained a large number of .303 bullet strikes (and others suggesting cannon strikes) in its tail unit, wings and fuselage. The enemy machine was on fire as it fell to earth and when it crashed, the impact was so great that wreckage was spread over a large area. Five MG15 machine-guns were recovered from the site, as well as a quantity of ammunition, but the Jumo 211 engines remained buried. It was noted that an MG17 machine-gun had been fitted in the bomber's tail.

Although it is by no means certain, it is possible that this aircraft was shot down by Pilot Officer H.S. Wyrill, with air gunner Sergeant Maul, in a Defiant of 255 Squadron, Kirton-in-Lindsey. They took off at 01.05 hours on 9 May to patrol the Hull area and they were at altitude 15,000 feet, to the north of Hull and flying eastwards when they saw a He111 abreast of them on the starboard side. At 01.25 hours the Defiant was on the dark side, with the Heinkel placed between the fighter and the moon. Maul immediately began intermittent firing at the enemy machine. His assault lasted for about one minute, during which Wyrill passed underneath the bomber so that Maul could also attack from the port side. Almost immediately, smoke began pouring from both engines; then flames began to flicker from the port motor. Wyrill observed Maul's bullets continuously striking home throughout the attack and saw, what appeared to be, a big explosion in the nose of the bomber before flames streamed down the forward part of the fuselage. At about the same time, Maul saw a large flash from the ventral gun position. During the course of the brief engagement, pursued and pursuer lost height to 9,000 feet. At that altitude, the Heinkel, apparently out of control, turned steeply over and dived straight towards the ground at a speed so great that Wyrill was unable to keep up. As the bomber fell away, Maul saw one German bale out but he did not see the parachute open.

Reinelt, Kalle and Lorenz were buried in Brandesburton churchyard, near Hornsea, where they still lie; Wulf was posted 'missing'.

8-9 May 1941 (Patrington)

Aircraft:	Heinkel 111H-5	A1+CW	w/nr 4042	6./KG53
Crew:	Uffz Helmut Teschke	pilot	pow	
	Gefr Willi London	observer	+	
	Gefr Johannes Kaminsk[1]	wireless op	+	
	Gefr Hans-J Steiglitz	mechanic	+	
	Gefr Hermann Decker	gunner	+	

Like the two previous aircraft, A1+CW was targeted on Sheffield but was shot down by a Defiant of 255 Squadron, Kirton-in-Lindsey. It crashed near Patrington, where Civil Defence observers reported that:

'At 01.40hours a fighter plane was seen to fire on an enemy plane over Winestead. The enemy plane crashed on the ground half mile NE Patrington station and 100 yards from the railway line. The aircraft burned itself out. Two dead airmen were found on the railway embankment.'[6]

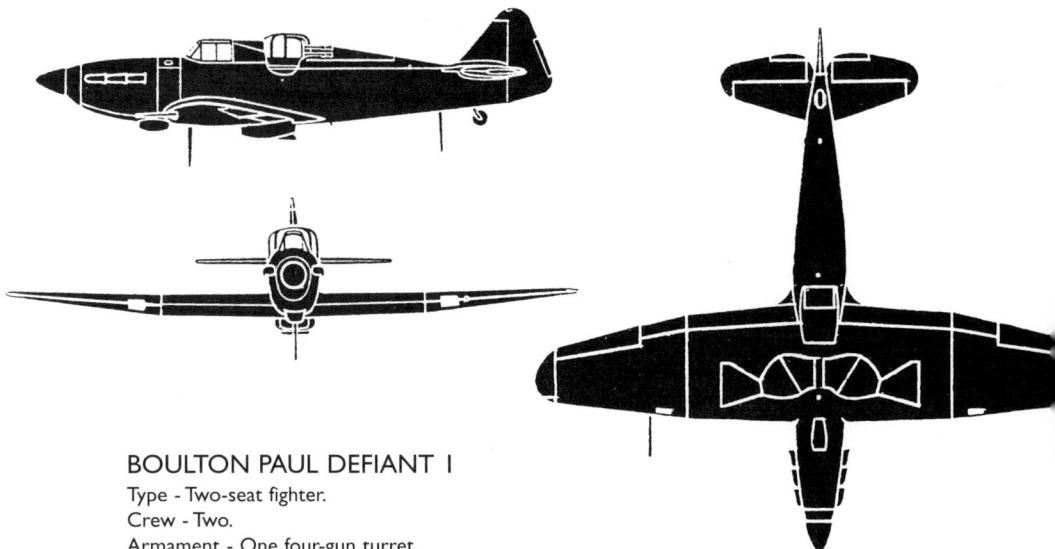

BOULTON PAUL DEFIANT I
Type - Two-seat fighter.
Crew - Two.
Armament - One four-gun turret.

Apparently the Heinkel had dived into a small stream and had exploded on impact, debris being spread over a large area. Air Intelligence investigators (who gave the military map ref. A7944) found a very large number of .303 bullet strikes and cannon strikes on pieces of wreckage. The extent of the destruction considerably limited the intelligence value of the wreck but four damaged MG15 machine-guns were recovered, as well as a MG17 machine-gun which had been fitted in the tail. The pilot, Helmut Teschke, was the only survivor from the crew of five: he escaped by parachute. His four comrades are buried in the churchyard at Brandesburton, near Hornsea.

Although it is not certain who was responsible for the demise of this aircraft, there is the possibilty that it was shot down by Pilot Officer Wynne-Wilson, with Sergeant J. Plant as air gunner. They had taken off at 01.06 hours on 9 May to patrol Hull. Twenty minutes later, when they were 15,000 feet above the Humber area, they found an eastward-bound He111 at the same altitude. At 01.28 hours Wynne-Wilson approached the bomber from the rear starboard quarter and closed to within 200 yards before Plant opened up with a two-second burst of machine-gun fire. Almost immediately, the Heinkel banked away steeply, its port engine on fire. The raider then levelled off some 3,000 feet below the fighter and commenced a series of clumsy evasive manoeuvres before the Defiant dived to deliver its second assault from the starboard quarter. Plant commenced firing at 70 yards, the De Wilde ammunition entering the nose of his victim and producing a brilliant explosion in the bomber's cockpit. The enemy machine then passed directly behind the fighter before diving steeply once again, this time with the Defiant in attendance. Plant managed one last burst of gunfire from 50 yards before the Heinkel began an 8,000 feet dive to destruction. The engagement was witnessed by several crews belonging to 255 Squadron, one of which also saw the enemy machine strike the ground and explode. One man was seen to bale out of the Heinkel and Pilot Officer Dale of 255 Squadron circled the German as he made his descent.

8-9 May 1941 (Hull area)
On the same evening that three German aircraft crashed on land in the area of Hull, claims were also awarded for two raiders alleged to have crashed in water. Among the claimants was Squadron Leader R.L. Smith, Officer Commanding 255 Squadron, Kirton-in-Lindsey. At this time, his squadron was in the process of changing from the single-seat Hurricane Mk.1 to the two-man Defiant and Smith was up in a Hurricane. Sometime after 01.20 hours on 9 May (Smith's combat report does not specify the time), he engaged an He111 at altitude 14,000 feet. He made a diving head-on attack, firing at close range (he estimated 200 yards closing to 30 yards) before breaking away. When he turned to re-engage, his quarry had disappeared. He informed Base of his encounter and was told that a Heinkel had dived into the Humber below him. He was credited with that aircraft and another, which he claimed 'damaged'. He engaged the latter, another He111, over the Hull area at 02.40 hours, shortly after he had seen it several thousand feet below him, prominent against the backcloth of Hull in flames. In the short exchange that followed his diving attack, Smith managed just one short burst – and saw his De Wilde ammunition striking home – before the German's return fire peppered the Hurricane's tail and starboard wing. He did not see that particular Heinkel again. The Luftwaffe Loss Returns show that 6./KG53 lost He111H-5 (A1+DP; w/nr.7045) on the Sheffield raid. The aircraft, with a crew of five and piloted by Feldwebel. Werner Scheer, failed to return from the operation and its crew was posted 'missing'. This *may* be the aircraft credited to Smith but, as yet, there is no evidence to suggest that it is.

On the same night, Pilot Officer J.D. Wright, with air gunner Sergeant R.I. Chesney, in a Defiant of 255 Squadron, chased a Ju88 twenty-five miles out from the East Yorkshire coast before engaging it at about 01.30 hours. Following a number of bursts of gunfire from Chesney, which seemingly disabled the Junkers' port engine, the bomber dived steeply towards the sea and the thin layer of cloud that masked it at 4,000 feet. Shortly afterwards, both Wright and Chesney saw a flash and a sustained red glow through the cloud and offered this as evidence that the enemy machine had been destroyed. Their claim was awarded. Withernsea and Tunstall Coastguards did subsequently report that a fighter plane was seen to fire a burst of gunfire into an enemy aircraft at about 02.00 hours and about four miles out to sea north-east of Withernsea. They also confirmed that pieces of the machine were seen to fall into the sea and the raider's engines stopped. However, although the time is approximately correct, Wright's encounter would appear to have been too far out to sea to have any connection with the Withernsea episode. Examination of the Luftwaffe Loss Returns shows that the only Ju88 report for the 8-9 May relates to a Ju88A-5 (w/nr.8199) of *Kampfgruppe 806*, which suffered fifteen per cent damage as a result of fighter attack while on operations to Sheffield.

9-10 May 1941 (off Whitby)

At 23.25 hours on 9 May 1941, Squadron Leader Meagher took off from Catterick in a Spitfire of 41 Squadron to patrol the Whitby area. There was 9/10 cloud at 6,000 feet but above that a full moon gave excellent visibility. At about 00.15 hours on 10 May, when Meagher was some 7,500 feet above the Yorkshire fishing port, his aircraft was briefly illuminated by searchlights through a gap in the cloud. Almost at the same time, an aircraft opened fire on him from 150 yards to port but the shots went over the Spitfire and caused no damage.

He reported the occurrence to his Controller, who instructed him to retaliate as there were no radar plots in the vicinity other than that for the Spitfire. Seeing nothing, Meagher continued on the same course, but a minute later he was attacked again from the same position. When he swivelled round to his left he caught a glimpse of an aircraft, either Ju88 or a Blenheim – he was not sure which. Given that the attacker might be a friendly aircraft, Meagher asked Control for permission to open fire, even though he (Meagher) could see not see the Resin lights which would have identified his attacker as 'friendly'. His Controller agreed. Once Meagher got a visual on his attacker, he had no further trouble in holding it in view because there was a full moon and visibility was good. In spite of evasive tactics by the other aircraft, Meagher managed to get in a two-second burst which hit his assailant but the flash from his guns momentarily affected his night vision. When that was restored, he saw the aircraft spiralling downwards. He followed and gave a further two-second burst from 50 yards dead astern and then continued his assault until his victim plummeted into the sea off Whitby. So engrossed was Meagher in his task that he almost followed suit and he had to pull away sharply to avoid a similar fate. He was, however, near enough to the impact for a piece of wreckage to strike his windscreen. On his return to Catterick, Meagher claimed – and was awarded – one Ju88 destroyed. However, examination of the Luftwaffe Loss Returns has so far revealed no likely candidate for this claim.

15 May 1941 (off Spurn Head)

Aircraft:	Junkers 88A-5	V4+GP	w/nr 6263	6./KG1
Crew:	Oblt Karl Schröder	pilot	+	
	St. Fw Ernst Wingenfeld	observer	pow	
	Uffz Josef Friedel	wireless op	pow	
	Obfw Willi Dietsch	gunner	+	

The Blitz, then and now. Vol 2 (1988) states that this aircraft was shot down by the naval patrol boat *Protective* and that it crashed into the sea off Spurn Head at 00.32 hours on 15 May. However, this is at variance with the version of events subsequently given to Air Intelligence personnel by the Luftwaffe survivors, Ernst Wingenfeld and Josef Friedel.

Seemingly the Germans had set off from Rosières-en-Santerre on an armed reconnaissance sortie against shipping off the Humber. At 00.25 hours, when they were flying up the Humber at about 200 feet altitude, Dietsch reported tracers being fired at their aircraft from astern. However, no fighter was seen and it was therefore assumed that the gunfire was ground-based light anti-aircraft fire. The pilot, Karl Schröder, banked sharply to the left in a defensive manouevre but in so doing he allowed the Junkers to lose height on the turn and the port wing touched the water. The Ju88 crashed at the mouth of the river (mil. ref. A8531) off Spurn Head. Both survivors maintained that their aircraft was not struck by gunfire.

After the crash, Wingenfeld managed to climb out of the wreckage and make his way towards the dinghy, which was floating nearby. En route he saw Friedel struggling to free himself from the wreckage and was able to assist the wireless operator and then help him into the rubber boat. The survivors were picked up by a barrage balloon drifter at 01.00 hours. Understandably, both were said to be suffering considerably from shock. The Luftwaffe Loss Reports give the names of the gunner and the wireless operator as above; *The Blitz, then and now. Vol 2* (1988) gives Dietzsch and Fridel.

2-3 June 1941 (near Whitby)

Aircraft:	Junkers 88C-4	R4+LK	w/nr 0570	2./NJG2
Crew:	Lt Johann Feuerbaum	pilot	+	
	Gefr Gerhard Denzin	wireless op	+	
	Gefr Rudolf Peters	gunner	+	

This Ju88 night-fighter crashed on Skelder Moor, four miles north of Whitby, at 00.30 hours on 3 June while on a night intruder sortie. The

The wreckage of Ju.88C-4 (R4+LK) of 2./NJG2, which crashed on Skelder Moor on 3 June 1941. [Author's collection].

military map reference is given as V3228. Seemingly, Feuerbaum's intended targets were RAF bombers returning to their Yorkshire bases after raiding Düsseldorf. Bad visibility is believed to have been the cause of the crash for there was no local report of any action in the vicinity; the Junkers simply crashed into the hillside. The machine disintegrated on impact and pieces were scattered over a wide area. A careful search of the heather subsequently revealed three 20mm shell guns, three MG17s and one MG15, all of which had probably been mounted in the nose. Eight unexploded 50kg bombs were found among the wreckage. A canvas case for signal cartridges was also found and was marked with British roundels. There were pockets for eight different two-colour recognition cartridges. It contained one cartridge marked 'white/green'. A further three cartridges were found on the moor, two being 'yellow/green' and one being 'white/green'. These were intended for use to fire off the 'colours of the day' used by RAF aircraft - and thus confuse or mislead defenders if challenged.

9-10 July 1941 (Staithes, near Whitby)

Aircraft:	Junkers 88A-5	M2+EK	w/nr 2227	Ku.Fl.Gr.2/106
Crew:	Oblt Edgar Peisert	pilot	+	
	Lt Rudolf Belloff	observer	+	
	Gefr Gerhard Vogel	wireless op	+	
	Fw Karl Kinder	gunner	+	

Ju88 M2+EK was one of three aircraft of Ku.Fl.Gr 106 that took off from their base at Schipol (Holland) with the intention of carrying out anti-shipping patrols between Whitby and Holy Island. En route the trio encountered mist patches and became separated. All three subsequently crashed in coastal areas. M2+EK came down at the North Yorkshire fishing village of Staithes; the others (M2+AL and M2+CL) crashed at Speeton (see below).

It seems that Peisart had reached his patrol line and was on the south-bound leg when disaster struck. Bernard Ward has lived in Cowbar, just across the stream from Staithes, all of his life. In conversations with the writer in 1991 he recalled that raiders destined for inland targets often crossed in over the small fishing village:

'On a still night you could hear them coming from Germany. Way out to sea. Droning for ages. Used to come straight over here. That night the air raid siren had sounded and I was outside the house. It was foggy. I could hear the plane coming from the north; it was low and close inshore. The sound of the engines, partly masked by Cowbar Nab as the plane approached, became much louder as he flew past the bay – then it was masked again. Then there was a crash and everything went quiet. A few seconds later, the smell of aviation fuel drifted back to us.'

Whether visibilty allowed Peisart to be fully aware of his position can only be guessed but immediately after passing Staithes he banked to starboard, presumably to resume his run to the north. His turn took him

Ju.88s of the type that struck east coast cliffs on the night of 9-10 July 1941.
[Author's collection].

Acklam Cemetery, Thornaby-on-Tees. The graves of the crew of M2+EK that crashed at Staithes on the night of 9/10 July 1941. [Trevor Smith].

into Brackenberry Wyke, a small bay fringed by high cliffs just to the south of the village. He may have realized the danger and tried to climb out of it: a few feet higher and he would have succeeded. However, the tail unit clipped the cliff edge at the north end of the bay. The Junkers broke in two: the tail plummeted down the cliff; the rest disintegrated across the high shoulder of upland of Quarry Bank (military map ref. V2838) and the fields of Cliff Farm beyond. There was little left of the aircraft to examine, although ammunition drums and portions of three MG15 machine-guns were found, as well two 500kg bombs and two 250kg bombs. The four members of the crew were subsequently buried in Acklam Road Cemetery, Thornaby, where they still lie.[7]

9-10 July 1941 (Speeton, near Filey)

Aircraft:	Junkers 88A-5	M2+AL	w/nr 4386	Ku.Fl.Gr. 3/106
Crew:	Hptm Heinrich Moog	pilot	pow	
	Lt Werner Blome	observer	pow	
	Obfw Alfons Wiese	wireless op	pow	
	Fw Heinz Riehme	gunner	pow	

9-10 July 1941 (Speeton, near Filey)

Aircraft:	Junkers 88A-5	M2+CL	w/nr 3245	Ku.Fl.Gr. 3/106
Crew:	Lt Helmut Sinz	pilot	+	
	Fw Harald Beuting	observer	+	
	Ufz Wilhem Quodt	wireless op	+	
	Fw Otto Donder	gunner	+	

These two Ju88s were part of the trio of three aircraft of Ku.Fl.Gr 106 that took off from their base at Schipol (Holland) with the intention of carrying out anti-shipping patrols between Whitby and Holy Island. However, they crashed behind the cliffs at Speeton, between Filey and Bridlington. Both came in low from the sea in misty conditions and were lucky to clear the precipice.

Local legend has it that the planes collided – and the proximity of the crash sites perhaps tends to support this belief – but there is no other evidence to substantiate the claim. Moog's aircraft hit the ground at a shallow angle in a field (military map ref. A6594) just behind the cliff and about 1,000 yards south east of Speeton coastguard station. He and his

1946 POW Camp, Sheffield. Friedrich-Wilhelm Koch (3./KG4) stands 1st left on the back row. His He 111 (5J+EL) was shot down off the Humber on 1 July 1940 by three Spitfires of No. 616 Squadron, Leconfield. Heinrich Moog (front, 2nd from left) was the pilot of a Ju 88 (M2+AL) of 3./Ku.Fl.Gr. 106 that crashed at Speeton (East Yorks) on the night of 9-10 July 1941. Also shown is the U-boat ace Otto Kretschmer (front centre). [F-W Koch].

Fw Harald Beuting, observer of the Ju.88(M2+CL) that crashed at Speeton on the night of 9-10 July 1941. [Karl Beuting].

crew survived, uninjured, and were apprehended by soldiers of the York and Lancaster Regiment. Sinz and his crew, whose aircraft came down a mile further west, did not fare so well. His stricken plane took off the top of the barn of Philip Jackson's Millholme Farm, Speeton, and then careered in front of the farmhouse, the starboard wing clipping one corner in the process. In almost the same instant, the Junkers struck the ground and disintegrated in the field alongside the house. Philip Jackson and his sister were at home at the time but suffered no physical injury; there were no survivors among the German crew.

Sinz's aircraft is believed to have crashed at 23.45 hours on 9 May. Moog's aircraft is believed to have come down at about the same time, although Air Intelligence investigators (who registered M2+AL as a Ju88A-1 variant) reported that M2+AL crashed at 01.00 hours on 10 May. However, search parties spent some time searching for Moog's aeroplane and it is more likely that the investigators' report gives the time that the Junkers was actually found. Moog set fire to his aircraft and it was the blaze that ultimately led searchers to the site. However, when they got there, there was little to salvage. Four MG15 machineguns were found, as well as two 500kg unexploded bombs; one 250kg bomb is said to have exploded when the plane was burned. The site at Jackson's farm yielded three MG15s, one unexploded 500kg bomb and two 250kg unexploded bombs.

The bodies of Helmut Sinz and his crew were initially buried in Bridlington Cemetery but in the 1960s they were transferred to the German Military Cemetery at Cannock Chase.[8]

EYE WITNESS
Germany Calling! Germany Calling!
- from Marske-by-the-Sea

When Reg Bell lived at Horse Close Farm, Marske, Teesside, during the early years of the last war, his radio could always pick up the German station *Radio Bremen* far more strongly than it could pick up the BBC in

Horse Close Farm Meacon site from the air c. 1946. [Author's collection].

Artist's impression of the Horse Close Farm Meacon site by Stuart McMillan.

London. He always wondered why, but he never found the reason. If he had been told the truth – that the German broadcasts were being transmitted from his farm – he probably would not have believed it. And yet it is true: Lord Haw Haw's propaganda programmes were transmitted from Horse Close Farm – and it was the RAF who was responsible. However, there was a patriotic reason for this seemingly treasonable activity.

In the early years of the war, Britain had virtually no defence against the Luftwaffe's night bombers. Anti-aircraft guns were not particularly effective at shooting down raiders, and we had no efficient nightfighter aircraft that could do the job and so night bombers came and went almost as they pleased. The RAF used Direct Reckoning navigation to strike at targets in Germany. But the method was notoriously inaccurate at night, because of restricted sightings of landmarks to check progress, and crews did not always arrive at their intended destinations. The Luftwaffe was far more resourceful. Ground stations in Germany and Occupied Europe transmitted navigational radio beams that were directed over targets in Britain. German night bombers flew along the beams and were thus accurately guided to their targets. After dropping their deadly cargoes, the bombers followed another transmission beacon on the Continent to take a bearing and so 'fix' their own geographical position before making the flight back.

In the early days, the RAF simply tried to 'jam' the beams so that they could not be intercepted by the bombers. But it was soon realized that it would be far better to mask the enemy transmission beacon by picking up its beam signal and re-broadcasting it. This masking of the beacons was known as *meaconing*. Horse Close Farm was a Meacon station, one of seventeen dotted around the country

Wilf Priestnall , was a radio-mechanic at Horse Close Farm, having been posted there in 1941, when the site was being built. He remembers that:

> *The transmitter at Horse Close used to work in conjunction with a receiving station at Brotton, on the site of what is now the Hunley Hall golf course. Brotton picked up the signal coming in from the German transmitter and sent it down to Horse Close Farm by a dedicated land-line. Marske then re-transmitted the signal on the same radio frequency as the German station.*
>
> *German aircraft came in following their own beam but then picked up the stronger Marske signal, which they followed (believing that it was their own). The Marske operators slightly shifted the 'route' of the original beam signal and in this way the raiders were led away from their intended targets and, hopefully, bombs dropped where they could do little harm.'*

The same system was used to confuse Luftwaffe crews returning home over the North Sea after bombing raids. Returning crews used the transmissions of the German beacons as aids for the flight home. But the Marske/Brotton Meacon sent out exactly the same signal as the German station. If the returning aircraft were nearer to Marske than to its German station, then the aircraft's direction finder gave the bearing for Marske as being the way home. And the crew of the bomber had no way of knowing that this was wrong.

Wilf Priestnall says that the system was so secret that Marske operators were never told of any successes they might have had. However, it is on general record that a number of *Luftwaffe* crews became hopelessly lost as a result of Meacon activity and crashed in the North Sea or elsewhere when they finally ran out of fuel.

When the Germans realized that their signals were being meaconed, they 'hid' their beam signals in transmissions of programmes by the German Broadcasting Service. But when the RAF realized this, Brotton adjusted its receivers, which then automatically picked up such broadcasts and transferred them to Marske for re-transmission. Thus when Reg Bell listened to Lord Haw-Haw coming through loud and clear on *Radio Bremen,* he probably did not recognise the significance of the occasional morse code signal among the propaganda. And he certainly did not know that the source of such good reception was over the hedge in the next field.

However, Reg does suspect that the Germans knew that something was going on at the Marske site even if he did not. He claims that one night he was listening to *Radio Bremen* when Lord Haw-Haw sent 'Greetings to Reg Bell, of Horse Close Farm, Marske,' and promised that 'The Luftwaffe will shortly be paying you a call.' Reg swears that incendiary bombs and high-explosives fell near Horse Close Farm a couple of nights later. If that was the case – and if the farm was, in fact, their target – then it was lucky for Reg that all of the bombs missed.

11 July 1941 (off the Humber)

Aircraft:	Heinkel 111H-5	5J+ES	w/nr 3956	8./KG4
Crew:	Fw Lothar Weitz	pilot	pow	
	Uffz Friedrich Pätztel	observer	pow	
	Obgfr Josef Ruhl	wireless op	pow	
	Obgfr Leopold Reisinger	gunner	+	

The Luftwaffe Loss Returns show that this aircraft failed to return from operations against Hull. *The Blitz, then and now. Vol 2*(1988) claims that it crashed off the Humber for reasons not known. In fact, 5J+ES ditched in the sea some twenty miles off Flamborough Head at 02.30hours on 11 July 1941 after being attacked by a fighter.[9]

Seemingly the whole of III./KG4 attacked Hull that night and 5J+ES was at 8,000 feet and running up to its target when the approaching fighter was noticed simultaneously by Ruhl and Reisinger. Wietz held his course until his observer had dropped the bombs and then he began evasive action while the gunners, Ruhl and Reisinger, attempted to dissuade their attacker. The fighter carried out five assaults in all, the third one of which seems to have done most damage: the Heinkel was hit in the fuselage and the port engine and was forced down to 700 feet of altitude as it flew out over the sea. The last two attacks by the fighter were thought to have been ineffective, although the German gunners believed that on those occasions they had managed to inflict some damage of their own. Shortly afterwards, the bomber's port engine burst into flames and Weitz was forced to ditch in the sea.

Both Pätztel and Ruhl were injured in the crash and it is believed that Reisinger was drowned as the crew attempted to release the dinghy. The survivors were subsequently picked up a minesweeper and landed at Hartlepool.

The identity of the fighter that engaged 5J+ES is currently not known for certain by the writer but it might well have been a Defiant (T3995) of 255 Squadron, Hibaldstow, crewed by Sergeant J.C.Cox (pilot) and Sergeant Fitzsimmons (gunner). This crew had engaged, what Cox thought was, an He111 at some 8,000 feet altitude ten miles north of Hull at 02.03 hours. The exchange of fire that followed resulted in Fitzsimmons being wounded in his right arm but he returned fire and saw strikes on the bomber's fuselage and cockpit area before the raider fell away and was lost. Cox landed back at Hibaldstow at 02.30 hours and submitted a claim for one 'damaged'. His was the only claim submitted by 255 Squadron that night.

2 August 1941 (off Flamborough Head)

Aircraft:	Junkers 88	S4+LH	w/nr 723	Ku.Fl.Gr.1./506
Crew:	Fw Alfons Eckardt	pilot	+	
	Lt z See Ernst Rupp	observer	missing	
	Obgfr Andreas Zanussi	wireless op	+	
	Fw Hans Braun	gunner	+	

The Luftwaffe Loss Returns show that Ju88 S4+LH failed to return from operations to the Humber estuary on 2 August 1941 and it seems highly likely that this was the aircraft shot down sixty miles off Flamborough Head at 16.05 hours that day by two Spitfires of 129(Mysore)Squadron.

Flight Lieutenant R.R. McPherson, Red 1, and Pilot Officer D.O. Cunliffe, Red 2, took off from Leconfield at 15.48 hours with orders to patrol their base. When airborne,

Küstenfliegerstaffel 1./506.

they were given a vector of 110° but at 15.56 hours this was changed to 100°, with information that there was a 'bandit' eight miles ahead at 2,000 feet altitude. They subsequently sighted an enemy machine six miles ahead, flying at about 1,200 feet altitude and north-east of a convoy. The sky immediately above the Spitfires was clear, but in the area above the enemy aircraft there was an 8/10 cloud layer at 2,000 feet. No doubt having seen the danger, the German climbed into the cloud. When the Spitfires arrived at the approximate position where the raider was last seen McPherson instructed Cunliffe to go below cloud, while he himself remained above it. When Red 2 emerged from the cloud base he found a Ju88 about 50 yards away on his port side.

As Red 2 manoeuvred into position astern and slightly below the Junkers, the German jettisoned four bombs just before Cunliffe opened fire with a two-second burst at 100 yards closing to 50 yards. During that first engagement, the bomber executed a number of fish-tail swerving movements to enable its gunners to reply, and Cunliffe saw return fire from both the dorsal and ventral gun positions – but all shots passed wide of their mark. The fighter's bullets, however, struck the raider's port engine, which started to smoke as the Junkers momentarily slipped into cloud. Red 2 followed and, on emerging into sunlight, found his quarry 400 yards ahead. He commenced his second foray at 150 yards range with a burst of gunfire lasting some four seconds. As he broke away, he noticed that the return fire appeared to have lessened and that the German's starboard engine was also smoking. The Junkers turned steeply to starboard and was once again lost momentarily in drifting cloud. When it re-emerged, Cunliffe closed in astern for his third assault – but before that attack could be pressed home, return fire from the bomber hit the Spitfire's oil tank and oil obscured the fighter's windscreen. Cunliffe broke away and turned for home, sixty miles to the west: he landed at Leconfield at 16.35 hours with a dead engine and survived without injury the crash that followed.

Cunliffe's attacks had covered a period of some three minutes. During that time McPherson had been in the vicinity but not in visual contact because of the thick cloud patches. Thus he did not see the combat but he did arrive on the scene in time to see Red 2's final break away and to see the Junkers smoking heavily. In endeavouring to close in on the crippled machine, McPherson twice lost the raider in drifting clouds. He eventually did get close enough to attack with two short bursts from 200-150 yards, but he did not consider that his gunfire had any damaging effect on his quarry. Shortly after that attack, during which some height was lost, the enemy aircraft once again gained the protection of a cloudbank but by then it was in difficulties. When McPherson caught sight of it again, the Junkers was down to 500 feet altitude and although its engines had ceased smoking it was descending in a steady glide. As McPherson watched, the bomber made a good touchdown but sank quickly. He noted three men – possibly four – in the sea with a dinghy that was not inflated. He then climbed to 3,000 feet and transmitted for a fix, which put his position – and that of the men below him – approximately sixty miles east-south-east of Flamborough Head. Then he headed for Leconfield, where he landed at 16.43 hours. It was later learned that at 16.09 hours the Royal Navy had intercepted a signal from the Junkers to its home station reporting that it was force landing on the sea.

8 August 1941 (east of Flamborough Head)

Aircraft:	Messerschmitt Bf 110C-5	4U+XH	w/nr 2306	1.(F)/123
Crew:	Oblt Friedrich Mende	pilot	missing	
	Fw Martin Pietras	wireless op	missing	

This aircraft failed to return from operations to Hull and was very probably shot down sixty-five miles south east of Flamborough Head by two Spitfires of 129 (Mysore) Squadron, Leconfield.

Flight Lieutenant R.H. Thomas, Blue 1, and Sergeant H. Bowman, Blue 2, took off from Leconfield at 12.35 hours. When airborne they were given a vector of 100° on which they flew at 2,000 feet until 12.45 hours, when it was changed to 80°. After about two minutes the vector was changed again, to 360°, with information that an enemy aircraft was in the vicinity at about 20,000 ft altitude. Blue 1 and Blue 2 flew on this vector for some five minutes, after which they sighted a Messerschmitt Bf 110 with an additonal fuel tank fitted underneath the wing on the outside of each engine. The enemy machine was flying west towards Flamborough Head and towards a convoy which was visible just off the coast. When the German saw the approaching fighters, he swung around, first to the south and then to the east, diving at the same time at a speed of about 430mph.

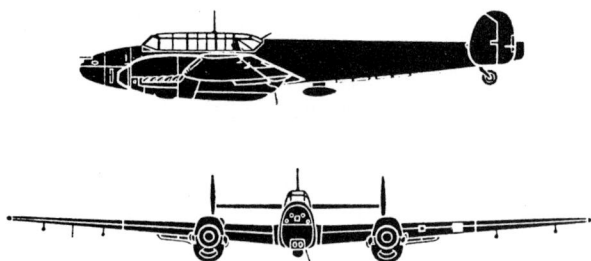

MESSERCHMITT Bf 110 C5
Type - Long-range fighter.
Crew - Two.
Armament - Two fixed cannon, four fixed machine-guns and one movable machine gun.

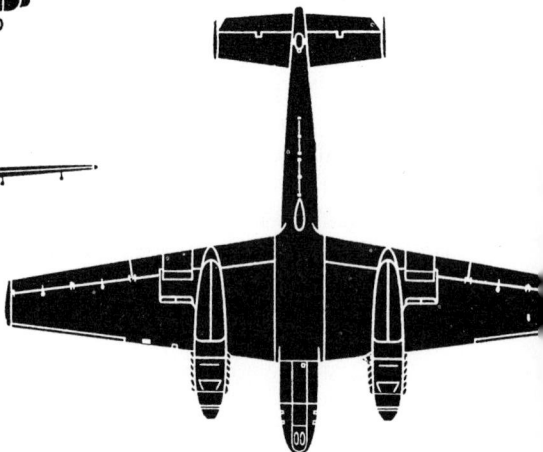

Blue 1 and Blue 2 followed the Messerschmitt in the descent but Thomas, being on the off-side position, was behind in the dive and lost sight of the enemy machine in the thin haze which lay over the sea up to a height of 1,000 feet. This haze also caused Blue 2 to temporarily lose sight of his quarry so he pulled up to 3,000 feet, from where he could get a clearer view of what lay below. After a short search he saw the raider about fifty ft above sea level and dived to give chase. Bowman opened fire with a two-second burst from 250 yards astern on the port side. He saw his first bullets hit the water slightly ahead of the fleeing target but with a slight correction of aim, his bullets then began to find their mark. Crossing over, Bowman delivered a similar attack from the starboard side of the enemy aircraft and registered another series of hits but he did not notice any return fire.

The Messerschmitt continued to fly close to sea level with Blue 2 one hundred yards dead astern and firing off regular bursts of .303 bullets from 100 yards. The German attempted evading action by making wide swinging movements – but, at least on one occasion, he must have been reminded of the danger of such manoeuvres at low altitude when the tip of his starboard wing actually touched the water. However, such risks ultimately failed to pay dividends for Bowman's tenacity was relentless and his aim accurate. His first bursts from astern caught the German's starboard engine and extra fuel tank: black smoke began pouring from the engine and petrol started streaming from the extra tank. Shortly afterwards, the port engine and extra tank were hit with similar results. Then Bowman saw flames alongside his own aircraft, but he had not been hit: he was so close to his target that petrol from the German's punctured fuel tanks was being blown against the Spitfire's exhaust pipes and was igniting.

With his ammunition virtually exhausted, but in the knowledge that his foe was now fatally damaged, Bowman fired a final burst into the smoking fuselage and then positioned himself 1,000 feet above the Messerschmitt, and slightly astern of it, to watch developments. He saw his victim slow down as the port and starboard propellers stopped in quick succession seconds before the German made a good touchdown on the water:the strength of the impact tore off both of the extra fuel tanks. He also saw two men scramble out in the minute or so it took the Messerschmitt to sink: only one was wearing a Mae West and Bowman did not see a dinghy.

Flight Lieutenant Thomas, who had lost contact with Bowman and the German early in the encounter, arrived on the scene in time to see the demise of the Messerschmitt and to see its crew alone in the sea and sixty-five miles from land. Seemingly, one of them raised his arm in salute as Bowman climbed to 3,000 feet to give a verbal fix of his position. But with that done, Blue 1 and Blue 2 returned to Leconfield leaving their foes to their fate. The writer does know whether the Germans survived.

10 November 1941 (Ravenscar, near Scarborough)

Aircraft:	Junkers 88A-4		S4+HK	w/nr 1409	Ku.Fl.Gr2/506
Crew:	Oblt Heinz Weber		pilot	missing	
	Obfhr Karl Schültze		observer	+	
	Obfw Werner Hanel		wireless op	+	
	Uffz Artur Gräber		gunner	missing	

S4+HK was shot down by gunfire from the escort destroyer HMS *Quantock* while attacking a convoy off Ravenscar, North Yorkshire. At 17.23 hours on 10 November 1941, the north-bound convoy FN528 was ploughing past Ravenscar in conditions of Gale Force 8, heavy seas, low cloud and slight drizzle when a Junkers 88 appeared out of cloud in a shallow dive about 1,500 yards to seaward of the convoy, which had the escort vessel HMS *Quantock* on its starboard quarter. The bomber passed close to the escort HMS *Kittiwake* and was about to attack the rear merchant ship of the convoy, some 1,000 yards away on *Quantock's* port bow, when the destroyer opened fire with all guns. Numerous hits were scored by the ship's forward and aft Pom-Poms and the effect was sufficient to force the Junkers to climb steeply away without dropping bombs. It flew westwards and shortly afterwards burst into flames before crashing at the foot of the cliffs at Blea Wyke Point (military map ref.

c.1991. Part of the engine of Ju.88 S4+HK jammed among rocks at Blea Wyke Point, Ravenscar. [Bill Wedgewood].

V4721), below the coastguard station just to the south of Ravenscar. In view of the very heavy sea running at the time, coupled with the possibility of other enemy aircraft being in the vicinity, no attempt was made by any of the escort vessels to leave the convoy and pick up survivors, assuming there were any.

Geoff White, of Bent Rigg Farm, Ravenscar, remembers that the Junkers came down in a most isolated and inaccessible spot, just below a narrow shore line of rocks and large boulders at the base of cliffs some 200 feet high. Air Intelligence investigators salvaged a little of the wreck but within two or three days the tide had broken up the remainder. However, the engines remained wedged among the rocks at least until the 1980s and smaller pieces could still be found in the 1990s.

The bodies of Karl Schultze and Werner Hanel were recovered and buried at the Acklam Road Cemetery, Thornaby-on-Tees. Heinz Weber, the Staffelkapitän of 2./506, and Arthur Gräber remain listed as 'missing' but it is thought that the bodies of these two airmen are also in Thornaby, in the two graves marked '*Ein Deutsche Soldat*'.

27 December 1941

RNLI Records at Poole, Dorset, show that on 27 December 1941, lifeboats from both Redcar and Hartlepool were launched to go to the aid of an unknown German aircraft said to have landed on the sea some eight miles east north east of Saltburn. Neither boat rendered service – but whether that was due to a false alarm or because the aircraft and its crew had sunk is not known.

Luftwaffe Loss Records show that Ju88 S4+HL (w/nr. 1144), piloted by Oberleutnant zur See Wolfgang Scholz-Tautz of KGr.506, failed to return from operations that day but the cause and location of the loss is not given.

Although there is no direct evidence to connect this aircraft with the RNLI report,. Franz Kurowski[10] states that Ju88s of KGr.506 were operating against shipping along the North East coast on this day. On that basis, it might well be that one of them was responsible for the sinking of the SS *J.B. Paddon* (570GRT), which was bombed and sunk at 53°55'N/00°16'E (one and half miles off Skipsea, East Yorks). Another of these aircraft flew to a secondary target at Scarborough. Kurowski goes on to say that on this occasion, S4+HL dived too close to the ground and was destroyed. However, if the aircraft had crashed on land, there would have been a record of it but to date the writer has failed to locate one. Thus the connection between S4+HL and northern lifeboats remains a matter of conjecture.

NOTES

1 Roger Hall: *Clouds of Fear,* Purnell Book Services 1975 pp134-141

2 See Bill Norman: *Luftwaffe over the North.*Leo Cooper/Pen & Sword. 1993 pp90-95.

3 WO166/2280 in Public Records Office.

4 Ken Wakefield: *Pfadfinder: Luftwaffe Pathfinder Operations over Britain, 1940-1944.*Tempus. 1999. P162.

5 CD/95 Bombing Incidents(Withernsea), 1939-1945 [East Yorks County Archives, Beverley].

6 CD/95 Bombing Incidents(Withernsea), 1939-1945.[East Yorks County Archives, Beverley].

7 A full account of this incident is given in Bill Norman: op.cit p102-106.

8 A full account of this incident is given in Bill Norman : ibid.

9 AIR40/2406.Prisoner of War debrief report 390/1941.in Public Records Office.

10 Franz Kurowski: *Seekrieg aus der Luft.* E.S. Mittler Verlag. 1979 p186.

3

INCREASING STRAIN
(1942)

From June 1941 to the early months of 1942, there was little activity over mainland Britain. The emphasis reverted to the mining of sea lanes and estuaries along the east coast as far north as Newcastle upon Tyne, scattered attacks on coastal shipping, raids on convoys, and occasional night attacks on harbours and ports, including Hull. Attacks on shipping targets were often carried out in daylight by single aircraft, while the number of bombers participating in night attacks on ports rarely exceeded thirty. These endeavours were aimed at the destruction of shipping, interference with the regular inflow of supplies to Britain via the ports and the deflection of at least some of Britain's war effort from offensive operations to those of a more defensive nature. Such operations proved to be widely scattered and highly disruptive, and they did tie down a lot of defending aircraft and manpower in Britain that could have been used in other theatres of war.

> 'This effort was increased when, during the summer of 1942, small numbers of long-range bombers operated singly over widespread areas of England in daylight and in cloudy weather, when British fighters could not operate. This effort, directed largely at causing maximum possible disturbance to industry with the minimum of aircraft, was also not without effect. Whilst physical damage to plant was negligible, the time wasted by factory staffs stopping work in the path of each aircraft certainly warranted the German expenditure of effort. German losses in those actions, too, were negligible.'[1]

Throughout 1941, the Luftwaffe favoured the anti-shipping campaign for they believed that satisfactory tonnages of shipping were being sunk or damaged for relatively low losses of aircraft. However, the situation changed radically in early 1942, by which time increasingly effective defensive armament of merchant vessels and improved fighter protection led to increased Luftwaffe casualties. Consequently, attacks on ships by day were abandoned in favour of the element of surprise in suitable (cloudy) weather conditions by day, and during the half-light of early morning and late evening.

April 1942 saw a reversal of policy regarding Luftwaffe strategy in the

West following the increasingly destructive raids by the RAF on German towns and cities. The raid on Lübeck on the night of 28-29 March 1942 triggered the Luftwaffe's reprisal Baedeker raids on a number of Britain's historic towns, including York, in April 1942, the participants including operational units from *Luftflotte* 3 as well as training units and operational units temporarily assigned from other theatres. Destructive raids against Middlesbrough were carried out on three occasions in July that followed, while in more southern parts of the county Hull, Leeds, Pontefract, and Doncaster were visited in the months of August and September. However, by then successive improvements to Britains's nightfighter defence force were reducing successful Luftwaffe attacks to a minimum. By the end of 1942, the raids that did occur required the time over the target to be necessarily shorter (ten-fifteen minutes' duration) to reduce risk of interception by airborne defenders. For the same reason, incoming raiders crossed the North Sea at minimum height to escape radar detection and climbed to attack height only when nearing the English coast. Then the target area was approached with a precautionary series of violent evasive manoeuvres – with consequent effects upon navigation – before bombs were dropped in diving flight to facilitate a faster escape from the danger area. But many were caught and as 1942 drew to a close, the operational strength of the German Air Force was falling further as the replacement rate of crews increasingly failed to make up for those lost on operations.

By late 1941 and early 1942, the British night-fighter was emerging as the scourge of the night bomber. In the early years of the bomber war, the night-fighter was in its experimental infancy and generally ineffective. By late 1941 the initial problems had been largely overcome. VHF radio had been developed and gave greater clarity and range; blind flying instruments had vastly improved; aerodromes were better lit and good runways had been installed at nightfighter bases. In addition, the heavily-armed Beaufighter, which was equipped with an increasingly refined airborne radar (A.I) to seek its prey, was working in conjunction with Ground Control Interception (G.C.I) ground stations to exact an ever mounting toll on raiders.[2]

By 1942 the British nightfighter was the most dangerous threat faced by German bombers in the West – and not only over the United Kingdom. In fact, by 1942 German aircraft could be harassed by British night-fighters at almost every stage of a bombing operation against the British Isles and there were many occasions when bomber crews would see comrades shot down, sometimes before an operation had even got underway. British 'intruder' nightfighters used to operate over Holland at times when German bombers were taking off from their bases and would endeavour to shoot them down, sometimes with success. It was not a beginning that inspired confidence among bomber crews waiting their turn to move down the runway. The pressure continued as bombers made their way out over the sea and towards their objective. KG2 used to exit from the continental mainland via the radio beacons at Texel and Den Helder but the British night-fighters used to circle there too. They also used to lie in wait over the North Sea and up to one hundred miles off the English coast, as well as operating over target areas. The danger was always present and inevitably had a psychological impact on bomber crews.

Even if Luftwaffe crews managed to avoid the hazards of the outward flight and the run over the target, danger still lurked elsewhere. The night bomber had to run the gauntlet of the return trip, which usually mirrored the hazards of the outward journey – and nightfighter 'intruders' also lay in wait when bombers returned to their continental bases. In the latter instance, airfield controllers usually responded by switching out all lights and directing returning bombers, which were often low on fuel, to go round again. This practice exposed returning aircraft to the dual effect of increasing the risk of attack by prowling 'intruders' and also offered the possibility of running out of fuel before they could touch down. Many returning crews were lost close by their own airfield, having overcome every challenge except the final one.

By mid–June 1942, the three *Gruppen* of KG2, regularly aided by II./KG40 and with occasional help from two coastal reconnaissance units, were the only units carrying the war to Great Britain. On paper, their total operational strength was 170 twin-engined bombers; in reality, serviceability problems reduced the number of available aircraft to something in the order of half that number. The aircraft that they did have were flown around the clock to give the impression that the Luftwaffe had more aircraft in the West than was actually the case. To this end, several crews often shared one aircraft, crews sometimes flew two sorties in twenty–four hours, and on occasion two sorties in one night. Bomber units were also frequently moved around to create an impression of operational strength. For example, targets on the English east coast were attacked from bases in Holland; targets on the south and west coasts were raided from bases in France. However, it was usually the same bomber units that carried out operations in both areas. Specific *Gruppen* did not attack specific areas. Instead, the *Gruppen* were regularly moved around for particular operational purposes and thus the location of any one *Gruppe* determined which geographical areas it would operate against. An additional ruse aimed at creating a false impression of bomber resources was to temporarily transfer bomber *Gruppen* into Europe from other operational theatres for short periods to participate in large–scale attacks on the United Kingdom. But even then the average raid strength was no more than forty–seventy aircraft.

Inadequate resources, coupled with the demands placed upon Luftwaffe crews, exacted their price. In January 1942, KG2 was understaffed when it had eighty–eight crews, but by September 1942 it was expected to meet its increasing operational demands with just twenty-three crews. It was an impossible task. By September-October 1942, destructive raids on British towns were progressively abandoned in order to spare the units. After that, the chief activity of the bomber was to carry out nuisance raids and mining operations.

NOTES

1. *The Rise and Fall of the German Air Force*. Arms & Armour edition. 1983. p195. For an example of such an operation over Yorkshire see Bill Norman: *Luftwaffe over the North*.Leo Cooper/Pen & Sword. 1993. pp144–159.
2. The radar equipment of GCI stations could guide a nightfighter to within one–two miles of its quarry and thus within range of the fighter's airborne interception radar. An excellent account of the nightfighter war over northern England is given in Lewis Brandon: *Night Flyer*.William Kimber. 1969

Losses
January 1942 - December 1942

13 January 1942

A Ju88 made a low-level raid on Warrenby steel works, near Redcar, and dropped four bombs. The plant suffered some damage but works-based anti–aircraft defences engaged the enemy aircraft, which was seen to be on fire as it flew out to sea.

15 January 1942 (South Bank, Middlesbrough)

Aircraft:	Dornier 217E-4	U5+HS	w/nr 5314	8./KG2
Crew:	Fw Joachim Lehnis	pilot	+	
	Lt Rudolf Matern	observer	+	
	Uffz Hans Maneke	wireless op	+	
	Obfw Heinrich Richter	gunner	+	

On 15 January, *IX Fliegerkorps* despatched sixteen bomber aircraft on armed reconnaissance and anti-shipping patrols along the east coast of England. Although fifteen of these aircraft were subsequently detected by British radar, it seems that there was no interception by British fighter aircraft.

It is believed that one of the participants, Do217 (U5+HS), dropped two bombs on Skinningrove Ironworks (on the North Yorks.coast) at about 17.30 hours and one bomb on Teesside's Eston Jetty at about 17.55 hours before dive-bombing the steamship *Empire Bay* (2824 GRT), which was anchored one mile off Hartlepool and waiting to

Kampfgeschwader 2 (Holzhammer)

*The crew of Do 217 U5+HS (8./KG2) who were lost when their aircraft crashed at South Bank, nr Middlesbrough on 15 January 1942, **L-R:** Fw Joachim Lehmis (pilot), Uffz Hans Maneke (wireless operator); Lt Rudolf Matern (observer); Obfw. Henrich Richter (gunner).* [Kurt Matern].

Ltn Rudolf Matern, observer, Do 217 U5+HS. [Kurt Matern].

join a south-bound convoy which was steaming down from the north. The bomber straddled the ship with five or six bombs, causing structural damage which eventually caused the vessel to sink. The Dornier reportedly suffered engine damage in an exchange of gunfire, after which it flew inland, towards the Tees balloon cordon, losing height and belching a long plume of black smoke. Minutes later it collided with the anchor cable of a barrage balloon flying 4,000 feet above the North Tees' jetties. The bomber lost a substantial part of its starboard wing in the collision and crashed on to the private railway sidings of Dorman, Long & Co. 100 yards east of South Bank railway station, on the LNER Darlington–Saltburn line. (see 'South Bank Dornier' below)

EYE WITNESS
South Bank Dornier: 15 January 1942

A World War Two German Dornier 217E–4 bomber that had crashed fifty-five years earlier was 'rediscovered' at South Bank, Cleveland, on 26 November 1997. The first pieces of wreckage were found just below the surface of the ground by Northumbrian Water Board workers laying sewers for a business park development. Following the discovery, full excavation of the site was undertaken by a team of Royal Engineers working with specialists from 5131 Bomb Disposal Squadron, RAF Wittering.

The aircraft, which was subsequently identified by makers' plates as U5+HS (w/nr. 5314) belonged to 8./KG2(*Holzhammer*) and was based at Schipol (Amsterdam). It crashed in the early evening of 15 January 1942 after being damaged by anti–aircraft fire from a merchant ship before colliding with a barrage balloon named 'Annie'.

Barrage balloons were an integral part of Britain's air defences during the Second World War and Teesside had its fair share. Forty-eight of the hydrogen-filled gas bags – 62 feet long and 25 feet in diameter – were dotted around the area (including ICI Billingham) in a random pattern and were usually flown at a height of 4,000 – 5,000 feet. The prime purpose of these 'flying elephants' was not to bring down raiders: their principal function was to keep enemy aircraft at altitudes which made

118

accurate bombing difficult while also keeping raiders at heights which allowed better targets for anti–aircraft defences and home-based fighter aircraft. However, there were times when aircraft *did* stray into balloon cordons: sometimes they were lucky; sometimes they were not.

Any aircraft crew finding itself in such a predicament, particularly in darkness, was in a potentially very dangerous situation because collision with the cable that held the balloon in position would invariably stop the aircraft in its tracks and send it crashing to earth. Of course, the Germans were aware of this and thus it was most unusual for any low-flying raiders to approach barrage balloon areas in darkness. Whenever bombers attacked Teesside, which was usually at night, they generally flew at heights exceeding 5,000 feet. However, the occurrence on 15 January, 1942, was to prove a costly exception to the rule.

On 15 January 1942, aircraft of KG2 were detailed to launch a late afternoon attack against shipping and port installations along England's eastern seaboard. An estimated twelve enemy aircraft were in the vicinity of the Tees balloon cordon between 17.34 hours and 18.58 hours[1] and among them was Dornier 217E-4 (U5+HS) of 8./KG2 crewed by Feldwebel Joachim Lehnis (pilot), Leutnant Rudolf Matern(observer/bombardier), Unteroffizier Hans Maneke (radio-operator), and Oberfeldwebel Heinrich Richter (gunner).

Lehnis had been ordered to attack a convoy which was travelling eastwards of Middlesbrough but it is believed that this aircraft might also have dropped two bombs on Skinningrove Ironworks Works (on the North Yorkshire coast) at about 17.30hours and one bomb on Teesside's Eston Jetty at about 17.55 hours before dive-bombing the coaster *Empire Bay* (2824 GRT), which was anchored off the port of Hartlepool.

The reason why *Empire Bay* was in such an exposed location was due to the fact that Hartlepool was a tidal port and sea-going traffic could use it only when the tide allowed. Furthermore, such traffic could sail in and out only during daylight hours: night-time use was prohibited because lights were forbidden by the blackout regulations. Thus the steamer had left port when the tide and regulations allowed and was waiting to join a south-bound convoy which was sailing down the coast from the north. In the late afternoon of 15 January 1942 *Empire Bay* was in a potentially dangerous situation for any merchant vessel in wartime: it was sitting at anchor and in daylight, without the protection a convoy might offer, and prey to any marauding enemy bomber – but there was little option.

Empire Bay had been waiting off Hartlepool for some time when the ship's crew heard the wail of Hartlepool's town siren which, according to Chief Steward John Cavanagh, was '...the only indication that a raid was a possibility...'. Shortly afterwards, the members of the crew were called to action stations but it was some time before they heard the dull drone

John Cavanagh, chief steward of the steamer Empire Bay, which was attacked off Hartlepool, 15 January, 1942. [John Cavanagh]

of engines approaching from the south-west. John Cavanagh was manning the twin-Lewis gun on the port side of the bridge:

'We heard the plane and it was not long before we saw it approaching from the south–west and diving towards us from the landward side. I wanted to start shooting there and then but the captain, a veteran of the Dover Patrol in the First War, kept shouting: "Guns, hold your fire! Hold your fire!" The plane was getting bigger with the passing of every second as it flew towards us. I thought that it was going to hit us before we got the chance to fire. I think I'd have emptied my pan of ammunition before he'd reached us, had it been left to me. But, as it turned out, the captain knew what he was doing... .'

John estimates that the Dornier was 200 feet high when it flashed across the *Empire Bay* and dropped a number of bombs towards the steamer.

'It was so vivid. I could actually see the Germans in the plane. I could see them. Then we saw the bombs dropping and I fired about a 15-second burst at him as five or six bombs straddled the ship. I don't recall the aircraft strafing us. It might have done, but in the excitement and confusion – the twin-Lewis made quite a racket and there was the explosion of bombs and huge fountains of water – who knows? Anyway, he broke away and started going back towards the land: by then he was losing height and trailing a plume of black smoke.'

The Dornier flew inland towards the Tees balloon cordon. Minutes later, it collided with the cable of a balloon flying 4,000 feet above the Tees

Tees pilot cutter W.R. Lister went to the aid of the steamer Empire Bay on 15 January 1942. [Author's collection].

jetties and shortly afterwards the crushed remnants of the bomber's tangled wreckage were blazing ferociously on the railway sidings (OS.534213) of the steelworks of Dorman, Long & Co. 100 yards east of what is now South Bank railway station, on the LNER Darlington-Saltburn line.

The airman in charge of 35 Tees Barrage–Balloon site (O.S. 531221) was Leading Aircraftsman Walter Myers, who now lives in Sedgefield, Co. Durham. In 1943, the Government's Ministry of Information booklet *Roof over Britain* (HMSO 1943) published Walter's version of the events that night.

> 'It was just getting dark when we got orders to fly our balloon. In a few minutes she was off the bed and aloft. We were rather pleased with ourselves, the boys and me, for we had put it up in extra quick time. I remember saying to one of our blokes, "If we don't get Annie up soon we'll probably be too late." I was only joking, really, because we had put our Annie up scores of times before without even hearing an enemy plane.

Tees pilot Bill Young, skipper of the cutter W.R. Lister on the night of 15 January 1942.
[Author's collection]

> 'Well, when she was up we trooped back to our hut, leaving the duty picquet on guard. We'd just started listening to the radio when we heard the plane coming low – very low, it was; much too low for my liking – so we decided to go outside and get a bit of cover. We'd no sooner got outside than the noise of the plane changed to a whine. It seemed as if it was diving right on top of us.

> "Jenny Macke!" says one of our airmen, an Irishman who says things like that when he's roused. "Jenny Macke!" he says, "He's going to machine-gun us."

> "No, he isn't," says I. "He's going to hit the cable." And he did. He went smack into it. There was a crash and the winch jumped as she took the strain. The cable sawed through the wing like a grocer's wire goes through cheese. That fixed him. Off came the best part of the starboard wing and we knew we'd got him.'

The nine-foot section of severed wing fell into an adjacent balloon site: the Dornier was destined not too travel much further.

Mr C.V. Evans, warden of Grangetown Boys' Club, was in South Bank at the time and heard the plane travelling '...very low and very fast...'. When it collided with the cable there was a yellow flash and the engine note immediately changed. His first thought was that South Bank was going to be dive–bombed, but he was mistaken. Clearly out of control,

121

The wreckage of the Do217(U5+HS) of 8./KG2, which crashed at South Bank, Teesside, on 15 January 1942. [Author's collection].

the Dornier came screaming low over the housetops and then plunged into the coal sidings at Clay Lane, South Bank. It crashed with a thunderous roar and in a sheet of flame which momentarily turned night into day. Then it began to burn like a Brock's Benefit, its supply of Verey cartridges popping off and arching skywards in a macabre fireworks' display. Instinctively, Evans ran towards the blazing wreck, but the heat was so intense that he could not get near. In any case, his was a futile gesture: the fliers were already beyond help

The crash site was examined the next day by Air Ministry investigators, who subsequently reported that the bomber had crashed at 18.10 hours. Seemingly, there was very little wreckage above the ground and most of that was burnt. Thus the investigators decided not to fully excavate the crater, largely because the aircraft had dived on to an important double–track railway siding 'which was needed immediately for work of national importance', but they did retrieve one 13mm machine-gun as well as ammunition for 15mm and 20mm calibre weapons before the hole was filled in and a new track laid. Three badly burned corpses were also recovered from the wreck and were subsequently buried at the Acklam Road cemetery, Thornaby, under the names of Joachim Lehnis, Rudolf Matern and Heinrich Richter. The body of the fourth member, believed at the time to be that of wireless operator Hans Maneke, was not found.

It might well be that the Dornier was not the only Luftwaffe loss over the Tees that night for the Hartlepool lifeboat crew spent three hours searching Tees Bay after a score of red and white distress signals were seen by Observer Corps and coast-watchers. At the time it was generally believed that the signals were discharged by downed aircrew, but it was a wild night and there was a high sea running. The search yielded nothing. If the flares had been fired by aircrew in distress then men and machines must have sunk without trace. The crew of the *Empire Bay* had better luck.

Fifty-six years on, John Cavanagh could not remember whether the bombs had actually hit his ship but he believes that they certainly exploded close enough to rupture the sides of the vessel. The damage would eventually sink her, but that final event was destined to take some hours. *Empire Bay* settled first by the stern, the raised bow held high by the anchor chain, and hung there for quite a while until the increasing weight of water within the hull finally began to ease the ship below the waves. As evening wore on it became increasingly clear that there could be only one outcome. At 19.30 hours, as the balloon crew set about their task of replacing their charge, the Tees pilot cutter *W.R. Lister* slipped her moorings to answer an urgent appeal for assistance from the crippled steamer. A contemporary report of the incident by Pilot W.H. 'Bill' Young, the duty skipper of the cutter, described what happened.

'The vessel had been bombed and seriously damaged. The Empire Bay *was sinking, but we were unaware of this fact. To locate the ship without lights under such conditions was a trying affair. Moreover, the cutter performed every giration short of capsizing. After thirty minutes of steaming, a flame was sighted away to northward. The course was altered and shortly afterwards we came upon* Empire Bay *plunging to her anchor and awash from quarter to poop. The Hartlepool and Tees Examination vessel was in the vicinity and she contacted us by loud-hailer. She informed us that she considered it unsafe to launch either of her boats but that she would be willing to give us plenty of light by means of her searchlights if we intended any rescue. This we readily took advantage of and closed the* Empire Bay *on her starboard quarter very cautiously.*

'*After one or two determined attempts to wreck herself among the upturned boats, rafts, fathoms of lifeboat falls, and empty davits swinging drunkenly outboard, the cutter was coaxed alongside the quickly settling vessel. We were now on the starboard side, which was swept continuously by heavy seas, lifting and falling, crashing and jarring. But one by one the men jumped and fell aboard the cutter. Soon they were safely aboard and, making them as comfortable as limited accomodation permitted, we proceeded towards the Tees entrance.*

'*During the whole of the operation I was ably assisted by Tees pilots C.*

Gray, G. Pounder and J.C. Swinburne and my crew, including the engineer and apprentices Franklin and Cook.'

The matter-of-fact nature of this report belies the drama of the situation – and the danger that men were willing to face in order to go to the aid of strangers in distress. It was not a new phenomenon: others had performed similar acts before and others would do so afterwards. As it happened, the *Empire Bay* incident proved to be one of the most notable rescue feats effected by Tees pilots during the war years: it appears to have passed virtually unnoticed.

John Cavanagh and his shipmates were landed ashore and spent the night at a local hospital, largely for observation purposes.

'While we were there we heard that Annie the balloon had got her first victim, but it was ours. Mind you, it didn't really matter who got the credit. We'd survived and the plane was down, that was the main thing.'

Following the 're-discovery' of the wreck on 26 November 1997, a full excavation of the site by a team of Royal Engineers working with specialists from 5131 Bomb Disposal Squadron, RAF Wittering, ultimately yielded some five tons of wreckage, including a large quantity of small arms ammunition, a number of machine guns, two parachutes in surprisingly good condition, a wooden propeller, parts of the undercarriage (oleo legs and wheel) and parts of the fuselage. The discovery of fragments of a military uniform and a small number of human bones quite early in the investigation gave rise to the belief that the fourth member of the crew had been in the Dornier when it crashed, but at the time of the discovery it was not certain that the remains were those of Hans Maneke.

The doubt was resolved later, when other,'substantial', human remains

November 1997. The Do 217 site at South Bank before the main excavation began.
[Author]

The burial of Obfw Heinrich Richter, 8./KG2, Thornaby Cemetery, 14 October, 1998. Heinz Möllenbrok, representing the KG2 Old Comrades Association, stands middle right with the garlanded wreath. [Stuart McMillan].

October 1998. Hans Maneke's grave was given a headstone 56 years after he was buried in Thornaby cemetery, Teesside. [Stuart McMillan]

were unearthed much deeper in the excavation and close by what would have been the ventral gunner's position. The discovery of part of a Luftwaffe battledress blouse bearing the collar insignia of three eagles near the remains led investigators to speculate that the remains were those of the pilot, Feldwebel Joachim Lehnis. However, subsequent forensic examination revealed that a fourth eagle was missing from the badge of rank. A coroner's inquest, held on Teesside in June 1998, therefore concluded that the remains were those of ventral gunner Oberfeldwebel Heinrich Richter and pointed to a confusion of identities half a century ago, Maneke having been buried under Richter's name in 1942. That error was corrected on 13

LAC Walter Myers, who was in charge of 35 Barrage Balloon site alongside the river Tees on the night of 15 January 1942. [Walter Myers]

Former Luftwaffe 3./KG2 bomber pilot Heinz Möllenbrok, who was KG2s representative at Richter's funeral. He was shot down and seriously wounded on 16 August 1940, while flying a Do.17 over Kent. [Heinz Möllenbrok]

October 1998, when Hans Maneke's grave was marked with a new headstone and that of Richter was removed pending its relocation over the new grave.

The following day, Heinrich Richter was buried alongside his comrades at Thornaby during a ceremony attended by the German Consul–General to Britain, the German Air Attache, three local mayors, the representatives of twenty-two ex-Serviceman's associations and some two hundred members of the general public. Attempts by the German authorities to trace surviving relatives of Richter and Maneke had met with no success but among those present was Heinz Möllenbrok, a former Dornier 17 pilot of KG2 who had been shot down during the Battle of Britain, and who had travelled from Germany to represent the KG2 Association. He laid the first wreath.

The number of local people who attended the burial ceremony and the church service that preceded it made a distinct impression on Heinz Möllenbrok and on Hans Mondorf, the German Consul-General. Addressing the funeral congregation at St. Peter's Church, South Bank (the nearest church to the crash site), Herr Mondorf said:

'I was quite moved and surprised by the sympathy that this case attracted with the population here. I have travelled very long distances in Europe. It is not uncommon still to have hatred towards former enemies, especially towards Germans. This is understandable, particularly in countries where the Germans had been in occupation; where people suffered from the Gestapo and SS. It is not the case here. I attribute this attitude to the sense of fair play which the British soul enshrines. Let us honour all of those who tragically lost their lives during this cruel war. Let's hope that nothing similar ever happens again.'

At the graveside, seventy-eight year-old Heinz

126

Möllenbrok voiced similar sentiments when he appealed for the spirit of reconciliation to continue through future generations. For this writer, at least, that spirit was amply demonstrated by an elderly lady who came forward to place her own small bouquet of flowers after the official wreaths had been laid. It transpired that she had been a member of the Belgian Resistance when her country had been under German occupation during the last war. Her husband of two weeks had been shot by the Gestapo. In those dangerous days, she had not been able to place flowers on her husband's grave but, she said, she hoped that someone had done so on her behalf.

Local legend has it that some time after the cessation of hostilities in 1945, a German lady visited South Bank and sought the location of the crash site. It is said that she told people that her son had been one of the crew of the Dornier but that he had never been found. If the story is true, the lady must have been the mother of Hans Maneke, for by then the wireless operator's three colleagues had been given graves in Thornaby cemetery. Sadly, she could not have known that an error had been made; and if she visited Thornaby and stood by the graves of her son's friends, she would not have known that she was standing within six feet of her son.

There were no members of Heinrich Richter's family present when he was buried on 14 October 1998, and it seems that any trace of Frau Maneke was lost long ago. However, they were represented on the day – by a grey-haired

Obfw. Heinrich Richter, gunner of Do.217(U5+HS) of 8./KG2, who was killed when his aircraft crashed at South Bank , Middlesbrough, on 15 January 1942. His body was retreived from the wreckage in November 1997. [Werner Feige].

old lady who had refuted justifiable reasons to feel bitter and whose spontaneous floral tribute made a far deeper impression on many of those present than did the impressive, and faultless, official arrangements.

Postscript. The claim that Lehnis might have bombed Skinningrove Works prior to engaging the *Empire Bay* is challenged by Franz Kurowski, who states that a Ju88A–4 (S4+EH) of *1./Kustenfliegergruppe 506* attacked the Works on the evening of 15 January 1942 and scored direct hits on the blastfurnace and hits on the coking plant and rolling mill. He also lists Ju88 S4+EH as missing on that operation[2]. The Luftwaffe Loss Returns show this aircraft (w/nr1612) as being lost on 15 January 1942 and gives the crew as: Leutnant zur See Dieter Andresen(observer), Unteroffizier Friedrich Pott (pilot), Unteroffizier Josef Scholze (wireless operator), and Feldwebel Franz Gruschka (gunner). *The Blitz, then and now. Vol 3* (1990)[3] claims that this aircraft was shot down off Tynemouth at 16.50 hours on 16 January 1942. Andresen's body was subsequently washed ashore at Tynemouth Haven and buried at Hylton cemetery, Sunderland. The crash date in *Blitz* (1990) is probably wrong but the recovery of Andresen's body near the Tyne suggests that the plane came down in that area. But was it on its way to or from Skinningrove? Air raid records in Cleveland County Archives show that Skinningrove was bombed at 17.30 hours on 15 January 1942. If the Ju88 crashed at 16.50 hours, as claimed in Blitz(1990), it seems unlikely that it did bomb the Works.

Empire Bay still lies on the seabed off Hartlepool, at 54°41' 08N"01°08' 36"W in a depth of some fifteen metres. She was dispersed to the seabed in 1946 by the Admiralty Wreck Disposal Organization. Much of the wreck was still intact in 1988.

19 January 1942 (east of Whitby)

Aircraft:	Junkers 88A-5		F6+PL	w/nr 440	3.(F)/122
Crew:	Uffz Franz Fichtinger	pilot	missing		
	Fw Gerhard Drassdo	observer	missing		
	Gefr Hans Blunck	wireless op	missing		
	Gefr Johann Bauer	gunner	missing		

This aircraft failed to return from operations on 19 January 1942. The Luftwaffe Loss Returns do not give the location or the cause of the loss but *The Blitz, then and now. Vol 3* (1990) claims that it crashed in the North Sea some twenty miles east of Whitby at 15.30 hours. The Junkers is believed to have been shot down by a Spitfire flown by Squadron Leader Tony Lovell DFC, the newly–appointed Commanding Officer of 145 Squadron, Catterick.

Lovell had taken off on a weather test at 15.15 hours in a Spitfire Vb. When he was some five miles east of Saltburn he was told of a 'bandit' coming down the coast from just off Newcastle. He was given two vectors and then sighted an aircraft two miles ahead, flying eastwards at cloud base, which was about 2,000 feet above sea level. Lovell was 1,000 feet below that altitude and so he climbed to cloud base in the hope of approaching the enemy aircraft unseen. However, in so doing he lost sight of his quarry and was forced to reduce height once more. When he regained visual contact, the 'bandit' was following the same course and

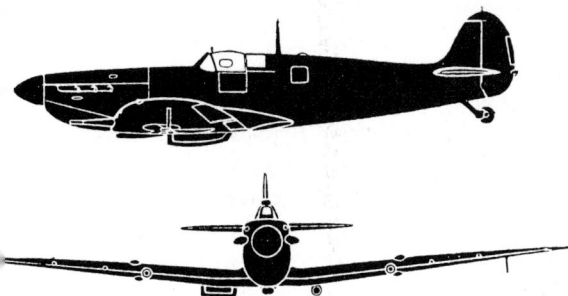

VICKERS-ARMSTRONGS SUPER-MARINE SPITFIRE VB

Type - Single-seat fighter.
Crew - One.
Armament - Two fixed forward-firing cannon and four fixed forward-firing machine-guns.

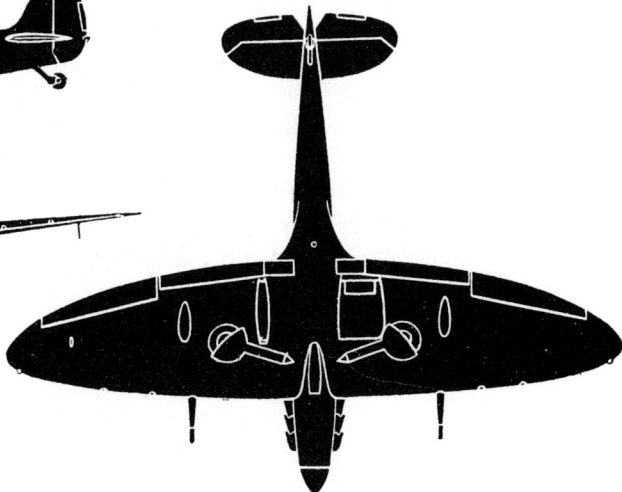

was at the same height. Lovell turned to port with the intention of cutting off the raider and flew in and out of cloud to mask his own approach. When he got within 1,000 yards, he recognized the aircraft as a Ju88. At that point he re-entered cloud and when he re–emerged he was 700 yards on the port beam of the Junkers and 300 feet above it. Lovell then banked to starboard and flew towards the bomber. With his sights set well ahead of his target, he opened fire with machine–gun and cannon from 500 yards, raking the Junkers from nose to tail with a four-five second burst. As he passed behind the tail of his victim at about 30 yards, he saw the starboard engine burst into flames and begin to shed debris. After continuing in level flight for a short time, and with the flames increasing in magnitude and ferocity, the Junkers turned to starboard and dived into the sea, where it exploded on impact.

18 February 1942 (off the Humber)

Aircraft:	Dornier 217E-4	U5+KR	w/nr 5342	7./KG2
Crew:	Lt Erich Palm	pilot	missing	
	Fw Rudolf Mühlbach	observer	missing	
	Uffz. Arthur Hoffmann	wireless op	missing	
	Obgfr Reinhard Kammerath	mechanic	missing	

On the night of 16-17 February the Humber was mined by KG2 without incident, while between 17-20 February KG2 sought shipping targets along the east coast – seemingly without much success. It was during one such operation that 7./KG2 lost U5+KR on 18 February. A Do217 (w/nr. 5348) of 9./KG2 was also shot up – although the cause is not known – but managed to return to Schipol, where it made a belly-landing. Returning crews reported that a large commercial vessel had been damaged and that an escort vessel had been sunk.

The German authorities listed U5+KR as missing off the east coast of England at 14.37 hours German time (13.37 hours British time). It is believed to have been shot down by Pilot Officer Y. Du Monceau de Bergandael in a Spitfire Vb of 609 Squadron, Digby. The Squadron's Red and Blue Sections (four aircraft in total) took off at 13.13 hours to patrol convoy CASING, which was steaming along the east coast, north-east of Mablethorpe. When the ships came under attack from individual Do217s, de Bergandael, who was flying as Blue 1 in Spitfire AD396, managed a short burst at one at 300 yards range and saw the port engine smoke and the starboard one emit a 'brilliant spray'. He did not see the enemy machine crash into the sea but soon after, the convoy reported that an enemy aircraft had been shot down by fighters. The shooting down was subsequently confirmed by Red 1, Flying Officer J.A. Atkinson, and de Bergandael was credited with the victory.

26-27 February 1942 (Humber area?)

Aircraft:	Dornier 217E-4	U5+ST	w/nr 1176	9./KG2
Crew:	Lt Josef Scharnbacker	pilot	missing	
	Uffz Sylvester Mischalla	observer	missing	
	Uffz Bruno Przybilla	wireless op	missing	
	Uffz Hans Kappenberg	mechanic	missing	

Thirty–one Do217s and two Ju88 (probably from KG6) laid mines off the Humber on the night of 26-27 February 1942. U5+ST failed to return from this operation but the cause and location of the loss is currently unknown to the writer.

27-28 February 1942 (Humber area)

Aircraft:	Dornier 217E-4	U5+AS	w/nr 5346	8./KG2
Crew:	Uffz Helmut Günther	pilot	missing	
	Obfw Karl Erber	observer	missing	
	Uffz Christian Pollok	wireless op	missing	
	Uffz Wolfgang Voltz	mechanic	missing	

There was a further mining operation over the Humber on the night of 27 February. Twenty-seven Do217s of KG2 took part and these were drawn from *Gruppe II* (Soesterberg) and *Gruppe III* (Schipol). The operation, which was considered a success, cost 8./KG2 the crew of Do217 U5+AS, piloted by Unteroffizier Helmut Günther. They were off the Humber when they were caught by ship's anti–aircraft fire and shot down into the sea but the location of the crash is not known. The Luftwaffe Loss Returns also show that Do217E-4 (w/nr. 5324) was damaged when it crash-landed at Soesterberg on return from operations after suffering engine problems.

8-9 March 1942 (Humber area?)

Aircraft:	Dornier 217E-4	U5+LT	w/nr 5335	9./KG2
Crew:	Oblt Helmut Hedler	pilot	missing	
	Uffz Heinz Stetler	observer	missing	
	Fw Günter Kowalski	wireless op	missing	
	Uffz Hermann Materne	mechanic	missing	

The Luftwaffe mounted a concentrated attack on the industrial installations and port facilities of Hull on the night of 8/9 March 1942 and 107 bombers were allocated to the task. One of those was Hedler's U5+LT which, according to the Luftwaffe Loss Returns, failed to return from the operation and may well have been lost off the Humber. However, that it is not certain because the cause and location of the loss is not stated in the Returns.

28-29 April 1942 (Coneysthorpe, near Malton)

Aircraft:	Dornier 217E-2	U5+KP	w/nr 1164	6./KG2
Crew:	Lt Karl Heinz Mühlen	pilot	pow	
	Uffz Otto Hacker	observer	pow	
	Uffz Fritz Kälber	wireless op	+	
	Fw Oskar Fussnecker	gunner	pow	

The series of Baedeker reprisal raids on medium–sized English towns, following the RAF's bombing of Lübeck on the night of 28-29 March, began in late April with attacks on Exeter and Bath. On the night of 28-

Lt Karl-Heinz Mühlen (centre) of 6./KG2, with Uffz Fritz Kalber(2nd left) and a second crew member Uffz Otto Hacker(right) with three ground crew and Do 217E-2 (U5+KP), which crashed at Coneysthorpe, near Castle Howard (North Yorks.) following a raid on York on the night of 29/30 April 1942. [K-H Mühlen via Heinz Möllenbrok].

Lt Karl-Heinz Mühlen, pilot of Do 217E-2 (U5+KP) of 6./KG2, which was shot down near Castle Howard on the night of 29-30 April, 1942. [K-H Mühlen via H. Möllenbrok]

29 April 1942 the target was the mediaeval walled city of York, which was also considered by the Germans to be an important rail junction with wagon–repair works, as well as a garrison town for the British Army's Northern Command. Seventy–four aircraft of *Luftflotte 3* were given the task of bombing these separate targets and participating crews claimed to have bombed as ordered and to have dropped ninety–five tonnes of high explosives and 158 racks of incendiaries over the York area. German Intelligence later estimated that fifty-five tonnes of bombs had actually fallen on the town, causing numerous fires and extensive damage, especially around the railway station. Seventy-two civilians were killed, ninety-two seriously injured and a further 113 received minor injuries. Three Do217s were lost in the attack, among them was Do217E-2 (U5+KP) of 6./KG2.

At 02.00 hours on 29 April a number of hostile plots appeared both overland and off the coast south of Catterick sector. It was apparent that York was the objective but a few enemy raiders travelled north off the coast of Scarborough to the mouth of the Tees and

Do 217E-4 of KG2 [K-H Mühlen via Heinz Möllenbrok].

about seven enemy aircraft were plotted within the sector. At 02.20 hours Flying Officer Furse (with Pilot Officer Downes) was scrambled in Beaufighter. R2389 and under Sector Control was vectored on a line from York east to Flamborough. At 03.20 hours, after being given several vectors that ultimately proved fruitless, Downes made A.I. contact with an enemy aircraft flying east at altitude 15,000 feet and on its way home. In spite of the German's violent evasive action and rapid loss of height, contact was maintained until a visual was obtained of a Do217E-2 at a height of 6,000 feet over the Yorkshire coast. Pursued and pursuer were just east of Bridlington when Furse closed in to 400 feet and fired a one-second burst from astern with all guns. Strikes were seen on both sides of the fuselage and the Dornier made a sharp climbing turn to port and disappeared. Neither Furse nor Downes saw the raider crash and thus it was claimed only as damaged. Later on, a Do217E–2 (U5+KP) was found to have come down at Coneysthorpe, near Malton. It crash–landed in a field some yards east of Thurtle Wood, just north-east of the North Lodge on the Castle Howard estate and just above the Coneysthorpe crossroads. Leutnant Karl–Heinz Mühlen (pilot), Unteroffizier Otto Hacker(observer), Unteroffizier Fritz Kälber(wireless operator), and Feldwebel Oskar Fussnecker (gunner) survived the crash but Fritz Kälber was severely burned and did not survive the night.

Following the interrogation of the prisoners, and after careful investigation of the wreckage, credit for the destruction of the Dornier was given to Furse. However, there is evidence to suggest that Mühlen was not Furse's victim. At the time of the York raid, German Summer Time(used by the Luftwaffe) coincided with British Double Summer Time (used by the RAF). Mühlen's account of his shooting down (see below) states that he crashed–landed at 02.15 hours, that is, five minutes before Furse took off from Scorton. Further evidence is provided by the fact that Furse claimed to have attacked only once, from astern; Muhlen, on the other hand, claims that he was attacked twice.

EYEWITNESS
A Luftwaffe pilot remembers an encounter with a night–fighter, 29 April 1942

'On 28 April I, Leutnant. Mühlen of 6./KG2, set out with my Do217 (U5+KP) on a night attack on military targets in York. It is two days to the full moon, cloudless and with very good visibility. We, Unteroffizier, Otto Hacker (observer), Unteroffizier, Fritz Kälber (wireless operator) and Feldwebel, Oskar Fussnecker (mechanic), are all in good spirits and thinking of anything but the dreadful disaster that we would encounter two hours later.

'The first half of the attack goes off smoothly, just like our previous

eighty-four sorties over enemy territory. Long before we reach the target, we can see the town burning. After dropping the bombs I turn and climb. The bombs have gone and with them the prickly feeling of tension. Nothing else can happen to us – or so we think. Our thoughts are once again on the beauty and pleasantness of our home base at Soesterberg.

'*Suddenly, all hell breaks loose. The devil himself is in our cockpit, complete with fork and glowing pointed talons. The aircraft trembles beneath the cannon and machine-gun fire of the night-fighters. It splinters and cracks. The cockpit is full of pungent smoky powder. Communication is out immediately. With the bullets and shells exploding around us, I swing my aircraft to the right. The smoky cloud disappears. I keep the machine turned. The fuel tanks are fast running out. Oskar makes himself visible and swings his left hand, still hanging together by the bones, in front of my eyes. My signals to Otto to watch out for further attacks from behind are not understood.*

'*The night-fighter attacks a second time and deals our poor 'KP' the death blow. I press myself against the armour plating. A nerve-shattering hit and a hard bang travels through the machine; one hole after another appears in the left-hand panel next to my captain's seat. It is literally like a sieve.*

'*The fighter plane came from above on the left and hit the left engine so that it is without power, although the propeller, driven by the wind, is still turning… .*

'*I am at 1,500 metres. Hoping that the second attack had destroyed no vital parts, I make a tight 360° turn to the left. I turn the machine over to try and shake off my persistent opponent. Behind me, I see the coast beckoning. At 200 metres I begin to straighten out. From this point, everything happens very quickly. The plane still reacts to the elevators, but not as normal. I look at the airspeed indicator – 250km per hour. That cannot be right after a fall of 1300 metres. I pull the joystick back hard into my stomach. However, the plane continues to go downwards. I pull the right side rudder right over but the crate still pulls to the left. What else can I do? I think and then yell: 'Jump!'. Then I look at the altimeter, which shows 150 metres, and shout: 'Stay in there!' The crate is getting spongy and wants to slide to the left – Full throttle on one (starboard) engine.*

'*In the moolight I see before me a narrow valley with no trees. Throttle down; brake slightly; landing flaps down. The cockpit hits the ground, is thrown high in the air, and then slides and ploughs through the earth; the cockpit windows are broken and soil is forced in. I hang there in my harness; the pressure falls – and we are standing! It is 02.15 hours. There is silence for a second – Nature holds her breath – then there is a massive explosion in the right main tank. A jet of flame lights everything up as bright as day. My momentary fear passes: 'Everybody out!' is my only thought… .*

'I release my seatbelt and parachute harness, squeeze between the seat and the steering column, which is stuck fast, and stand up. Hot, choking air and greedy bright red flames coming down through the radio operator's turret hit me. My thoughts are in turmoil… Then I see the emergency handle of the upper exit hatch and pull the handle down. Somehow I climb up and throw off the canopy – and as I do so a big, hot flame jumps at me and eats at my face. I roll to the right over the edge of the exit and drop between the gun turret and the left engine. I pull myself up and run for some ten metres before I come to and regain control of myself.

'Where are my comrades? Gigantic flames are shooting out of the plane: are they still in there? Then Oskar falls into my arms. He groans and curses: 'Everything is over. I must die. My hand…' I take his bleeding left arm and lead him over to the edge of the ploughed field, where I force him down and try to comfort him. My nerves are on edge and I am shivering. I bandage his arm as best I can. It looks horrible. It is undamaged but the tendons and nerves are torn and the hand is hanging from only one bone and a few strips of flesh. I see immediately that the lower part of his forearm and his hand must be amputated.

'While I am bandaging Oskar, I hear a weak cry from Otto. He is lying on the ploughed field and can go no further. I hurry over to him. He's been shot in his right thigh. I cut away his trousers and underpants with my knife and bandage his wound with my field dressing.

'I hear shouts for help for a second time in these dramatic, unforgettable minutes. In the hissing and crackling flames of my burning plane and amid the numerous exploding bullets, which often go off with a bang and a fantastic shower of sparks, I search for Fritz – the only one it can be who is calling. As I run towards the voice, I see in the pale moonlight a picture I'll never forget; a picture seared forever in my mind… . I see a groaning, swaying figure tottering towards me. At the top of his harness a still-gleaming strip of his burnt–off uniform: it shines fiendishly in the pale moonlight. This poor, destroyed person sinks down at my feet. What should I do? What useful help can I give him? I can do nothing but undo his helmet, which is fastened close round his head and neck. The heat of the fire has stuck the leather together. I also free him from his harness – and burn my hands because it is red hot.

'In this awful situation, Fritz tells me that he knows he is going to die. This soldier, this brave man who will fight for the Fatherland to his last breath, thinks only about the radio codes which are in the right pocket of his flying suit. But the flying suit is burnt on his body: I can't find the codes but I tell him that I have found them and pretend to tear them up. His stifled groans and powerfully restrained despair break my heart. My God, if only I could help him! I lay him along the furrow and promise to get *help. My nerve breaks. I run back to the others.*

'*They are lying side by side. Oskar has dragged himself the twenty metres to Otto. It's wonderful to see. These indestructible men are smoking like chimneys again. It is a touching picture: dirty, covered in mud, clothes ripped and torn, sprayed with dried blood mixed with dirt, the two comrades lie there and smoke a crushed cigarette. I renew Oskar's pressure pad. Otto says his right leg has gone cold. I tell him I'll get help. He gives me his pistol; I fire a few shots but nothing moves... .*

'*I drift around the countryside. Where is there a person? Where is there a house? Where do I get help from? Where should I go in this ghostly landscape? I climb over a fence, go through a narrow, sparse wood, come to a field that I zig-zag across, and see a footpath that I follow. At last there is a house! I circle it. Nothing moves. These stupid, short-sighted people! They shut themselves in and don't move out of fear. I'm here shouting loud and need help urgently for three comrades. My swearing doesn't help. I have to go on, along the footpath. I must have gone round my burning plane in a half circle for I can see nothing more of the fire. Dazed, I go on further. On the right is a street. The slope down towards it goes on and comes to a gate that is set in an out-of-proportion stone wall – the height of a man – which disappears in a bend in the distance. A notice asks you to close the gate or the farmer will have to walk 1^1/$_2$ miles to close it. I go through the gate and into a dark, gloomy wood which the stone wall edges. The road winds through it. I see a hut (or a house) and I'm still 50 metres away when I see a car being driven away. I want to shout but it is too late. I get nearer, go through a big iron gate and shout in front of the house, where a dog is howling. I find myself surrounded by ten men armed with rifles who are very excited. I don't trust myself to even blink – otherwise a gun might go off. As they came nearer, I classed them as armed farmhands or 'Home Guards'. Soon after it turned out that they were regular troops.*

It was about 05.30 hours when they took me prisoner. As first priority I spoke about my comrades who were lying in the cold, inhospitable night and in need of urgent help. They assured me that help was on the way. The Tommies were soon convinced that I was harmless and fetched me soap and water to wash my burnt mud-stained face. I didn't feel any great pain. After that, they gave me the place of honour in the hut: an old grandfather's chair, dirty and greasy.

There was a stumbling but lively conversation. For the first time, I was speaking English with English people. Is there such a thing as white bread in Germany? What are your war aims? What do you think about Churchill? About the RAF? Hitler? Luftwaffe? The Dutch coins I had in my pocket were soon shared out as souvenirs of the capture of a German Luftwaffe officer. I showed them my Iron Cross First Class and my uniform under my flying suit. Both were admired, as were my fur boots.

As soon as the news of my capture had been radioed in there were soon people and a doctor on the spot who bandaged me up. Only then did I discover that I had been wounded in the left calf. They spread burn cream on my face... (He was then taken under three–man escort to the military hospital at Malton, where he discovered that his crew had been found and seen by a doctor). *However, help came too late for my true comrade, Fritz Kälber. I will never forget him.*

Lt. Karl-Heinz Mühlen, pilot,
Do217(U5+KP), 6./KG2

28-29 April 1942 (east of Whitby?)

Aircraft:	Junkers 88A-5	3Z+AV	w/nr 0289	11./KG77
Crew:	Lt Armin Körfer	pilot	missing	
	Uffz Heinrich Müller	observer	missing	
	Uffz Fritz Ernt	wireless op	missing	
	Obgfr Hermann Schleising	mechanic	missing	

It is possible that this aircraft was shot down by Pilot Officer A.G. Lawrence(with Sergeant H.J. Wilmer) in Beaufighter T3034 of 406 Squadron, RCAF. Lawrence was scrambled from Scorton at 03.08 hours on 29 April and was initially directed to the Saltburn area to intercept a raid travelling south-west – without success. However, at 03.33 hours, when the Beaufighter was under G.C.I. *(Ground Control Interception)* control, Wilmer made A.I. *(Airborne Interceptor)* contact with a raider. At the moment of contact, both aircraft were at 11,000 feet altitude and Wilmer managed to keep the link when the German took evasive action and lost height rapidly. Lawrence pursued the contact some eighty miles out to sea before gaining a visual of his quarry, which turned out to be a Ju88. Both aircraft were 3,000 feet above the sea when the Beaufighter closed in to 300 feet. Lawrence fired a six–second burst from his cannons, followed by another of three to four seconds before flames started licking their way along the fuselage of the enemy machine and the starboard engine began to belch orange flame and smoke. Shortly after that, the Junkers turned over on its starboard wing and plummeted into the sea some eighty miles east of Whitby. Lawrence landed back at Scorton at 04.35hours and claimed one Ju88 destroyed, which was later confirmed.

The Blitz, then and now. Vol 3 (1990) states that IV./KG77 lost one Junkers 88 on the York raid.[4] Scrutiny of the Luftwaffe Loss Returns for that date shows 3Z+AV to be the only relevant Ju88 loss but neither the aircraft's intended target nor the location of the loss is given in the Returns. If *Blitz* (1990) is correct, it would seem that Lawrence's victim was 3Z+AV but at the time of writing this can only be conjecture.

28-29 April 1942 (near York)

Aircraft:	Junkers 88D-1	M2+CH	w/nr 1334	Ku.Fl.Gr.1/106
Crew:	Lt Werner Boy	pilot	+	
	Uffz Karl H. Kugler	observer	pow	
	Gefr Willi Schindler	wireless op	pow	
	Gefr Heinz Müller	gunner	pow	

This aircraft was on a sortie to York when it was shot down by Free French pilot Warrant Officer Yves Mahé, in a Hurricane IIc (BN292) of 252 (Hyderabad State) Squadron, Hibaldstow (Lincs.). It crashed at Crockey Hill (mil.ref. A.1066), three and a half miles south of York, seemingly at 03.00hours on 29 April[5] – although the Frenchman allegedly did not launch his attack until 03.15 hours.

Mahé took off from Hibaldstow at 02.50 hours on 29 April and was vectored to York with instructions to orbit the city at 6,000 feet. While en route northwards, he sighted a Ju88 flying south but failed to intercept it. Then at 03.15 hours, while he was on station over York, he saw a trail of flares dropping to the south-west of his position and from about the height at which he was flying. He proceeded to the spot at full throttle and sighted an enemy machine some 1,000 yards to his port side and flying approximately south-south-east. Mahé made a diving turn in pursuit and initially positioned himself 2,000 feet below the enemy machine and very slightly astern of it. Shortly afterwards, he eased the Hurricane upwards until he was sitting on the enemy's tail. He had difficulty identifying his quarry – because the fighter's windscreen was oiled up – and speculated whether it was a Ju88 or a He111 before opting for the latter option. Then he delivered a two-second burst that set fire to the raider's starboard engine. The enemy machine went into a steep spiral

Ju 88D-1 (M2+CH; w/nr. 1334) of Ku.Fl.Gr. 1./106 which crash-landed at Crockey Hill, near York, in the early hours of 29 April 1942. [Author's collection].

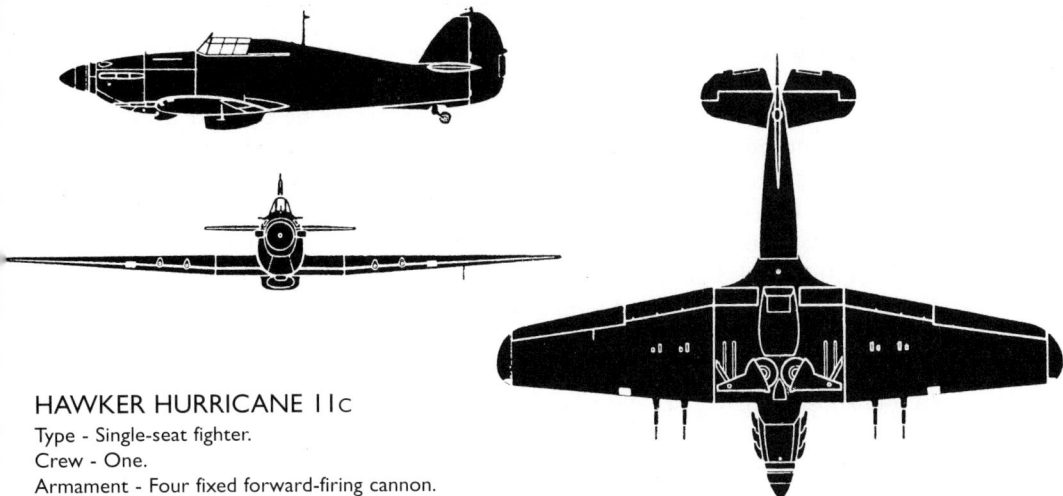

HAWKER HURRICANE IIc

Type - Single-seat fighter.
Crew - One.
Armament - Four fixed forward-firing cannon.

dive and although the Frenchman managed to follow for a while, he lost his victim at 3,000 feet. By that time, the flames had been extinguished but the bomber was still diving at some 300mph. As soon as Mahé had fired his burst, he informed Control that the raider was going down. The 'fix' that Control took approximated to the position where Ju88 M2+CH was found and the Frenchman was later given credit for its destruction.

Leutnant Werner Boy had already made one run over the target that night but his bombs had failed to drop and so the nineteen year-old pilot had decided to go around again. He was on his second attempt when the fighter was seen approaching from astern and to starboard. The German survivors of the encounter subsequently reported to their captors that Karl Kügler had jettisoned the bomb load at almost the same time that the fighter opened up with one short burst of cannon fire. The shells struck home, damaging the controls and forcing the Junkers to dive from its approach altitude of 6,000 feet to 3,000 feet, at which point Werner Boy gave the order to bale out. His crew managed to evacuate the aircraft with time to spare and survived to become prisoners of war but the pilot, who was still on board when his aircraft crashed, was killed.

After his encounter with the Junkers, Mahé returned to his patrol line and was to the north-west of York at 03.52 hours when he saw a stick of bombs falling east of the city. Assuming from the line of explosions that the bomber must be flying a north-south route, the Frenchman flew an intercept course over York and obtained a visual on, what he thought was, a Heinkel 111. The enemy machine was accelerating away from the target when Mahé dived to catch up. When he had done so, he repeated his earlier strategy, positioning his Hurricane some 2,000 feet below the raider and then easing his fighter up until he was close to the tail of the German.

He got within seventy yards of the bomber before he opened up with a two–second burst from dead astern. As his bullets found their mark, the enemy machine peeled off very sharply to port and then plunged earthwards in a vertical dive. Mahé followed and managed to squeeze off another short burst using slight deflection. At altitude 1000 feet and with the bomber and fighter still diving steeply at 400mph Indicated Air Speed, the Frenchman fired a three-second fusillade before the danger of hurtling into the groud forced him to break away. By then, he estimated that they were twenty miles east of York and the enemy machine was still in a fairly steep dive. He did not see it again.

19–20 May 1942

One hundred and thirty-two aircraft from *Luftflotte 3* were allocated to raid Hull on the night of 19-20 May 1942. In total, they carried 154 tons of high explosives and 14,200 incendiary bombs. Approximately one hundred aircraft were later reported to have operated over the Hull area, where thirty tons of bombs reportedly fell on port installations. Several large fires broke out in the port area, including Alexandria Docks and the King George Docks, both of which suffered a number of direct hits, and a fire at the Victoria Dock was not brought under control until 23 May. Ulf Balke states that 2./KG2 lost one Do217E-46, while *Blitz, then and now. Vol.3* (1990) claims that Ku.Fl.Gr.1./506 lost two Ju88s[7.]

Examination of the Luftwaffe Loss Returns shows that Do217E-4, coded U5+JK, (w/nr.5362) of 2./KG2, piloted by Leutnant Heinz Scholz, failed to return from the attack on Hull. The same record also shows that Ku.Fl.Gr.1./506 lost two Ju88A-4s: S4+BH (w/nr. 1610) piloted by Feldwebel. Hans Bleek; and S4+AH (w/nr.1514), piloted by Hauptmann Alfred Rumpf. In each case, the date of loss is given as 20 May 1942 but the causes and locations are not stated.

6-7 July 1942 (east of Whitby)

On the night of 6-7 July 1942 *Luftflotte 3* dispatched fifty-two bombers against targets on the Tees. During the course of the raid, twenty-eight tons of high explosives and nineteen tons of incendiaries were dropped over the area, and the Luftwaffe subsequently claimed to have inflicted damage on ICIs chemical works at Billingham, Dorman, Long's steelworks in Middlesbrough, and the yards of the Furness Shipbuilding Co at Haverton Hill. The raid cost KG2 at least one Dornier 217, which is believed to have fallen victim to a Beaufighter of 219 Squadron, Acklington.

Squadron Leader J. Topham (with Flying Officer H.W. Berridge) took off from Acklington in Beaufighter X8221 at 01.15 hours on 7 July and later claimed a Do217(perhaps U5+BT of 9./KG2) off Amble. The Squadron had further success some two hours later, when Flight Lieutenant John Willson(with Pilot Officer D.C. Bunch) in Beaufighter. V8325 claimed a Dornier damaged in a combat which began twenty miles east of Seaham Harbour and ended fifty miles east of Whitby. Willson took off from Acklington at 03.55 hours on 7 July. Under Ouston Control, he was ordered to climb to 13,000 fee on vector 90° before being handed over to Northstead GCI at 04.06 hours. Six minutes later, when the Beaufighter was twenty miles east of Seaham Harbour and still under Northstead's guidance, Bunch got an A.I. *(Airborne Interceptor)* contact on 170° at 13,000 feet altitude and crossing from starboard to port at four miles' range. Bunch then guided Willson close enough to get a visual of a Do217, to starboard and 1,000 feet above the night-fighter.

The German gunners were alert and opened fire with twin guns from the lower (ventral) turret as Willson made his approach. That gunfire was the prelude to a series of violent evasive actions – jinking and diving from 13,000 feet to 4,000 feet – which were taken by the bomber and which prevented the Beaufighter from ever getting closer than 400 yards. Willson held his fire for as long as possible in the hope of closing the gap, but when he realized that he was not going to get any nearer he opened fire at 400 yards with four short bursts and one long one with both cannon and machine-gun. The Dornier crew retaliated strongly, mostly with tracer, from both the dorsal and ventral twin gun positions and the Beaufighter received hits on the tail and on the port main plane. However, Willson also had some success and strikes with explosive cannon shells on the bomber's tail and mid-fuselage were soon followed by plumes of black smoke. After that, there was no further defensive fire from the Dornier, which dived to 300 feet before being lost by its pursuers. Willson was fifty miles east of Whitby when he broke off the combat. When he landed at Acklington at 04.53 hours he claimed one Do217 'damaged'. The writer believes that this aircraft may have been a Do217E-4 (w/nr. 1199) of II./KG40, piloted by Oberfeldwebel Alfred Voigt, that crashed near Soesterberg, killing Voigt and two others.

7-8 July 1942 (off Scarborough or the Tyne?) see Discussion below

Aircraft:	Dornier 217E-4	U5+BM	w/nr 5465	4./KG2
Crew:	Fw Johann Grandl	pilot	+	
	Lt Johannes Bredtmeyer	observer	missing	
	Uffz Horst Müller	wireless op	+	
	Uffz Franz Meindl	gunner	missing	

At 00.40 hours on 8 July 1942, some twenty-five raiders appeared seventy miles east of Scarborough, flying north-west at altitudes varying

from 12,000-14,000 feet. When east of the Tyne, they turned south-west and made landfall between Seaham and Scarborough, losing height to 6,000-10,000 feet. Four or five enemy aircraft operated between Seaham and Middlesbrough and three others between Middlesbrough and Scarborough. The remainder concentrated over the Middlesbrough area, where the ICI works at Billingham was probably one of the main objectives. High explosive bombs and incendiaries were dropped, mainly in the Middlesbrough, West Hartlepool and Billingham areas, where damage was done to a dockyard, power-house and warehouse. The ICI works at Billingham suffered damage and a large fire was started at an oil storage site alongside the Tees.

In June 1942, 406 Squadron RCAF moved from Ayr, Scotland, to Scorton , North Yorkshire, and it was from there that Wing Commander D.G. Morris(with Pilot Officer A.V. Rix) took off in a Beaufighter at 00.56 hours on 8 July under Sector Control and with instructions to patrol sixty miles off the coast. After five unsuccessful attempts to intercept targets, Morris was two miles out to sea with Middlesbrough slightly to starboard when he was advised that there was a raider two miles south at a height of between 10,000 feet and 14,000 feet. Shortly afterwards, the north–bound enemy passed nearly vertically below the nightfighter at a range of 2000 feet. Morris dived hard to port in pursuit and gradually overtook the enemy machine, which appeared to be taking no evasive action but was slowly reducing height. After ten minutes, visual contact was obtained at a range of 1,500 feet, with the German slightly to starboard and 200-300 feet above the Beaufighter, which was flying at an altitude of 12,500 feet. Morris identified it as a Dornier 217. He approached to within 500-600 feet below his target and then slowly climbed before edging up to 300 feet range. Using the German's port engine exhaust as his aiming point, Morris fired one burst of two seconds duration with cannon and machine-gun fire. Vivid strikes were seen at the root of the port wing, just before the port engine burst into flames and began to burn furiously. In spite of the damage inflicted on it, the enemy aircraft continued for a time on a straight and level course and returned very accurate fire from a distance of 100 yards, the Beaufighter receiving two hits. Then the Dornier slowed, its port wing and nose dropped, and the aircraft started down in a left-hand turn. Burning parts were seen to fall off the aircraft as it disappeared in a steep spiral through clouds 5,000 feet-6,000 feet below. Although the bomber was not seen to strike the sea, a bright glow was seen reflected through the clouds for a time before it faded out. Morris gave the location of the crash site as being seventy miles east of the Tyne. Fifty minutes later, at 02.55 hours, the nightfighter landed back at Scorton, where Morris was credited with one Dornier 'destroyed'. There is a possibility that Dornier U5+BM, piloted by

Feldwebel. Johann Grandl, was shot down by Morris.

No.406 Squadron RCAF, claimed four other successes (including one damaged) on the night of 7-8 July: Pilot Officer R.H. Harrison accounted for two of them. Harrison (with Pilot Officer E.P.A. Horrex) took off from Scorton at 00.55 hours under Sector Control before being handed over to GCI and then vectored towards the target area of Middlesbrough. At 01.20 hours, when the Beaufighter was at 16,000 feet altitude, Horrex obtained an A.I. contact at maximum range on an enemy aircraft approaching head-on at 1,000 feet above. Harrison got a visual when the enemy aircraft was directly overhead. The nightfighter turned hard to port and gave chase, Harrison following visually but being aided by A.I. At range 1,500 feet, keeping slightly to port of his quarry and with the raider clearly silhouetted against the northern sky, Harrison identified it as a Do217. When the nightfighter had closed to 1,000 feet, the bomber started taking the most violent evasive action, eventually turning hard to port and diving on a straight run over the target area. At approximately 01.35 hours, Harrison fired one short deflection burst followed by a longer burst of three seconds from above and with his would-be victim silhouetted against almost daylight conditions during its run over the target. The German responded with some fairly accurate return fire, which did not find the nightfighter. In the brilliance of the searchlights, bomb bursts and incendiary flashes over the target, it was difficult for the Beaufighter crew to detect strikes on the Dornier but immediately after the second burst the enemy machine pulled over sharply to port in a very steep dive. It was last seen at 3,000 feet, diving towards the sea at an angle that increased to the vertical. It was impossible for the Beaufighter to follow and so Harrison gave up the chase and returned to Sector Control. He was subsequently awarded a 'probable'.

After his combat over Middlesbrough, he returned to Sector at 01.45 hours and was given vector 140. Horrex got an almost immediate contact on an aircraft well below and 10° to starboard: the enemy machine was reducing height and flying at an Indicated Air Speed of 280mph. Using full throttle, Harrison slowly gained ground. The fighter was at 12,000 feet altitude when Harrison got a visual sighting at 1,500 feet range and identified the silhouette as that of a Dornier. At 02.00 hours, with both pursuer and pursued at 7,000 feet altitude, Harrison eased to within 300 feet of the raider and, in the face of fairly accurate defensive fire from the enemy machine, managed to squeeze off a three-second burst from his cannons. Immediately, a large cloud of white smoke billowed from his victim and that was followed by a vivid explosion. Oil sprayed over Harrison's windscreen as the bomber went into a steep dive with sparks streaming from its starboard engine. The speed was too great and the angle too steep for Harrison to follow and thirty miles south–east of

Hartlepool he was forced to give up the chase. Seemingly, he did not see the Dornier crash but after he had landed at Scorton at 02.35 hours he was credited with one Do217 destroyed.

406 Squadron's fourth claimed success of the night was provided by Wing Commander G.G. Stockdale (with Flight Sergeant W.R. Dibden DFM), who took off from Scorton at 01.05 hours under Sector Control. At 01.37 hours when at a height of 12,000 feet, Stockdale was handed over to GCI and vectored north-west. After a number of vectors, contact was obtained on an enemy aircraft in a head on position, going to port. It was at maximum range and at 8,000 feet altitude. Stockdale turned hard left in pursuit and increased speed to 240mph. In spite of evasive action by the German, contact was maintained for thirty-eight minutes. At 02.15 hours, when both machines were at 6,000 feet altitude, Stockdale got his first momentary visual, which was soon lost in dark cloud. Dibden, however, kept A.I. contact and minutes later a second sighting was obtained and Stockdale identified his quarry as a Dornier 217, which he recognised by the position of its exhausts and by its silhouette. Closing in to 400 feet, he squeezed off a two-second burst from astern and slightly below. Immediately, the Dornier emitted a shower of sparks and then a huge sheet of flame. Burning fiercely, it turned to starboard in a slow climb and fell spinning into the sea. Stockdale landed back at Scorton at 03.20 hours to be credited with one Do217 destroyed. Grandl's Dornier (U5+BM) was the only one acknowledged by the Luftwaffe as having been lost over the North on the night of 7-8 July – and Stockdale was the only claimant who saw his victim crash. Thus there is the possibility that it was he, rather than Morris, who caught Grandl.

No. 406 Squadron's fifth claim was submitted by Pilot Officer A.G. Lawrence (with Sergeant H.J. Wilmer), who took off at 01.15 hours and claimed to have destroyed a Heinkel 111 over Hartlepool at 01.30 hours. Lawrence was freelancing at 10,000 feet when Wilmer got an A.I. contact at maximum range and some 600 feet below the Beaufighter. The unidentified aircraft, a 'bogey', was intercepted and when the Beaufighter was 1,500ft astern and 300 feet above Lawrence indentified the silhouette as that of a Heinkel 111. Closing to 400 feet, Lawrence fired two short bursts of one second each from dead astern. No results were obtained other than the enemy aircraft turning slowly to port. Following a further burst of gunfire, this time of three seconds, the bomber swung slowly to starboard. At no time was there any return fire. Then Lawrence saw a flash from the starboard engine immediately prior to the raider going into a spin. Lawrence followed his victim down to 8,000 feet before the Heinkel went into a steep spiral dive. It was followed visually until it disappeared into clouds at 3,000 feet, still spinning. The bomber was not seen to crash but Lawrence claimed one He111 destroyed when he landed back at Scorton at 02.40 hours.

Examination of the Luftwaffe Loss Returns shows no Heinkel loss for this date. However, two Ju88s of Ku.Fl.Gr.106 returned damaged from operations but it is not certain that they took part in the raid on the north east.

Luftwaffe Losses for 7 July 1942

4./KG2	Do217E–4	U5+BM	w/nr.5465 pilot – Fw. Johann Grandl
9./KG2	Do217E–4	U5+BT	w/nr.4270 pilot – Oblt. Günter Lanz
II./KG40	Do214E–4	?	w/nr.1199 pilot – Ofw. Alfred Voigt
			Crashed near Soesterberg on return from ops.
Ku.Fl.Gr.106	Ju88A–4	?	w/nr.140022 pilot – unknown.
			Returned to base with 25% damage
Ku.Fl.Gr.106	Ju88A–4	?	w/nr.1650 pilot – unknown
			Returned to base with 25% damage

DISCUSSION

There seems to be a good deal of confusion regarding Luftwaffe losses over the north-east of England on the nights of 6-7 and 7-8 July, with acknowledged authorities putting forward almost diametrically opposed views regarding what happened.

Middlesbrough was raided on the consecutive nights of 6–7 July and 7-8 July. *The Blitz, then and now. Vol. 3*[8] states that the raid on the night of 7-8 July 1942 resulted in the loss of two Do217s by KG2: U5+BT – piloted by Oberleutnant Günter Lanz of 9./KG2 – which crashed into the sea off Middlesbrough, and one from 4./KG2 which crashed off the Dutch coast on its return to the Continent. *Blitz* also claims that 406 Squadron RCAF, Scorton, was responsible for the demise of U5+BT. On the other hand, Ulf Balke states that two Do217s, U5+BT (piloted by Lanz) and U5+BM (piloted by Feldwebel Johann Grandl) were shot down on the night of 6-7 July[9]. However, Balke seems to be in error for the List of Aircrew Losses (*Verlustliste*) at the Deutsche-Dienststelle, Berlin, shows that Grandl and his crew took off from Eindhoven at 23.34 hours on 7 July 1942 – and thus could not have been shot down the night before!

Balke also claims that Squadron Leader John Topham, of 219 Squadron, Acklington, was responsible for shooting down both U5+BM and U5+BT. It is known that Topham made a claim (but only one) for a Do217 on the night of 6/7 July (which was seen to crash off Amble, Northumberland) and that Flight Lieutenant John Willson (also of 219 Squadron) made a claim for one Do217 damaged[10]. Thus 219 Squadron did submit two claims for the night of 6-7 July 1942, but not quite in the form stated by Balke

The situation is not helped by the fact that the Luftwaffe Loss Returns for that time show that *Luftflotte 3* lost three aircraft on operations on 7 July (which could embrace the nights of 6-7 *and* 7-8 July), and might include aircraft claimed by 406 Squadron for 7/8 July. Luftwaffe records show KG2 as having lost two Do217s on 7 July: U5+BM and U5+BT, while II./KG40 is shown as having lost one (w/nr.1199). The latter crash-landed near Soesterberg on return from operations, killing the pilot Oberfelwebel Alfred Voigt and two of his crew. However, it is not certain that this aircraft took part in the Middlesbrough attack, although II./KG40 regularly accompanied KG2 on operational sorties. No operational losses for *Luftflotte 3* could be found for 8 July 1942.

What can be said is that the Luftwaffe's Loss Returns show three Do217s lost on 7 July, one of which crashed in Holland. 219 Squadron claimed one destroyed, which was seen to crash, and one damaged on the night of 6-7 July. 406 Squadron claimed *four* destroyed on the night of 7/8 July, only *one* of which was actually seen to crash, namely, the Do217 claimed by Wing Commander Stockdale (although Morris observed a glow which he interpreted as eminating from his a crashing victim). Thus the combined claims do not match the Loss Returns but the 'sighted' claims do match. However, although the writer has offered possibilities regarding victors and victims, it cannot be said with certainty which claim relates to which loss.

21 July 1942 (off Spurn Head)

Aircraft:	Dornier 217E-4	U5+IH	w/nr 4260	1./KG2
Crew:	Ofw Heinrich Wolpers	pilot	missing	
	Hptmn Walter Frank	observer	missing	
	Fw Karl Schmidt	wireless op	missing	
	Ofw Arnim Eyrich	mechanic	missing	

U5+IH was lost off the east coast whilst on a reconnaissance mission and is believed to have been shot down some fifty miles off Spurn Head by a nightfighter of No.151 Squadron, Wittering. Hauptmann Frank was Staffelkapitän of 1./KG2.

23-24 July 1942 (off Flamborough Head?)

On the night of 23-24 July 1942, a combined force of forty-five Do217s drawn from KG2 and II./KG40 raided Bedford. As a precaution against scattered raids in Fighter Command's No.12 Group area entering No.13 Group territory, three Beaufighters of 406 Squadron RCAF, Scorton, were ordered to patrol the Humber area. One of those crews was Pilot Officer A.G.Lawrence (with Sergeant H.J.Wilmer) who took off at 23.17

hours and thirty-five minutes later claimed a Ju88 destroyed thirty miles off Flamborough Head.

Lawrence took off under Sector Control but shortly afterwards he was handed over to GCI and instructed to climb to 10,000 feet. After several vectors, Wilmer obtained an A.I. contact at the same time that his pilot saw an aircraft 1,000 feet below and crossing from port to starboard. Lawrence turned hard to starboard and lost height while Wilmer maintained A.I. contact with the target aircraft, which by then was using violent evasive action. Both aircraft were at 9,000 feet altitude when Lawrence closed to 300 feet and, from astern and slightly below, identified his quarry as a Ju88. At 23.52 hours he squeezed off a one-second burst of combined cannon and machine-gun fire. There was an immediate violent explosion at the point where wings joined fuselage and the Junkers fell into the sea in flaming pieces. No return fire was experienced in that brief encounter. Lawrence continued to orbit the Humber area until he was ordered to return to base. He landed back at Scorton at 01.20 hours

Examination of the Luftwaffe Loss Returns for this date shows no relevant Ju88 loss.

28-29 August 1942 (east of Whitby?)

Aircraft:	Dornier 217E-4	U5+FH	w/nr 5341	1./KG2
Crew:	Lt Josef Weigl	pilot	missing	
	Uffz Hans-Joachim Hanisch	observer	missing	
	Obgf Maximilian Reitter	wireless op	missing	
	Obgf Wilhelm Schlesinger	mechanic	missing	

Dornier bombers of KG2, augmented by several aircraft from I./KG77, were detailed to attack Sunderland with twenty–one tons of bombs on the night of 28-29 August 1942. In total, fourteen aircraft of *IX Fliegerkorps* took part in the operation. Balke claims that twelve aircraft reached their target, with two others attacking alternatives in Middlesbrough and County Durham[11]. However, it would appear that the raid was more scattered than intended. The Operations Record Book of the Scorton–based 406 Squadron, RCAF, records that about twelve enemy aircraft made a sharp attack on the north-eastern coastal area from Hartlepool to Alnwick between 22.09-23.50 hours and that bombs were dropped in the Sunderland, Seaham, Alnwick and Acklington areas. 406 Squadron scrambled Flight Lieutenant J.R.B. Firth (with Pilot Officer R.G. Harding) in Beaufighter X8222 at 23.00 hours.

The attackers lost two aircraft on the operation: a Junkers 88 (3Z+CB) of 3./KG77 and a Dornier 217 (U5+FH) piloted by Lt Josef Weigl. It is believed that the Ju88 crashed off Sunderland, but it is not known for certain what happened to the Dornier, although it is likely that it fell to Firth. The Operations Record Book of 406 Squadron, Scorton, shows that soon after take-off, Harding obtained an A.I. contact which quickly led to a visual sighting by Firth. A stiff combat followed, ending with the destruction of an enemy aircraft thirty miles east of Whitby, the wreck being observed burning on the water. The Beaufighter was damaged in the engagement and Firth had to return with his starboard engine dead. On his return to Scorton a heavy ground mist increased the hazard of landing. The Beaufighter overshot and crashed into a house near the end of the runway at 00.15 hours. Firth and Harding were killed.

EYEWITNESS
Willi Schludecker, Dornier 217 pilot
Kampfgeschwader 2

Luftwaffe bomber pilot Feldwebel Willi Schludecker began operational flying in the spring of 1941, when he was twenty-one years old. Willi, who was awarded both the Iron Cross (First Class) and the Iron Cross (Second Class), made a total of 120 war operations flights and saw service in the Balkans, over Russia and over England.

During the course of his operational career, nine of his battle-damaged aircraft were written off in crash-landings, the last one of which, on the night of 23-24 July 1942, put him in hospital for six months and ended his operational career, though he later continued flying in an instructor capacity. He knows that he was lucky to survive the war.

Willi Schludecker's first operational flight over England – to Grimsby on the night of 7-8 April 1942 – was his seventieth operational sortie. He completed thirty-two war flights over England and was forced to abort five others, usually due to engine problems. All of those flights were made during April – July 1942 and included sorties to Sunderland, York, and Middlesbrough. Most of those missions were bombing operations but his flights also included mining sorties to the Thames, the Wash, and the Humber as well as a couple of attacks on shipping when, he said, nothing was hit '...because the targets were moving...'

At the time that Willi was operating over England, the Luftwaffe had relatively few aircraft for offensive operations in the West, the shortage being largely due to wide-ranging operational commitments in Russia, the Mediteranean and in the defence of Germany itself in the face of

Fw Willi Schludecker, when he was with 10./KG2, Spring, 1942 [Willi Schludecker]

148

increasing Allied raids. The aircraft that they did have were flown around the clock to give the impression that the Luftwaffe had more aircraft than was actually the case. To this end, several crews often shared one aircraft, crews sometimes flew two sorties in twenty-four hours, and on occasion, two sorties in one night. Bomber units were also frequently moved around to create an impression of operational strength. For example, targets on the English east coast were attacked from bases in Holland while targets on the south and west coasts were raided from bases in France. However, it was usually the same bomber units that carried out operations in both areas. Specific *Gruppen* did not attack specific areas. Instead, the *Gruppen* were regularly moved around for particular operational purposes and thus the location of any one *Gruppe* determined which geographical areas it would operate against.

Shortage of aircraft was not the only difficulty faced by the Luftwaffe at that time. Fuel supplies were always a problem. Thus, in order to conserve supplies, the fuel allocation per aircraft for each operational flight was carefully calculated and each aircraft was rarely given more than the calculated amount, even when England was the target. In addition, a rather questionable practice evolved to secure further economies. The Dornier 217 (the aircraft of KG2 in 1942) needed 400–600 litres of fuel to run up its engines prior to take–off. To avoid such 'wasteful' consumption, crews were ordered to use a cold start procedure, in which aviation spirit was added to oil in the engines in the ration of 1:4. The strategy certainly reduced the warm-up time of engines but it also wore them out more quickly. Willi believes that the practice accounted at least for some of his aborted flights.

Willi Schludecker flew with three separate *Staffeln* of KG2 during the time of his operations over England: 10./KG2, 6./KG2 and 3./KG2. His aircraft was the Dornier 217E–4, which usually carried a bomb load of 2,000kg, combined as follows: 4 x 500kg HE or 2 x 500kg HE +1 x 1,000kg HE or 1,000 x 2kg IBs.

When aircraft in his unit were setting out to raid England, they usually left at minute intervals and generally flew alone in order to reduce the risk of collision over the target, although on nights of a full moon aircraft sometimes flew in threes. British nightfighters were the most dangerous threat faced by German bombers in 1942. Thus Willi believes that, even though there were intervals between aircraft over the target, the fact that there were a number of bombers in the area at any one time had the effect of reducing the chances of night-fighter attack on any one raider. But such dangers did not lie solely over target area. In fact, by 1942, German aircraft were being harassed by British night-fighters at almost every stage of a bombing operation against the British Isles and there were many occasions when bomber crews would see comrades shot down, sometimes before an operation had even got underway.

British 'intruder' night-fighters used to operate over Holland at times when German bombers were taking off from their bases and would endeavour to shoot them down, sometimes with success. It was not a beginning that inspired confidence among bomber crews awaiting take–off. As Willi puts it:

> 'You are standing on the runway, waiting your turn to take off, and you see the first plane shot down in front of you – before you have even left the ground. That did not have a very calming effect on you!'

The pressure continued as bombers made their way out over the sea and towards their objective. KG2 used to exit from the continental mainland via the radio beacons at Texel and Den Helder but the British night–fighters used to circle there too. They also used to lie in wait up to one hundred miles off the English coast, as well as operating over target areas. The danger was ever–present and inevitably had a psychological impact on bomber crews, as Willi points out:

> 'You didn't see anything, but you knew you were being hunted – so you got nervous. Sometimes, somebody would think they'd seen something and shout 'Nightfighter!' and evasive action would be taken, even though nothing was there… .'

Of course, it was better to be safe than sorry, but even if Luftwaffe crews managed to avoid the hazards of the outward flight and the run over the target, danger still lurked elsewhere because the night bomber had too run the gauntlet of the return trip, which usually mirrored the hazards of the outward journey.

Willi remembers that in the early days of operations against England, raiders flew across the North Sea at 'very high' altitudes. However, the resultant exposure to British land–based radar and the subsequent alerting of GCI Beaufighters prompted a change of strategy by the middle months of 1942. Then the flights were made at very low altitude – often not more than sixty feet above the sea – in order to reduce the risk of detection by radar.

> 'We had electrical altimeters to measure precisely our vertical height above the water. But they gave an accurate reading only when the aircraft was not turning: when we were turning, it gave a false reading and showed the height to be greater than it was. So, before turning, we always had to climb a little, otherwise a wing could hit the water during the turn.
>
> We would start climbing to bombing height as we approached the coast. Over the target, I would decide the bombing height, depending on the nature and strength of the defences in the area. In my view, the most strongly defended targets were Southampton, the Isle of Wight and

harbours containing warships. In those cases, I always went in high.

'The night–fighter was the most dangerous threat bomber crews faced, followed by medium flak, which reached up to 3,000 metres and was barrage fire. High altitude flak was not so dangerous and was easier to avoid. My strategy was to have the crew watching the ground. When they saw a muzzle flash from artillery shooting at us, they would call out 'Mündungsfeuer!' I would then change course – and the shell missed.

'Barrage balloons also caused little problem: if we saw them, we simply climbed over them (but, of course, that was the purpose of balloons – to force aircraft to higher altitudes where they would be more exposed to fighters and flak and from where their bombing would be less accurate). If we were to actually hit a balloon, we hoped that the cutters on the leading edges of the wings would sever the cable before it did too much damage.

'Sometimes there were lots of searchlights over a target. Once they caught you, it was difficult to escape. When one caught you, immediately all of the others came, then it was very difficult to get away – usually, only by a full aerobatics programme! '

Fw. Heinrich Buhr, Willi Schludecker's mechanic and gunner. [Heinrich Buhr].

The wreck of Willi Schludecker's Do 217E-4 (U5+BL;w/nr.4252) that he crash land-ed at Gilze-Rijen(Holland) after his encounter with 'Peter' McMillan of 409 Squadron RCAF off the east coast of England on the night of 23-24 July 1942. [Willi Schludecker]

Although Willi was aware of the dangers presented by airborne defenders, generally speaking, he preferred to keep a straight course enroute to the target in order to maintain a precise flight. However, this was potentially very dangerous because his particular Do217 was not equipped with radar detection against night-fighters. Thus the members of his crew were always on the look-out and when a night–fighter was seen to be making an attack they would call out 'Nighfighter!' Willi's tactic was then to make a hard turn to the left, followed immediately by a steep dive into cloud (if there was any) – so steep that the nightfighters, which were usually Beaufighters at the time, were unable to keep up. He would then pull out of the dive near to the ground.

> '*Don't forget that the Do217 was a dive-bomber, although bombs were often released in level flight. It had two bomb-sights: one used by the observer (who was responsible for bombing when the aircraft was in level flight), the other used by the pilot (who was responsible for bombing when the aircraft did a diving attack). The Do217 was licensed to a diving speed of up to 750km (468mph) IAS, But on one occasion, while attempting to evade a night–fighter, I took my aircraft to 950km (594mph) IAS. I distorted the wing surfaces – but we got away!*'

During an attack on Sunderland on the night of 30 April-1 May 1942, Willi was threatened by a night-fighter as he neared the English coast. When the warning shout came, he instinctively dived for (what he thought was) cloud below but it was, in fact, sea haze. He was over land when he pulled out of his dive and immediately realized the potential danger of his situation when his aircraft narrowly missed some trees as it was restored to level flight. Shortly afterwards, he dropped his bombs on

Willi Schludecker's Do 217 (U5+BL), Gilze-Rijen, 24 July 1942. [Heinrich Buhr].

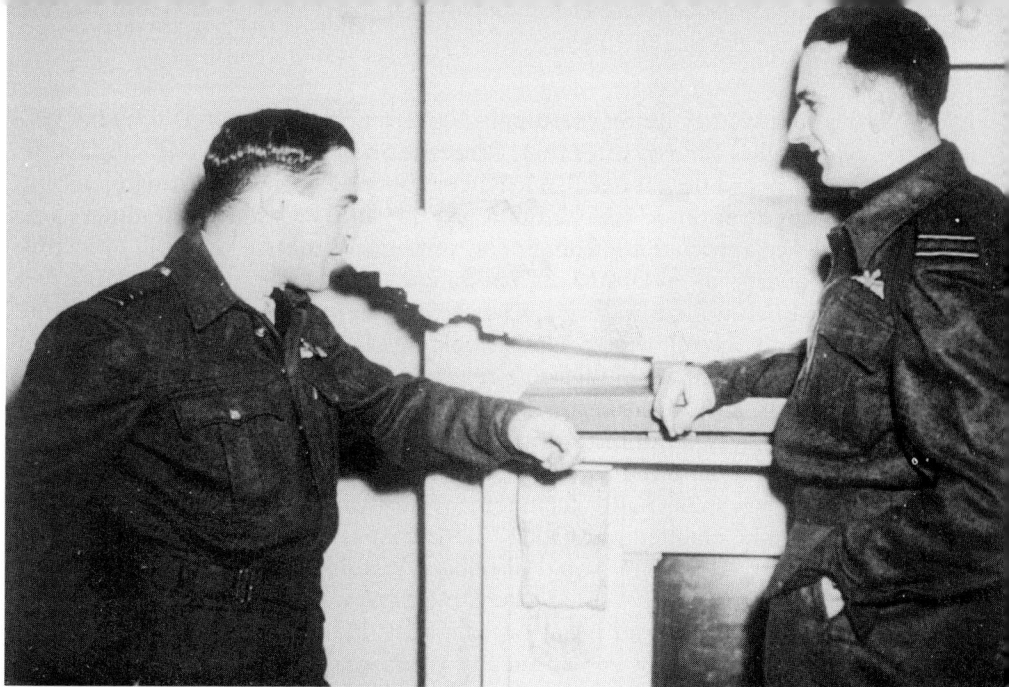

a railway line '...possibly in the area of Seaham...' and beat a hasty retreat. Willi Schludecker and his crew felt the heaviest impact of a night-fighter attack on the night of 23-24 July 1942, when they were approaching the east coast of England and en route to Bedford. For some time previously one of their machine guns had not been working properly and the mechanic-gunner, Feldwebel Heinrich Buhr, was testing it over the sea. The test eventually proved that the gun was working but it was shooting tracers and, they believe, the flashes attracted a patrolling nighfighter. Schludecker saw the fighter approaching for a stern attack but decided to allow it to get near enough to be shot down by the Dornier's gunners. As soon as the German gunners opened up, the Beaufighter returned fire with its four cannons and six machine guns. The combined muzzle flashes from the fighter's guns were so bright that the Dornier crew thought that they had hit their attacker and that it had exploded! They did not see it again but it had not been damaged.

Schludecker's assailant was Flight Lieutenant E.L. 'Peter' McMillan, in a Beaufighter Mk.VI (X8153) of 409 Squadron, RCAF. McMillan (with Sergeant Shepherd) had taken off from Coleby Grange (Lincs) at 23.05 hours on 23 July and had already shared in the destruction of one Do217 that night.[12] Peter McMillan's combat report records that after his first victory he resumed patrol and was given vector 100 by his GCI Controller. Shortly after that, Sergeant Shepherd got an A.I. contact 20° to starboard on a 'bogey'. McMillan obtained a visual sighting of a vague silhouette at range 1,500ft but it was not until he had moved much closer and was approaching from below and to port that he was able to identify his quarry as a Do217. When range had been reduced to 500 feet, McMillan pulled up level and astern of the raider and launched his one and only assault which almost coincided with a burst of gunfire from Heinrich Buhr, Schludecker's rear gunner, before the Dornier rolled to one side and dived vertically away. McMillan attempted to follow but decided to pull out of his dive when his altimeter was reading 4,000 feet. His aircraft suffered no damage in the encounter but he knew that some of his own shells had struck home. Thus when he landed back at Coleby Grange he claimed one Do217 destroyed and one Do217 damaged.

In fact, McMillan would have been justified in claiming two Dorniers that night for Willi Schludecker's machine was so badly damaged by the night–fighter's assault that he jettisoned his bomb-load and turned for home. It was only with difficulty that he finally reached base at Gilze Rijen, where he crash-landed his aircraft at three times the normal landing speed after making three approaches. It was his ninth crash-landing and the injuries he sustained in it put him in hospital for six months and ended his operational flying career.

Extract from Willi Schludecker's flying log–book [Kampfgeschwader 2]

Op	Date	Time up/down	Aircraft	Staffel	Base	Target
1	7/8.4.42	2201-0135	Do217/U5+AU	10./KG2	Achmer[1]	Grimsby. Bombed from 800m. Heavy flak.
2	15/16.4.42	2245-0205	Do217/U5+HP	6./KG2	Soesterberg	Sunderland. Bombed from 800m.
3	16/17.4.42	2400-0345	Do217/U5+HP	6./KG2	Soesterberg	Southampton. Bombed from 2,800m.
4	18.4.42	0044-0415	Do217/U5+HP	6./KG2	Soesterberg	Southampton. Bombed from 3,000m.
5	18/19.4.42	2221-0105	Do217/U5+HP	6./KG2	Soesterberg	Grimsby. Bombed from 2,500m
6	23/24.4.42	2204-0109	Do217/U5+HP	6./KG2	Soesterberg[2]	Exeter. Bombed from 800m. Flak and searchlights. (Baedeker raid)
7	24/25.4.42	2314-0321	Do217/U5+HP	6./KG2	Soesterberg	Exeter. Bombed from 1,500m. Flak searchlights and nightfighters. (Baedeker raid).
8	25/26.4.42	2203-0055	Do217/U5+HP	6./KG2	Soesterberg	Bath. Bombed from 1,200m. Flak, searchlights and nightfighters. (Baedeker raid).

9	26.4.42	0343-0642	Do217/U5+HP	6./KG2	Soesterberg	<u>Bath.</u> Bombed from 1,600m. Flak, searchlights and nightfighters. (Baedeker raid).
10	27.4.42	0042-0253	Do217/U5+HP	6./KG2	Soesterberg	<u>Bath.</u> Bombed from 2,800m. Flak, searchlights and nightfighters. Return flight on one engine.(Baedeker raid).
11	27/28.4.42	2333-0135	Do217/U5+HP	6./KG2	Soesterberg	<u>Norwich.</u> Bombed from 2,500m. Flak, searchlights, nightfighter. (Baedeker raid).
12	29.4.42	0154-0507	Do217/U5+HP	6./KG2	Soesterberg	<u>York.</u> Bombed from 1,000m. Hit gasometer. Nightfighters, flak and searchlights. (Baedeker raid).
13	1.5.42	0123-0527	Do217/U5+FP	6./KG2	Soesterberg	<u>Sunderland.</u> Bombed from 50m. following three nightfighter attacks.
14	4.5.42	0058-0322	Do217/U5+LP	6./KG2	Eindhoven[3]	<u>Exeter.</u> Bombed from 1,400m
15	4/5.5.42	2214-0014	Do217/U5+LP	6./KG2	Eindhoven*	<u>Cowes.</u> Bombed from 3,000m Heavy flak and searchlights
16	8/9.5.42	2348-0213	Do217/U5+LP	6./KG2	Eindhoven	<u>Norwich.</u> Bombed from 2,100m. Heavy searchlight activity. (Baedeker raid).
17	13.5.42	1947-2136	Do217/U5+LP	6./KG2	Eindhoven	Armed reconnaisance. Low altitude.
18	19/20.5.42	2225-0148	Do217/U5+LP	6./KG2	Eindhoven	<u>Hull.</u> Bombed from 2,000m. Heavy flak and searchlights.
19	24/25.5.42	2347-0223	Do217/U5+AL	3./KG2	Gilze Rijen[4]	<u>Poole.</u> Bombed 1,500m. Light flak.
20	28/29.5.42	2238-0143	Do217/U5+DL	3./KG2	Gilze Rijen	<u>Humber estuary.</u> Mining. 400m. 3 nightfighter attks. Fire combat.
21	29/30.5.42	2330-0313	Do217/U5+DL	3./KG2	Gilze Rijen	<u>Grimsby.</u> Bombed from 800-1,000m. Flak splinter in tail.
22	30/31.5.42	2337-0145	Do217/U5+LL	3./KG2	Gilze Rijen[5]	<u>Thames.</u> Mining from 800m. Nightfighter.
23	1.6.42	0030-0220	Do217/U5+AL	3./KG2	Gilze Rijen	<u>Canterbury.</u> Bombed from 1,700m. Nightfighters, flak, searchlights.
24	2.6.42	0147-0335	Do217/U5+AL	3./KG2	Gilze Rijen	<u>Ipswich.</u> Bombed from 800m. Nightfighters, flak and searchlights.
25	3.6.42	0155-0358	Do217/U5+AL	3./KG2	Gilze Rijen	<u>Poole.</u> Bombed from 1,800m. Nightfighters and searchlights. Return flight on one engine
26	8.6.42	2253-0245	Do217/U5+AL	3./KG2	Gilze Rijen	<u>Isle of Wight.</u> Mining from 800m. Flak and searchlights.
27	13.6.42	0015-0349	Do217/U5+CL	3./KG2	Gilze Rijen	<u>Isle of Wight.</u> Mining from 500m.Flak and searchlights.
28	15.6.42	2340-2400	Do217/U5+AL	3./KG2	Gilze Rijen	<u>Isle of Wight.</u> Mining. Aborted. Engine problems.
29	21.6.42	2317-0254	Do217/U5+CL	3./KG2	Gilze Rijen	<u>Southampton.</u> Bombed from 1,800m. Flak and searchlights.
30	24/25.6.42	2326-0250	Do217/U5+AL	3./KG2	Gilze Rijen	<u>Birmingham.</u> Bombed from 1,600m
31	27.6.42	0039-0309	Do217/U5+CL	3./KG2	Gilze Rijen	<u>Norwich.</u>Bombed from 600m. Searchlights, nightfighters, flak and barrage balloons.

32	27.6.42	2350-2351	Do217/U5+CL	3./KG2	Gilze Rijen[6]	Weston-S-Mare. Crashed NW of Evreux after RH motor failed on take–off. 60% damage to aircraft.
33	2.7.42	0051-0137	Do217/U5+AL	3./KG2	Gilze Rijen[7]	Bristol. Aborted. Engine problems.
34	6/7.7.42	2347-0331	Do217/U5+BL	3./KG2	Gilze Rijen	Middlesbrough. Bombed from 800m. Flak, searchlights, barrage balloons. Flak in u/carriage
35	12.7.42	2330-0040	Do217/U5+BL	3./KG2	Gilze Rijen	Thames estuary. Mining. Aborted. Engine problems.
36	13.7.42	2400-0140	Do217/U5+BL	3./KG2	Gilze Rijen	Thames estuary. Mining from 700m. Searchlights.
37	23.7.42	2200-0039	Do217/U5+BL	3./KG2	Gilze Rijen	Bedford. Damaged by nightfighter off English east coast. Aborted. Crash–landed in wood at Gilze–Rijen.

1. Transferred to Schipol for the attack.
2. Transferred to Evereux on 23.4.42 for the attack and stayed there until 27.4.42(pm). All Soesterberg operations were mounted from Evereux in the period 23–27.4.42.
3. Transferred to Evereux for the attack. Eindhoven* operations against Cowes also mounted from Evereux.
4. Transferred to Evereux for the attack.
5. Transferred to Deelen for the attack.
6. Transferred to Evereux for the attack.
7. Transferred to Evereux for the attack.

September 1942. The wreck of Me 210A-1 (2H+CA; w/nr.2348) of 16./KG16 in a field alongside the Redcar reservoir, New Marske, and close to New Buildings Farm. The tail unit landed in the field between the trees on upper right. [Author's collection]

1 September 1942

The Luftwaffe Loss Lists (*Verlustliste*) at the Deutsche-Dienststelle, Berlin, shows that Do217 F8+EN (w/nr. 233) of 5./KG40 failed to return from operations against Leeds on the night of 1 September 1942. The crew of Oberfeldwebel. Karl Schnieder (pilot), Oberfeldwebel. Gerhard Schmidt (observer), Feldwebel. Fritz Wengel (wireless operator) and Obergerfreiter Eduard Schösser (mechanic) were listed as 'missing'. The cause and location of the loss is not given in the lists and currently the writer can shed no further light on the incident.

6 September 1942 (New marske, near Redcar)

Aircraft:	Messerschmitt 210A-1	2H+CA	w/nr 2348	16./KG6
Crew:	Fw Heinrich Mösges	pilot	+	
	Obgfr Eduard Czerny	wireless/op	+	

6 September 1942 (Near Robin Hood's Bay)

Aircraft:	Messerschmitt 210A-1	2H+HA	w/nr 2321	16./KG6
Crew:	Oblt Walther Maurer	pilot	pow	
	Fw Rudolf Jansen	wireless/op	pow	

These aircraft were on reconnaissance over the Tees area when they were intercepted by two Typhoons of 1 Squadron, Acklington. Typhoon pilots Pilot Officer Perrin and Pilot Officer Bridges had been scrambled from Acklington at 11.16 hours and had patrolled the Farne Islands and Blyth before being vectored along the coast towards Teesside.

At about 11.46 hours, when they were at 28,000 feet and to seaward of Redcar, Perrin and Bridges saw the Messerschmitts to starboard and gave chase. The raiders crossed the coast near Redcar, where they escaped anti–aircraft fire, and were over Lackenby when they realized the danger fast approaching from behind. They jettisoned four bombs over Lackenby before separating. Perrin dived in pursuit of Mösges (in 2H+CA); Bridges broke hard right to follow Maurer (in 2H+HA).

Perrin closed to 250 yards before squeezing off a two–second burst of cannon fire from astern and slightly to port, damaging the intruder's port engine in the process. He then crossed over to fire another two–second burst from astern and slightly to starboard. Pieces flew off the raider's engines as the shells found their target. Perrin's third and final burst at the faltering Me210 was delivered from 100 yards, decreasing to 50 yards from dead astern. His cannons blasted away part of the tail of his victim and caused flames to lick around what remained of the rudder. The stricken aircraft turned on its back to commence a vertical dive earthwards at full power. At 3,000 feet the tail of the Messerschmitt broke off just forward of the leading edge of the fin and the plane started spinning to its final fate in the manner of a sycamore seed.

Whether Obergefreiter Eduard Czerny baled out or whether he was ejected by his aircraft's gyrations can only be guessed but when eight–year old Stanley Hill, of New Buildings Farm, New Marske, saw him falling '...feet first and ramrod straight, as if standing to attention...' his parachute had 'roman candled' and the German wireless operator was in trouble. The silken canopy that would have saved him never fully deployed and the luckless airman plummeted to instant death one hundred yards from the schoolboy. His pilot, Heinrich Mösges was destined to fare no better. Stan Hill remembers that as the spinning Me210 neared the ground close by the small reservoir between New Buildings Farm and Fell Briggs Farm,

'..a second man came tripping out of the aircraft and plunged into the middle of the pool a split–second before the aircraft tucked into the ground just beyond the north wall of the reservoir.'

Mösges did not survive.

Meanwhile, Bridges was in pursuit of Maurer, the Staffelkapitän of 16./KG6, as 2H+HA flew south towards Whitby. Initially, the Typhoon seemed to be making no impression on the distance that separated pursued and pursuer but then Maurer turned to port and Bridges immediately noticed the distance decreasing. As the Me210 began diving south–eastwards, Bridges closed rapidly and fired several short bursts at 200 yards from the port quarter astern. His shells struck home between the Me210's port engine and the fuselage as well as on the cockpit cover. As Maurer began to weave violently, Bridges saw pieces fly off the damaged engine shortly before it began to emit white smoke. A second burst of cannon fire from Bridges caused the Me210's port engine to catch fire and then the Messerschmitt slowed down and dived away steeply to port. The raider was over Robin Hood's Bay when Maurer and Jansen baled out. Shortly afterwards, at 11.50 hours, the Messerschmitt

Oblt. Walter Maurer, Staffelkapitän of 16./KG6, whose Me.210A-1(2H+HA) was shot down on 6 September 1942 over Robin Hood's Bay, North Yorks. by No.1 (Typhoon) Sqdn, Acklington.
[via Steve Simpson]

Me 210A-1 (2H+CA; w/nr. 2348) was shot down by a Typhoon of 1 Squadron, Acklington, on the morning of 6 September 1942 and crashed at New Marske, near Redcar (North Yorks). Pilot Fw. Heinrich Mösges and wireless operator Obgfr. Edmund Eduard Czerny did not survive and are buried in Acklam Road cemetery, Thornaby on Tees. [Trevor Smith]

crashed at Sunnyside Farm, Fylingthorpe, near Robin Hood's Bay.

Maurer landed in the sea, close inshore. Mrs Amy Collinson, one-time landlady of the Bay Hotel, Robin Hood's Bay, recorded the incident in her diary:

'A memorable occasion was September 6th 1942, when a German plane crashed in the field behind Sunnyside Farm. About mid–day, we saw a parachutist come from the land, over the old village and heading towards the sea. Immediately, the Olive, *Oliver Storm's boat, was launched through the barbed wire of the dock and along with Mr Storm were Reuben Bulmer and Jack Fewster. From our balcony we could see that the airman was in the water and there was a race towards him from a Whitby fishing boat and a Scarborough fishing boat. The Bay boat reached him first, but on seeing that it was a German airman the Bay boat did not pick him up but let the Scarborough boat take him to Scarborough. Jack Fewster, who was a Special Constable, had the authority to arrest the*

Manufacturer's plate from Me 210A-1 (2H+HA) of 16./KG6. [Author]

airman. *However, Reuben Bulmer had recently lost his only son at sea* (through enemy action, when the Whitby steamer SS *Kildale* was sunk by air attack on 3 November 1940) *and was very bitter towards Germans, so Jack gave way to the older man.*

Jansen made a safe landing in a large cow pasture near Middlewood Farm, Fylingthorpe, and was apprehended by Frank Roberts, a Hull journalist, who was brambling nearby with his children.

EYEWITNESS
A memorable day at Robin Hood's Bay
6 September 1942

'I was living at 'Holme Dene', New Thorpe, Robin Hood's Bay, from 1940 to 1945. On Sunday, 6 September 1942 I was waiting by the roadside outside the house for my school-friend, Ernest Brown, to deliver the Sunday newspapers. While I was watching him coming up the hill to our house, I could hear distant cannon-fire out to sea and to the north of the bay. However, I thought little of it because aircraft regularly tested their guns over the sea. When Ernest arrived at the gate, the gunfire appeared to be much closer and we both looked out to sea for a while but could see nothing unusual, although visibility was good and we were standing about 300ft above sea level. Eventually, we made out a twin-engine plane coming in from the sea, directly towards us. It was at about 1,000ft, with smoke trailing behind it. We could see no other plane in pursuit and as it drew nearer we could see that it was a fighter-bomber. As it approached Fylingthorpe village, two parachutes opened up below it

The aircraft lost height and crashed below the crest of the hill behind

Sunnyside Farm, at the top of Sledgates. There was an explosion, followed by dense smoke and flames and it was impossible to make out the exact spot where it had fallen. Ernest and I raced up the 1 in 4 hill as only two fifteen year-olds could and, upon arriving near Parkgate Farm, found the road littered with small pieces of aluminium debris from the plane, which by this time was burning fiercely in the small field behind Sunnyside. The stone wall that bordered the road up to the Park Gates had been flattened by the blast for several yards. Parts of the plane had evidently blown over the road into the garth opposite because there was also a large fire there. We knew that the main fuselage was behind the wall, however, because there were explosions coming from that direction as ammunition was ignited.

We kept under the cover of the shattered wall and were not foolhardy enough to approach any closer: it was obvious that there was little left of the aircraft... As we left the scene, I noticed that one of the small fragments of aluminium on the ground was oblong in shape. Upon picking it up, I was delighted to find that it was an identification plate from a piece of the plane's equipment. Upon examining this much later, I noticed the letters 'ME' and the numbers '210'. This puzzled me because I knew only of the Messerschmitt Me 110 and had never heard of the Me210. It was sometime later before details of the plane appeared in the spotters' books and I knew for certain what type it was.

Dennis Crosby, schoolboy, Robin Hood's Bay, 1942

23-24 September 1942 (off Flamborough Head)

Aircraft:	Dornier 217E-4	U5+FH	w/nr 4294	1./KG2
Crew:	Oblt Alfred Cornelius	pilot	missing	
	Uffz Werner Hawran	observer	missing	
	Fw Gerhard Hopf	wireless/op	missing	
	Uffz Otto Muxel	mechanic	missing	

Four Dornier 217s of KG2 took part in a raid on York on the night of 23-24 September 1942. A further machine attacked an alternative target at Beverley. Do217 U5+FH is believed to have been shot down during the attack by Pilot Officer R.Peake in a Beaufighter of 25 Squadron, Church Fenton.

Peake (with Sergeant T.R. Parry) took off in Beaufighter X7814 at 22.45hours. After a few practice interceptions with Easington Chain Home Low (CHL) radar station, they chased a 'bogey' and after closing range to 4,000 feet Peake got a visual sighting of a Do217. The Beaufighter subsequently closed to 2,000 feet range, at which the enemy gunners opened fire. However, the German bullets failed to find their mark and Peake followed the bomber round in a diving turn, closed to 600 feet and aimed a combination of cannon and machine–gun fire at his target while the enemy gunners offered spirited resistance. Peake then lost sight of his target while attempting to avoid the raider's defensive gunfire. It seems, however, that Peake's initial assault was effective because Pilot Officer Hill of the same squadron saw the bomber falling in flames before striking the sea, where its wreckage continued to burn for a short while.

It is believed that KG2 suffered a further loss when another Do217E-4 (w/nr.4244) crash-landed on its return to Eindhoven and suffered forty per cent damage. Peake landed back at Church Fenton at 01.30 hours.

17 December 1942 (Wheeldale Moor, near Goatland)

Aircraft:	Dornier 217E-4	U5+AK	w/nr 4348	2./KG2
Crew:	Fw Wilhelm Stoll	pilot	+	
	Obgfr Hans Röschner	observer	+	
	Obgfr Gerhard Wicht	wireless/op	+	
	Obgfr Franz Armann	mechanic	+	

17 December 1942 (Hawnby, near Helmsley)

Aircraft:	Dornier 217E-4	U5+GR	w/nr 4342	7./KG2
Crew:	Oblt Rolf Häusner	pilot	+	
	Uffz Sirius Erd	observer	+	
	Obfw Hartwig Hupe	wireless/op	+	
	Obfw Ernst Weiderer	mechanic	+	

Fifteen Do217s of KG2 carried out a 'revenge attack' on York on the night of 17-18 December 1942. At about 22.00 hours they dropped four tons of high-explosives and almost three tons of incendiaries from heights between 2,000 – 3,000 feet. Most of the bombs fell in the city area and a number of large fires were started, perhaps the most spectacular being caused by the crew of Oberleutnant Karl von Manowarda, who claimed to have hit the gasworks. The attack cost KG2 two aircraft: U5+AK, flown by Feldwebel Wilhelm Stoll, and U5+GR, piloted by Oberleutnant. Rolf Häusner.

U5+AK crashed at about 22.00 hours in an isolated location on Wheeldale Moor, high above Goathland, and was not discovered for some days. The four members of the crew were killed and were later buried in the Acklam Road cemetery, Thornaby-on-Tees. There were no signs of bullet strikes in the wreckage but there were indications of anti–aircraft fragmentation. Thus Air Intelligence investigators concluded that the aircraft had been engaged by anti-aircraft fire and had been sufficiently damaged to prevent it gaining enough height to clear the moors. It hit the flat top of a hill 2000 feet above sea level at a very shallow angle and completely disintegrated, spreading wreckage over 800 yards. Investigators later reported that both engines (BMW 801) broke off when the aircraft first touched down and although they rolled a long way, one was retrieved in comparatively good condition. The remains of a power turret containing an MG131 of 13mm were also traced. From ammunition found scattered round the crash site, it appeared that guns of 20mm and 7.9mm calibre had also been carried as armament. Two single-seat dinghies were recovered in addition to pieces of the normal four–seat dinghy. In this regard, the crash investigators were moved to note that the aircraft involved in the previous three Do217 crashes they had investigated had carried single-seat dinghies in addition to the normal large dinghy. From a captured document it was evident that such had become standard practice with certain long–range bomber units operating over the sea.

Obfw. Hartwig Hupe (right) wireless operator of Do 217E-4 (U5+GR;w/nr. 4342) of 7./KG2, which crashed at Crow Nest, six miles NW Helmsley (North Yorks), 17 December 1942. [via Ulf Balke].

U5+GR came down at 22.15 hours at Crow Nest, (military map ref. Z9909) near the village of Hawnby, six miles north-west of Helmsley, whilst en route to York. Various explanations have been offered as to the cause: Balke gives credit to anti-aircraft fire[14], while eye-witness William Woods, now of Ewe Cote Farm, Laskill, recalls that as a twenty-one year old living with his parents at Wethercote Farm, he heard machine-gun fire above him shortly before the aircraft crashed. On the other hand, Air Intelligence investigators thought that the crash had resulted from a flying accident *'for there were no reports of action in the neighbourhood at the time.'*

Whatever the cause, the machine hit a stone wall near the top of a hill 1,500 feet above sea level and entirely disintegrated, scattering wreckage over many acres and causing a number of small fires. Investigators subsequently deduced that the armament of the bomber had consisted of one MG151 machine-gun of 15mm calibre, one forward–firing Oerlikon 20mm(the ammunition being contained in 30-round drums), probably two MG131 machine–guns of 13mm and one or two MG15s of 7.9mm calibre. Four 50kg incendiary bombs of a new type 'Sprengbrand C.50'

Obfw. Ernst Weiderer (gunner/mechanic) and Obfw. Hartwig Hupe (wireless operator) were buried in Dishforth cemetery, near Thirsk (North Yorks) after their Do. 217 (U5+GR) of 7./KG2 crashed at Crow Nest, near Helmsley. Both were exhumed on 20 June 1962 and transferred to the German Military Cemetery at Cannock Chase, were they still lie. [Author]

(HE/Incendiary) were found near the crash, as well as several unused parachute flares. The remains of a single-seat dinghy were found in the wreckage in addition to the normal four-seat dinghy.

It is believed that the crew of four were killed. Ernst Weiderer was buried in Dishforth cemetery on 24 December 1942, alongside an 'unknown Hauptmann' from the same crash. The 'unknown' airman was later identified as Oberfeldwebel Hartwig Hupe – although the difference of rank raises a question. Both bodies were exhumed on 20 June 1962 and now lie in the German Military Cemetery at Cannock Chase.

EYEWITNESS
A Luftwaffe pilot remembers the night attack on York, 17–18 December 1942

'In spite of poor weather conditions, we got the order to make a reprisal attack on York. After briefing on the mission and weather conditions – at which the 'weather man' raised his eyebrows in doubt – we went to our planes. Rain spattered in puddles on the airfield and the wind whistled and sang around the aerials and wires of the camouflage nets. We set off at last at 20.05 hours. Strong squalls were trying to sweep us from the runway. The heavily-laden Do217 reared up and shook but it responded to the rudder. We drew free and climbed slowly.

'Flying on instruments, we went out over the North Sea. The air stream pushed the rain horizontally past the cockpit window and the white horses of the North Sea, whipped up by the storm, gleamed below us. On the right, the Dogger Bank flashed past and on the left Flamborough Head soon came into view. That narrow tongue of land with the now–extinguished lighthouse: it was there that my old squadron leader, Oblt. Cornelius, was killed on the 23-24 September in an air battle with a British night-fighter. Further south was the mouth of the Humber, and there was a dangerous flak battery at Grimsby. Over the Wash, our best gunner shot down his third nightfighter, which was set to attack from out of the protective darkness below. Every stretch of land in England held its own memories from previous difficult attacks. Finally, we reached Flamborough Head and from there we changed course for York.

In the late 1970s a substantial amount of the wreckage of Do 217 (U5+AK) still remained on Wheeldale Moor. [Norman Sudron].

'The coast swung blackly from the horizon and the first roofs, wet with rain, gleamed in the pale moonlight. The first nightfighter slipped past. On the left of our course there was a sudden bright glow of fire. We went further over England. Hailstones cracked against the cockpit and the fuselage. At last we reached the little river Ouse. We were flying in patches of cloud with brief glimpses of the ground as we approached the target.

'On the road that led straight to York, a lonely driver put his headlights on every few minutes: he obviously didn't like the swinish weather. The first houses in York started along this road. Bomb doors open! We climbed higher and made out the gas works first. The bombs fell. Before we could fly away in a left–hand curve, the plane jerked and a dazzling tongue of flame shot up as high as a church tower. The flame turned blood red. We must have hit the gas works. On the flight back, we could see the red clouds over York from ten kilometres away.'-

**Oberleutnant Karl von Manowarda, pilot,
Do217 3./KG2**

NOTES

1 Operations Record Book, 938 Balloon Squadron, 15 Jan.1942. AIR27/2281 in Public Record Office.
2 Franz Kurowski: *Seekrieg aus der Luft*. E.S. Mittler Verlag. Germany. 1979. p186.
3 Winston .G. Ramsey ed.: *The Blitz, then and now vol.3* Battle of Britain Prints(International. 1990. p94
4 Winston G. Ramsey ed: op.cit p121.
5 AI1(k) Report No.85/1942. AIR40/2410 in Public Record Office. Winston G. Ramsey ed: ibid. gives the location as Tree Farm, Elvington.
6 Ulf Balke: *Der Luftkrieg in Europa: die operativen Einsätze des Kampfgeschwaders 2 im zweiten Weltkrieg vol 2*. Bernard & Graefe Verlag. Koblenz.1990 p112.
7 Winston G. Ramsey ed: op.cit. p131.
8 Winston G. Ramsey ed: op.cit. p153.
9 Ulf Balke: op.cit. p128.
10 Bill Norman: *Broken Eagles 2:* Northumberland and Durham (to be published 2002).
11 Ulf Balke: op.cit. p147.
12 Do217E–4 (F8+CN;w/nr.4279) of 6./KG40, which crashed at Gedney Hill, Holbeach, at 2355hours. Credit shared with F/Lt H.H. Sweetman, in a Hurricane of 486 Squadron, Wittering. But see 'Disputed Kill' by Alastair Goodrum in *FlyPast* magazine April 2001.
13 This serial is taken from the Luftwaffe Loss Reports but Air Intelligence investigators stated that the serial no.5600 was painted on the fin.
14 Ulf Balke:op.cit. p181.

4

DESPERATE TIMES
(1943-1945)

By 1943, German forces had extended their control in France to include the southern half of the country, which previously had been unoccupied because of agreements with the Vichy Government. As a consequence, the burden on *Luftflotte 3* was increased further. By May 1943 it was responsible for covering Belgium, Holland and the whole of France. In January of that year, the Luftwaffe had only about one hundred bombers and fighter-bombers for operations in the West. In March 1943 the post of *Angriffsführer England* was created to strengthen that bomber force and develop an effective fighting force against England, but by September the force stood at 135 aircraft (mainly Do217s and Ju88s) and replacements were barely keeping up with losses.

Bombs fell on the East Riding in January 1943 and in March 1943, German bomber units (mainly KG2, with help from KG6) carried out a number of destructive attacks, mainly on targets near the coast – including Teesside and Hull – but only with minimal effect. By that time, the Luftwaffe had modified its offensive tactics on approaching targets. Because of the numbers of nightfighters waiting in those areas where incoming bombers climbed to attack height, low-flying approaches were abandoned and the climb was spread over the length of the entire flight across the North Sea. It was hoped that such a change would reduce the risk of interceptions while obviating the need for the precautionary evasive tactics which had previously made accuracy so difficult. Hull, the most frequently bombed town in Britain during the Second World War, continued to have visits from night bombers until well into the summer of 1943, bombs falling on the town on four separate instances in July and August. The same months saw bombs widely scattered throughout the county on two other occasions.

By then, the bomber war against England was virtually over, although Hull was visited briefly in April 1944, when raiders were over the area south of a line drawn between Scarborough and York. Bombs fell but little damage was inflicted. The last visit to the north of England by the Luftwaffe in strength occurred on the night of 3-4 March 1945, when Ju88 nightfighters infiltrated streams of RAF bombers returning to Yorkshire after an attack on Kamen, in the Ruhr. The RAF suffered forty-four aircraft lost or damaged.

Losses
January 1943 - March 1945

3 January 1943 (Skeffling, Spurn Head)

Aircraft:	Dornier 217E-4	U5+KT	w/nr 4314	9./KG2
Crew:	Uffz Anton Reis	pilot	pow	
	Obgfr Horst Küster	observer	pow	
	Uffz Arno Salz	wireless op	pow	
	Uffz Alfred Muschiol	mechanic	pow	

On the evening of 3 January 1943, *IX Fliegerkorps* assigned units of I./KG2 and II./KG2, as well as part of II./KG40 to attack port installations in Hull. In total twenty-three aircraft were detailed. Because of exceptionally severe weather – rain, hail showers and gusting winds – it proved to be a demanding task for crews and many found it difficult to locate the target. Three aircraft attacked alternative targets at Withernsea, Hornsea and an aerodrome near the coast; another three broke off the operation because of technical problems. Fifteen Do217s claimed to have been over Hull between 20.32-20.56 hours and part of the fourteen tons of high explosive and three tons of incendiaries that were dropped fell on the City Docks as well as in the adjacent areas of the town to the north and west. Returning crews reported 'numerous fires' in these areas but British sources reported the damage as 'small'. KG2 lost two aircraft on this operation. U5+KT was hit by flak in the area of Spurn Head while on its way to the target and at 21.30 hours made a forced landing on the east side of the Skeffling – Old Newton road, near Spurn Point. The four members of the crew were subsequently captured and taken to Withernsea police station – but not before they had set fire to their aircraft. KG2 lost a second aircraft on the return run when the Do217E-4 of Leutnant Guul (U5+MS; w/nr.5498) of 8./KG2 crashed at Harderwijk (Holland), killing all members of the crew. The cause of the loss is unknown.

15-16 January 1943 (Humber area)

Aircraft:	Dornier 217E-4	U5+AT	w/nr 4272	9./KG2
Crew:	Uffz Hans Unglaube	pilot	missing	
	Oblt Franz Holtz	observer	missing	
	Uffz Rudi Vögerle	wireless op	missing	
	Obgfr Heinz Bongardt	mechanic	missing	

U5+AT was one of fifteeen Do217s targeted on Lincoln and is believed to have been shot down in the Humber area by Flight Lieutenant J.

Singleton in a Mosquito of 25 Squadron, Church Fenton.

Singleton (with Flight Lieutenant C.J.C. Bradshaw) took off at 20.15 hours in a Mosquito Mk.II (DD752) and was vectored on to a hostile raid by Easington CHL. Contact was subsequently obtained on an aircraft at 7,000-8,000 feet altitude and flying an easterly course, crossing from starboard to port at 7,500 feet range. Contact was held until a silhouette and exhausts were seen at 400 yards range. Singleton identified the aircraft as a Do217, which was travelling very fast and weaving continually. Singleton closed to about fifty yards before firing his first burst of gunfire. Strikes were observed on the Dornier's tail unit, whereupon it dived away steeply to port.

Singleton followed and managed a second burst from 150 yards as the enemy machine crossed from starboard to port, but no result was observed. Immediately after that, while attempting to close from astern, the fighter was turned on its back – presumably by the enemy's slipstream – and was violently shaken. This shaking continued after the pilot had brought the nightfighter back to an even keel, by which time the bomber had been lost. When the Dornier was next seen it was 100 feet above the fighter and Singleton, his aircraft still vibrating very badly, eased the Mosquito to within fifty yards before squeezing off another burst as his quarry crossed from starboard to port. Bradshaw saw strikes on the Dornier's port wing root. before the night-fighter crew lost the bomber for a second time.

Singleton's aircraft was still vibrating very badly and as he tried to get it under control, he lost visual contact with the Dornier; Bradshaw also lost A.I. contact and that could not be regained because the CHL Controller was unable to give further help. Vectors were given towards another enemy machine but then the fighter's R/T failed and Singleton decided to return to base. He landed at Church Fenton at 21.25 hours, when it was noticed that the starboard undercarriage nacelle door had been damaged not, however, by enemy action but presumably by the high speed and the slipstream of the enemy aircraft. No return fire was experienced by the Mosquito crew during the engagement and a claim for one Dornier damaged was made.

3 February 1943 (Muston)

Aircraft:	Dornier 217E-4	U5+GL	w/nr 5462	3./KG2
Crew:	Obfw Karl Müller	pilot	missing	
	Fw Heinz Lewald	observer	missing	
	Uffz Friedrich Fruth	wireless op	missing	
	Uffz Heinrich Wilmsen	gunner	missing	

On the night of 3 February 1943, twenty Dornier 217s of KG2 set out to bomb the port installations at Sunderland. Three returned to base early because of technical problems and another two failed to find their target and bombed Hartlepool instead. The remaining aircraft were over Sunderland between 20.31-20.45 hours and dropped thirteen tons of high explosives and two and a half tons of incendiaries. The raid cost KG2 one Do217 (U5+GL) which was shot down by Flight Lieutenant John Willson (with Flying Officer Bunch) in a Beaufighter of 219 Squadron, Scorton.

Willson took off from Scorton in Beaufighter Mk.VI (V8552) at 19.50 hours and was on a training exercise when he was taken over by Seaton Snook GCI Control and ordered to patrol at 11,000 feet. Bunch subsequently got an A.I. contact on a target 5,000 feet below and to port at a range of two miles. Shortly afterwards, under directions from Bunch, Willson reduced his altitude to that of his quarry and obtained a visual sighting at about 1,000 feet range. During that time the enemy machine took violent evasive action consisting of dives, turns, complete orbits and variations of speed between 170-240mph. The chase lasted about five minutes, during which time Willson was able to close in and reduce range to 450-500 feet and to identify the target as a Dornier because of its two fins and a high mainplane. By then the aircraft were in the Filey area and the time was 20.30 hours. As Willson lined up to give the Dornier the benefit of his stealth, the bomber released a flare, which must have illuminated the Beaufighter. At almost the same time that Willson closed in from slightly below and astern and opened fire, the raider's gunners retaliated with orange-coloured tracer from both upper and lower turrets: none of the German bullets found its mark. Willson seems to have had similar luck with his first effort for he failed to see any strikes on the target, and so he continued firing. There was no doubt about his second fusillade, which was of four seconds duration and which found a critical mark. There was a fierce explosion as the target blew up before plummeting earthwards to crash at military map ref. 573985, between Hunmanby and Muston, near Filey, at 20.37 hours. The Dornier hit the ground at high speed and disintegrated, scattering wreckage over an area of some half a mile in length. No trace of the crew was ever found and Air Intelligence investigators assumed that they had baled out over the sea.

11 March 1943 (off Yorkshire coast?)

Aircraft:	Dornier 217E-4	F8+LP	w/nr 5313	6./KG40
Crew:	Uffz Erich Schuld	pilot	missing	
	Uffz Werner Beihofer	observer	missing	
	Uffz Walter Deihard	wireless op	missing	
	Obgfr Wilhelm Pyttel	gunner	missing	

On the night of 11/12 March 1943, fifty-one aircraft of *IX Fliegerkorps* took off in two waves to bomb Newcastle upon Tyne. The first wave consisted of twenty-one aircraft, fifteen of which bombed Newcastle between 21.49-22.10 hours. One crew attacked the alternative target at Tynemouth; the remaining four crews abandoned their allotted tasks because of various technical problems and night-fighter attacks. Crews reported that visibility over the target area was good, bombs were dropped according to orders and several fires were started in the target area. The second wave consisted of thirty aircraft, twenty-two of which bombed Newcastle between 23.18-23.45 hours. By then there was a heavy haze over the town and the bombing was widely scattered. Returning crews reported several small and large fires in the target area. As in the first raid, one Do217 attacked the Tynemouth alternative.

Aircraft from at least three Luftwaffe units – KG2, KG6 and KG40 – took part in the raid and each lost at least one aircraft. The Luftwaffe lost four aircraft in total and Beaufighter crews of 219 Squadron, Scorton, submitted claims for three enemy aircraft 'destroyed' and two 'probably destroyed'. Most of these victories were claimed over the more northern counties of Durham and Northumberland but, Sergeant Hollingworth (with Sergeant Alcock) of 219 Squadron, Scorton, claimed a Dornier 217 some fifty miles off the Yorkshire coast.

Hollingsworth took off from Scorton at 22.00 hours in a Beaufighter Mk. VI. At 23.45 hours, while operating under Goldsborough GCI, Alcock obtained an A.I. contact on an enemy aircraft flying at 2,500 feet altitude and at three miles range. The chase that followed lasted fifteen minutes, during which the enemy machine made slightly jinking manoeuvres from port to starboard, but employed no other evasive tactics. Hollingsworth eventually closed to within 1,500 feet and visually identified his quarry as a Do217. When the Beaufighter had closed to 600 feet, the German – perhaps having realised the danger – did a steep turn to port but Alcock maintained A.I. contact. Hollingsworth managed two short bursts of combined cannon and machine-gun fire from 600 feet and saw strikes on the bomber's port engine, which immediately burst into flames. The fire spread rapidly and the aircraft was soon transformed into a ball of fire as it spiralled down to the sea. The engagement was witnessed by Flight Lieutenant Hooper (of 219 Squadron) who also confirmed that Hollingsworth's victim crashed into the sea fifty miles off the Yorkshire coast. The author hazards a guess that the Dornier was F8+LP of 6./KG40.

EYEWITNESS
KG66: A Luftwaffe 'Pathfinder' crew 1943

Hans Altrogge joined KG66 at the time of its formation in the Spring of 1943 and stayed with it until the end of the war. In a letter to the author he recalled that KG66 recruited experienced personnel from existing bomber units. All of those chosen were above-average fliers who were highly motivated; '...determined and decisive airmen who were primarily individuals but who were capable of special teamwork...' This target-finding unit flew only a few operations against north-east England and were guided to their target by a radio beam (*Hyperbel-Verfahren*). Their progress along the beam was constantly monitored by a ground control station, which also instructed the aircraft when to drop their markers.

One of Altrogge's first operational flights with KG66 was to Hull (Victoria Dock) on 13 July 1943, which 'was a very tiring flight because we had to fly at low level to avoid British radar...' On 17 August 1943, he and his crew acted as a Pathfinder for the raid on the motor works at

Luftwaffe 'Pathfinder' crew of I./KG66 c.1943. L - R: Fw. Hermann(observer), Lt Hans Altrogge(pilot) and Obfhr. Grauenhorst(wireless operator). [Hans Altrogge].

Lincoln by KG2. He was flying a Junkers 188 – his first operational flight in one - and marked the target with flare bombs. The following Do217s of KG2 flew over the North Sea at altitudes of 170-300 feet before climbing to bombing height over the Wash. The attack on Lincoln was not made en-masse but was carried out by number of aircraft making an individual approach. 'This gave the English nightfighters a real chance and we saw seven aircraft shot down. We also saw several nighfighters but we were not attacked...'

Hans Altrogge, pilot,
Ju188 1./KG66, 1943

15-16 March 1943 (off Spurn Head?)

Aircraft:	Junkers 88A-14	3E+WK	w/nr 4532	2./KG6
Crew:	Uffz Arno Diemer	pilot	missing	
	Obgfr Heinz Kretching	observer	missing	
	Uffz Jochen Atzwanger	wireless op	missing	
	Gefr Albert Schmidt	gunner	missing	

15-16 March 1943 (North Thoresby, Lincs)

Aircraft:	Dornier 217E-4	U5+LP	w/nr 5590	6./KG2
Crew:	Oblt Hartmut Holzhapfel	pilot	pow	
	Ofw August Küpper	observer	pow	
	Fw Günter Stein	wireless op	pow	
	Fw Gerhard Dörr	mechanic	pow	

On the night of 15-16 March, *IX Fliegerkorps* attacked the port installations at Grimsby, the aiming point being the Royal Docks and the Alexandria Docks. Forty-four aircraft took off for the operation and thirty-two of those claimed to have operated over the town between 21.25-21.48 hours. The rest of the crews returned early because of night-fighter attacks or technical problems. Although it was a cloudless night, the raid was not successful because a heavy ground haze reduced visibility and prevented crews from finding their targets. The total bomb load of ten tons of high explosive and twenty-three tons of incendiaries was widely scattered and caused no damage worth mentioning. The attackers found night-fighters to be particularly active, with some raiders being intercepted up to 100 miles from the English coast as they made their way towards Grimsby. The raiders lost at least two aircraft on the operation: I./KG6 lost a Ju88 and 6./KG2 lost a Do217. Flight Lieutenant John Willson, of 219 Squadron, Scorton, was credited with the Dornier but he might also have caught the Junkers. He was credited with two victories that night but he believed that both of his victims were Do217. It is possible that he mistakenly identified the Ju88.

Willson (with Pilot Officer O. Holloway), took off from Scorton at

20.20 hours with instructions to intercept hostile aircraft entering the south of the Sector. At 21.15 hours, they were 'freelancing' 10,000 feet over the East Yorkshire coast north of the Humber when Holloway got an A.I. contact on an aircraft crossing from starboard to port at three miles range. Under Holloway's guidance, Willson closed to 3,000 feet and got a visual sighting of four exhausts. The raider appeared to see the Beaufighter at that point and turned hard to starboard and then to port, diving, climbing and increasing speed considerably. Willson eventually got within 1,000 feet range and identified the aircraft as a Do217. He had closed to within 800 feet of the jinking target when the German did a climbing turn to starboard and then started to dive. Willson gave a full deflection burst of two seconds and saw strikes on the Dornier's starboard wing and wing root before the bomber steepened its angle of descent to the vertical and disappeared. Willson did not see it again but he did orbit the area, scanning the scene below in the hope of an indication that the raider had crashed. He did not see the bomber hit the sea but he did note the time (21.20

(Left) Oblt Hartmut Holzapfel (6./KG2) whose Do 217E-4 (U5+LP/wnr.5590) was shot down by F/Lt John Willson, 219 Squadron, Scorton, on 15-16 March 1943. The Dornier crashed at North Thoresby(Lincs). (Right) Lt G. Pöpel (1./JG3) whose Me.109F-2 was shot down over Kent on 8 May 1941 by Hurricanes of 302 Squadron. [Hartmut Holzapfel]

hours) just in case ground-based observers had witnessed the fall. A minute later, he saw small fires on the sea below and he considered this to be the German aircraft in pieces. Thus he claimed one Do217 destroyed.

After that first engagement, Willson climbed away and, still 'freelancing', began searching again. Seeing heavy anti-aircraft fire to the south-west of his position, Willson decided to search there and, after informing his Sector GCI of his intention, he entered the heavy gun defended area around the Humber. Grimsby was under attack and there was much activity below. Holloway then got an A.I. contact to starboard and well above the Beaufighter's position. Climbing hard under Holloway's instructions, Willson got a visual on an aircraft being engaged by searchlights dead ahead at 4,000 feet range. At that moment, the enemy machine – identified as a Do217 – took violent evasive action, diving and climbing hard to starboard. The Beaufighter closed to a distance of 700 feet and when the bomber was above and just about on its back in a stall, Willson fired a two-second burst from cannons and machine-guns. The bullets were seen to hit their target and the raider burst into flames and then plummeted to earth in the searchlight belt around Grimsby. The bomber commenced its dive at 6,000 feet altitude and Willson followed it for 2,000ft - until he suddenly saw some barrage balloons ahead and decided to call it a day. As the night-fighter climbed above the balloons and made for home, it was constantly engaged by searchlights and Willson had to fire off the colours of the day twice to alert ground defenders and had to use evasive action in order to avoid their attentions.

Fw. Günter Stein, wireless operator of Do217 (U5+LP) of 6./KG2.
[Hartmut Holzapfel]

As in the first instance, Willson did not see his victim crash but, as before, he did note the time (21.40 hours). When the Beaufighter landed back at Scorton, its pilot claimed two Dorniers destroyed and before the night was out HQ Fighter Command had telephoned the aerodrome to confirm the claims. However, the Luftwaffe Loss Returns do not record the loss of two Do217s on the Grimsby raid, but they do record the loss of a Do217 (U5+LP) and a Ju88 (3E+WK). There is a possibility that Willson mistakenly identified his first victim on the night of 15-16 March and that it was, in fact, the Junkers; there is more certainty about his second claim of the night.

The Beaufighter's second victim of the night was U5+LP of 6./KG2, which crashed between Grainsby Halt and North Thoresby (Lincs.) railway station at 21.40 hours. Its pilot was Oberleutnant Hartmut Holzapfel, an experienced flier who was on his 101st operational sortie. His wireless operator (Feldwebel Günter Stein) had flown 196 war flights! U5+LP must have been among the first of the raiders to be attacked by fighters that night for Holzapfel and his crew were Pathfinders for the raid, tasked with the job of illuminating the target with flares and incendiaries for those who followed. They had crossed the North Sea at low level in order to reduce the risk of detection by British radar but when they were five minutes flying time from the English coast they climbed to 9,000 feet in preparation for their bomb run. Holzapfel claims that they were off the Humber when they were attacked.

Feldwebel Stein was facing backwards and when he caught sight of the nightfighter he called his warning: 'Nightfighter from left!' Hartmut Holzapfel thought that his wireless operator meant that they were being attacked from the pilot's port side and thus he pulled his aircraft hard round and into the direction from which he thought the attack was coming. It was an accepted defensive manoeuvre which would place the bomber on the inside of the fighter's line of approach and make it virtually impossible for the attacker to press home his assault – but Stein had meant that the fighter was approaching from his (Stein's) left (and thus from Holzapfel's *right*). When the wireless operator screamed to correct his pilot's attempted evasive action, Holzapfel flicked the Dornier into a tight curve to starboard just as cannon fire exploded in the area of his left engine. Fuel lines were ruptured and bright yellow flames erupted from under the engine cover.

Obfw. August Küpper, observer of Do217 (U5+LP) of 6./KG2. [Hartmut Holzapfel]

Holzapfel closed down the affected engine and pushed his aircraft into a prolonged dive in the hope that the artificially created wind would blow out the flames, but luck was not on his side: the fire did not go out. Instead, in his words, 'We became a bright, luminous torch; a prominent target for the nightfighter and without even the smallest chance of getting away...' Realising the futility of his situation, Holzapfel climbed to 3,000 feet and ordered his crew to bale out. Oberfeldwebel August Küpper (observer) and Feldwebel Gerhard Dörr (mechanic) went first: Holzapfel and Stein were not far behind. Seconds later, the blazing Dornier hurtled to its explosive destruction between Grainsby Halt and North Thoresby railway station, Lincolnshire (military map ref. 7618). It crashed at 21.40 hours.

Stein found his pilot near the burning wreck. The wireless operator had suffered a fractured ankle; Holzapfel had a sprained ankle. They made their way towards a nearby airfield. It is not clear whether their intention was to attempt to escape, but they subsequently hid in a haystack. The next morning, both of them being almost unable to move, they stopped a passing military vehicle and – still armed – were taken to the airfield, where they became prisoners of war.

Beaufighter crew. Scorton, 1943 - 1944

Jeff 'Dinty' Moore was a Beaufighter pilot with 604 Squadron during their time at Scorton, North Yorkshire, from April 1943 to April 1944. His NR (Navigator-Radar) was Jimmy Hogg. They flew Beaufighter Mk.VI aircraft fitted with Mk.VIII Air Interception (A.I.) radar. 'Dinty' Moore's account of the operational activities of Beaufighter crews provides an interesting insight into how night fighter crews prepared for nightly conflict.

'The crews would report to dispersal on the morning when their stint began, receiving their instructions and possibly doing night recognition training or tests. After lunch, they would take up their aircraft for a night-flying test of about thirty minutes. If any snags showed up on the air test, the ground crews would have time to service the faults – and a pretty good job they made of their tasks, I have to say. After tea, depending on what time the sun went down, the crews would return to dispersal ready for the night's activities. Our job was to patrol the east coast from north of Whitby down to Hull. We operated in pairs (of aircraft) for up to three hours under the control of G.C.I. (Ground Control Interceptor) stations. Seaton, Patrington and Goldsborough were the three G.C.I. stations which controlled our patrols.

'In the absence of an air raid we would practise interceptions on each other during the period of our patrol. The ground operators would try to bring the intercepting Beau on to the target Beau with a crossing flight at a range of about seven to eight miles. The idea of the crossing flight was to reduce the

Jeff 'Dinty' Moore, 604 Squadron, Scorton, 1943 - 1944. [Jeff Moore]

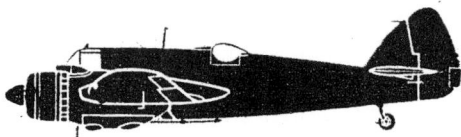

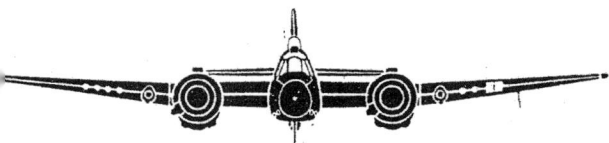

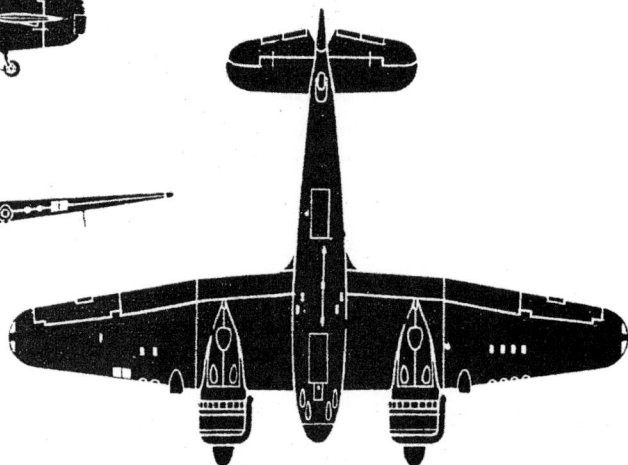

BRISTOL BEAUFIGHTER I
Type - Long-range fighter.
Crew - Two.
Armament - Four fixed forward-firing cannon and six fixed forward-firing machine-guns.

Flight Sergeant crews of 604 Squadron pictured on the village green at Scorton, early Summer 1943.
Back (L-R): S. Jameson, 'Dinty' Moore.
Middle (L-R): Len Ambrey, Pete' Catchpole.
Front (L-R): Jimmy Hogg, Jack Wilkinson. Crews: Jameson (P)/Ambrey (NR), Wilkinson (P)/Catchpole (NR) Moore (P)/Hogg (NR).
[Jeff Moore]

distance between aircraft more quickly and avoid a long stern chase with aircraft of similar speeds.

'When our NR had a good clear contact on his airborne radar he would take over the interception with the word 'Contact!' and would guide his pilot into the target using a fairly standard commentary used by all NRs. From a range of six to eight miles the target would be brought in as close as 300-400 feet, when the pilot would identify it visually – even on the darkest night. (Our night vision was of a high standard due to the fact that we trained regularly in a darkened room and, being competitive, we liked to get a high standard on tests.)

'The moment the target pilot heard the interceptor aircraft declare 'Contact!', that was the signal to start taking evasive action. Then a night-time dog-fight would ensue, with the target trying to lose the interceptor. In this way we all became proficient at our job of night interception. A pairing with 'Wingco' Maxwell (the Commanding Officer and a fine pilot) on patrol resulted in a very hectic flight and one would often arrive back at dispersal after the flight with sweat running down one's back.

'The Beaufighter was ten-and-a-half tons of very sturdy fighting machine carrying four 20mm cannons and six machine guns; an ideal gun platform, steady as a rock when air firing and a very robust aircraft indeed. It was a little self-willed on take-off and landing, and slightly tricky on one engine. The Beau. VI had feathering propellers that improved single-engined performance considerably, but I can honestly say that I never had an engine failure on a Beaufighter fitted with Hercules engines. One had a correct procedure for running down the engines after a flight and if this was done conscientiously – although it took ten minutes – these engines were most reliable. The Beaufighter Mk. II, fitted with Merlin engines, was a different proposition: it would swing violently on take-off and landing, and its single-engined performance was very bad. However, I only flew these aircraft in training, where I did have the doubtful pleasure of losing an engine - but, luckily, I had plenty of height and was able to make a 'straight in' approach to the runway.'

Jeff ('Dinty') Moore, Beaufighter pilot, 604 Squadron, Scorton, 1943 - 1944

13-14 June 1943 (east of Flamborough Head?)

Aircraft:	Dornier 217E-4	U5+BN	w/nr 4376	5./KG2
Crew:	Fw Friedrich Sünnemann	pilot	missing	
	Uffz Heinz Orchel	observer	missing	
	Fw Gerhard Duwe	wireless op	missing	
	Uffz Heinz Oesterle	gunner	missing	

On the night of 13-14 June 1943, a combined force of nearly seventy aircraft drawn from KG2 and KG6 attacked the port of Grimsby with high explosives and 42,500 incendiary bombs. Five Beaufighters of 604 Squadron, Scorton, were despatched to meet the threat but only Flying Officer D.B. Wills (with Flying Officer G.A. Ledeboer), had any conclusive success.

Wills and Ledeboer were on exchange from 68 Squadron, Coltishall and had taken off from Scorton at 23.58 hours (in Beaufighter V8738) to practise with the Goldsborough, North Yorkshire,CHL radar station. After about one and half hours of practice the fighter was diverted towards hostile raids that were reported to be approaching the Humber from the east and south-east at 5,000 feet. The Beaufighter was on a southerly course when Ledeboer got an A.I. contact to starboard at three and a half miles range. At range 6,000 feet, Wills got a visual of a silhouette. At 1,000 feet range he believed that his intended target was a Heinkel 177. It was 01.50 hours and Wills was two miles east of Flamborough Head when he closed to 600 feet behind his quarry. As he did so, he was unaware that the 'freelancing' Commanding Officer of .604 Squadron, Wing Commander Michael Constable Maxwell was investigating the same 'bogey'. Maxwell was trying to decide whether or not it was an RAF Wellington bomber when Wills came up from behind and opened up on the raider with a two-second burst of gunfire that must have given Maxwell at least a mild surprise before he dived away hard to avoid being either shot or damaged. Wills' shells found their mark and there was a large explosion in the bomber's forward fuselage and debris catapulted in every direction. Will's victim fell away to starboard in a mass of flames and was seen to go down into the sea, the debris continuing to burn on the water for some time.

When Wills landed at Scorton at 02.55 hours he claimed an He177 destroyed, although it seems that he did have some doubts about the type of aircraft. Wing Commander Constable Maxwell confirmed that Wills had scored but he, too, appears to have had reservations about the type. The Luftwaffe Loss Reports for this date do not record the loss of an He177 but they do show that Do217E-4 (U5+BN), piloted by Feldwebel Friedrich Sünneman, failed to return from operations that night. KG2 had two other casualties in addition to U5+BN: a Do217K-1 (w/nr 4439) landed at Vannes with forty per cent damage and a Do217M-1

W/Cdr M.Constable Maxwell (right) and F/Lt John Quinton in the cockpit of a Mosquito Mk VI of 84 Squadron in 1945. [via Alex Revell].

(w/nr. 40779) touched down at Eindhoven with fifteen per cent damage By the 1990s, at least, Michael Maxwell had come to the conclusion that Wills' victim was a Do217. Some years ago, he recounted the tale in an issue of the 640 Association Newsletter and highlighted the fact that the surprise delivered by Wills proved to be a persuasive argument to some of our American cousins. (see Eyewitness below).

EYE WITNESS
604 Squadron persuades some of our American cousins.
13-14 June 1943

'I got command of 604 in April 1943 at Scorton, my third posting to the Squadron. Six weeks later the Air Officer Commanding sent for me and told me an American Beaufighter squadron was coming shortly to Scorton and I was to train them, but without any authority from him. I asked him how this could be done if he could give me no authority over them. 'That's your problem,' he replied.

'When they arrived we gave them a good welcome. I asked their Commanding Officer if there was anything we could do to help in their training. "No, thanks," he replied. "We trained in the U.S. and spent a few weeks at an Operational Training Unit. We are a trained Night Fighter Squadron and want to get into action as soon as possible."

'Next day I saw him again and commiserated with him for the delay before his squadron became operational. I said I wondered if he would like to fly with me one night just in case he was able to see an enemy aircraft. He was delighted and agreed to his own people doing the same.

'A few nights later, he came up with me and Johnnie Quinton and we were soon told of 'trade' approaching Hull. I put revs and boost to maximum. On the Beau. this was allowed for five minutes only. After twenty minutes I saw him looking anxiously at the revs. I gave the controls another shove forward to make sure we were flat out, and told him not to worry, we were going as fast as possible. In fact, the saving of a few seconds might mean catching a bomber before it reached its target, and Hercules engines were marvellous.

'John picked up the target on his radar and directed me towards it until we saw it some 40° above and ahead. It was an enemy aircraft and we started pulling up into firing position about one hundred yards behind. Then John shouted, "Look out, there's a Beau behind us!" [this other Beau. was being flown by F/O Wills - (see 13-14 June 1943)]. Battle of Britain instincts took over immediately – I had been shot down four times in Hurricanes – and did an immediate half roll and out of the way. While inverted, with the American, needless to say, standing on the floor of the aircraft with his feet vertically above his head, we had a perfect close up *view of the Dornier blowing up. Another American was standing behind Flying Officer Wills and, of course, saw everything. For some reason, neither of them saw us!*

'*On the way home we had a cheerful dog-fight. Our guests had previously thought of the Beaufighter as more of an airliner than a fighter and on landing could only keep saying, "Well, God Damn!"*'

'*Next day, the American C.O. very generously had all his crews together and said that whatever anyone in 604 told them they were to do. There were no half measures about our friends!*'

Wing Commander Michael Constable Maxwell , DSO DFC
CO 604 Squadron, April 1943 - July 1944

12-13 July 1943 (off Humber estuary?)

Aircraft:	Dornier 217K-1	U5+EM	w/nr 4478	4./KG2
Crew:	Lt Hans Saliger	pilot	missing	
	Gefr Hans Dähler	observer	missing	
	Uffz Walter Labinschuhs	wireless op	missing	
	Uffz Kurt Nürnberger	gunner	missing	

The port installations at Grimsby were raided again on the night of 12-13 July 1943. Thirty-seven Do217s of KG2 were detailed for the operation, but two returned early because of technical problems. Those that followed through to attack dropped forty-eight tons of bombs over the target area. The last crews to leave reported numerous fires in both the port and the town. In total, some fifty fires were started, some of which were not brought under control until the next morning, and parts of the docks and the adjacent town areas suffered severe damage.

Four Mosquito nightfighters of 410 Squadron, RCAF were scrambled from Coleby Grange (Lincs) to intercept the raiders. Among them was Squadron Leader A.G. Lawrence DFC (with. Flight Sergeant H.J. Wilmer DFM), who took off shortly after midnight on 13 July. At 00.52 hours, while operating under GCI control, Lawrence was vectored on to his first 'bogey' of the night and subsequently obtained a visual sighting of a Do217 10,000 feet above the Humber. Although the German pilot took violent evasive action, Lawrence followed him down to 5,000 feet, closed in and gave him a short burst of gunfire but no strikes were observed. Shortly after that, as both aircraft entered the target area, a combination of flares, anti-aircraft fire and searchlights ensured that the visual was lost.

Lawrence then climbed to 8,000 feet and was given vector 090. Shortly afterwards, Wilmer got an A.I. contact at range 7,500 feet almost at the same time that Lawrence obtained a visual on a Do217 crossing in front of him. The time was 01.01 hours when he turned his Mosquito sharply to port and closed in from behind. With the Mosquito following astern, the bomber performed a series of climbing turns to port and starboard, and its gunners fired inaccurate tracer, before Lawrence managed to fire a short burst, seemingly without effect. The one-second burst he followed up with was more destructive: there was a huge flash, followed by plumes of smoke from the raider's starboard engine and then the Dornier plummeted seawards. Lawrence followed and saw it crash into the sea some ten miles east of the Humber. The Dornier is believed to have been U5+EM of 4./KG2, the crew of which were never found .

Ulf Balke claims that Saliger's Dornier (U5+EM) was shot down over the Humber either by a Beaufighter of 307 Squadron or by a Mosquito of 605 Squadron[1]. However, given that 307 was operating out of Fairwood Common, Glamorgan (Wales) at that time and that No.605 was based at Castle Camps, Essex, Balke's suggestion seems highly unlikely.

13-14 July 1943 (east of Scarborough?)

Aircraft:	Dornier 217M-1	U5+EL	w/nr 56153	3./KG2
Crew:	Uffz Willi Spielmanns	pilot	missing	
	Fw Herman Richter	observer	missing	
	Uffz Hans Concemius	wireless op	missing	
	Uffz Walter Wickel	gunner	missing	

KG2 targeted the port installations at Hull on the night of 13-14 July 1943. Between 23.05-23.35 hours fifty Do217s of I./KG2 and II./KG2 took off from bases at Eindhoven and Soesterberg and set course for Hull's Albert Dock and Queen Victoria Dock. Although weather over Holland was satisfactory, that was not the case over East Yorkshire. Deteriorating weather conditions, as well as lively searchlight activity in the target area, made it difficult for crews to find their targets. Some did not find them at all and of the fifty aircraft that set out from Holland, only forty-four crews subsequently reported that they had reached their objective, on which they unloaded a total of fifty-four tons of bombs and caused in excess of fifty fires.

The crew of U5+EL (the 'oldest' crew of 3.Staffel) were on their sixteenth operation to the Humber when they were shot down by a nightfighter. Balke states that U5+EL crashed into the sea some ten miles east of the Humber and he attributes the loss to a Mosquito of 410 Squadron RCAF, Coleby Grange[2]. However, examination of 410 Squadron's Operations Record Book shows no account of a victory that night. On the other hand, Warrant Officer D.W. Wray (with Warrant Officer G. Wallace) in a Beaufighter of 604 Squadron, Scorton, did register a claim for a Do217, which was seen to crash in the sea ten miles east of Scarborough. It seems likely that this was U5+EL.

Wray had taken off from Scorton at 23.50 hours for a practice session with the Chain Home Low radar station at Goldsborough (North Yorks). After practising for about forty-five minutes, the Controller ordered Wray to investigate a 'bogey' and the fighter was vectored on to an easterly course but Control was unable to give any heights. The Beaufighter was at altitude 6,000 feet when Wallace got an A.I. contact on a target crossing from starboard to port at three and a half miles range. When the range had been reduced to one mile, the 'bogey' started taking very violent evasive action and Wray was of the opinion that the German crew must have detected the fighter's approach. The fighter pilot did not get a visual sighting of his quarry until the range had closed to 2,000ft, when a silhouette – still taking violent evasive action - was spotted well above the Beaufighter. Wray increased height to 9,500 feet and got close enough to identify the silhouette as that of a Do217. Easing still closer, Wray positioned his aircraft 200 yards dead astern of the enemy machine and opened fire with a three-second burst of cannon. Strikes were seen on the Dornier's starboard engine, which immediately burst into flames. Then the bomber turned slightly to starboard and then flicked hard to port before it dived vertically towards the sea. By then its starboard engine and its mainplane were a flaming mass but Wray delivered one further short burst of cannon with full deflection as the luckless raider fell away. The enemy machine was last seen by Waller as it disappeared into 5/10 cloud at an altitude of 5,000 feet. The demise of the Dornier was later confirmed by Observer Corps spotters, who saw it crash into Scarborough Bay at 01.25 hours

On the same night, Squadron Leader W. Hoy (with Warrant Officer E.F. Le Comte), also of 604 Squadron, claimed one enemy aircraft damaged thirty miles east of Patrington after engaging in a combat in which Hoy's Beaufighter was subject to a good deal of return fire and was suspected of having been hit. Fortunately, this proved not to have been the case, although all necessary precautions were taken for his return to Scorton.

The loss of Willi Spielmann's Do217 was not the only one suffered by KG2 that night. Over Hull the Do217M-1 (U5+IL; w/nr.56122) of Stabsfeldwebel Wolk (3./KG2) collided with an unknown nightfighter and wireless operator Unteroffizier Hugo Pankuweit[3] was killed when he was thrown out of the machine by the force of the impact: the rest of the crew aborted their mission and returned safely to base. However, dangers did not cease once the raiders had left the target area because British long-range night-fighters lay in wait near the Luftwaffe's aerodromes in Holland. Unteroffizier Hauck's Do217M-1 (U5+CK; w/nr.56050) was on its landing approach to Eindhoven when it fell to the guns of a Mosquito of 605 Squadron (Castle Camps). The aircraft was lost but the crew managed to bale out in time. Nightfighters may also have accounted for the Do217K-1(U5+FM; w/nr. 4530) of Feldwebel Detlef Krüger (4./KG2), which crashed due to unknown causes while on its approach to Soesterberg. In that instance there were no survivors.

Luftwaffe Losses on operations to Humber on 21-22 and 22-23 September 1943
Locations not always known

13th	3./KG2	Do217M-1	U5+EL;	w/nr 56153 FTR Uffz Willi Spielmann(pilot). 4 missing. Believed to have crashed 10 miles east of Scarborough.
	4./KG2	Do217K-1	U5+EM;	w/nr 4478 FTR Lt Hans Saliger(pilot). 4 missing. Believed to have crashed 10 miles east of the Humber.
14th	3./KG2	Do217M-1	U5+ IL;	w/nr.66122 Collided with nightfighter over Hull. Stfw Wolk (pilot). 1 killed.
	2./KG2	Do217M-1	U5+ CK;	w/nr.56050 Shot down nr Eindhoven by nightfighter on return from ops. Uffz Hauck(pilot). 2 injured.
	4./KG2	Do217K-1	U5+FM;	w/nr 4530. Fw. Detlef Krüger(pilot). Crashed nr Soesterberg on return from ops. Cause unknown. 4 killed.

(Luftwaffe Loss Returns 16-17 July 1943)

Observant readers will have noticed that the above shows Do217 (U5+EL) and Do217 (U5+EM) as having been lost on 13 July 1943. This information is taken from the Luftwaffe Loss Lists pages 118 and 126, which show the losses incurred by *Luftflotte 3* during the period 12-14 July. British nightfighters in northern England made two confirmed claims (both for Do217s) during this period – and the Loss Returns show only two relevant losses. Having said that, it is currently not known for certain which nightfighter claimed which bomber and thus the details for 12-14 July should be treated with some caution.

EYEWITNESS
Operations to the Humber
with KG2 and KG66

Luftwaffe pilot Ernst-Karl Fara, who flew with KG2 and with the Pathfinder unit KG66, made his first operational flight on 12 June 1943, when he went to Plymouth with 2./KG2, which was then based at Eindhoven (Holland)

He flew on a number of bombing raids over the north of England during his time with KG2, including Grimsby (13 June 1943 and 12 July 1943) and Hull 24 June, 13 July, 25 July and 20 October – all in 1943 – and 20 April 1944, when he was a target marker with 2./KG66). He also flew on mining operations to the Humber estuary and to Spurn Head. In

*Ernst-Karl Fara and his crew among the wreckage of their Ju 188 (Z6+AK) of 2./KG66 after they had baled out near Dunkirk on 28 March 1944. **L-R**: Leo Häusler(Truhe-observer), Hermann Visarius(mechanic), Ludwig Konietzka(observer), Ernst-Karl Fara(pilot) and Gerhard Pfeifer(wireless/op).* [Ernst-Karl Fara].

a letter to the author nearly sixty years later, he recalled some of those wartime flights:

'Attacks from the sea were always good with regard to observation; we could more easily find the target. Crossing the sea, we flew at low altitude (10-15metres) to avoid British radar and nightfighters. Near the target we would climb in circles to our attack height.

'On 13 July 1943 we followed our usual route to Hull. We took off from our base at Eindhoven and flew at altitude 200-300metres to the radio beacon at Den Helder. We then set course for Spurn Head, crossing the sea at 10-15 metres to reduce the risk of radar interception. When we were in visual range of Spurn Head, we climbed in a circle to attack height – about 4,000 metres – before taking course to the target. I remember that Hull was already burning when we got there. On 13 July 1943, I had 4 x 500kg fragmentation bombs and four containers of C50 incendiary bombs on board. The bombs were dropped either horizontally or in a dive. After the attack, we dived towards the sea and pressed hard, flying at 600km per hour at altitude 10-15 metres, until we arrived.

'For us, operations near Spurn Head and the Humber estuary were always mining operations. We used to use Spurn Head to mark the launch point. We always flew from such a start point on land, say Spurn Head or a lighthouse. Then we would fly from that start point for a designated time before releasing the mines. There used to be a sound locator at Spurn Head and we used to manipulate it by running our engines out of synchronization and thus influence the control of the searchlight which was also there. By allowing one engine to run at fewer revolutions, the searchlight was made to move in the direction where the sound was louder (i.e. more to the right or to the left). For mining operations, we would cross *the sea at low altitude (10-15 metres). Near the target we would climb to attack height, which for mine-laying was 800 metres.*

Ernst-Karl Fara subsequently transferred to KG66, a target-marking unit formed from experienced and reliable crews from operational bomber units. He and his crew had flown twenty-two operations over England when they moved to the Pathfinder unit 2./KG66.

'In 2./KG66 we flew to our targets using the 'Hyperbel-Verfahren' (called by us the 'Truhe-Verfahren') radio beam guidance system. Other Staffeln used the X and Y beams to fly to targets. An additional radio signal was received from the ground control station for 'Bomb-doors open', which was followed by the 'Drop bombs' signal.'

Fara and his crew had brushes with both British nightfighters and British flak defences during sorties over Britain. On 7 October 1943, during a sortie to Norwich, a night-fighter caught him over the target. The fighter's gunfire exploded a container of 500 incendiaries in the bomb bay of Fara's aircraft. Some of them ignited and began to burn on the bomb-doors. A quick-thinking member of his crew managed to crank open the doors by hand and jettison the container, after which Fara returned to base and landed safely. However, his landing following a second encounter with British defences was a little more traumatic.

'On 28 March 1944 I was a target marker on a raid to Bristol. I was flying a Ju188 (Z6+AK) and we were hit by flak on approach to the target. The compass was so disturbed by the damage that I began to fly to France. An hour later, I was over London. From there I flew by the stars (Orion) towards the east. We had to bale out near Dunkirk because of a fuel fault.'

Given his difficulties with the compass, one is tempted to think that his aircraft may have been targeted by a meacon station (see p102)

**Ernst-Karl Fara, pilot,
2./KG2 and 2./KG66, 1943-44**

24-25 July 1943 (off Humber)

Aircraft:	Dornier 217M-1	U5+HK	w/nr 6058	2./KG2
Crew:	Uffz Otto Querlich[4]	pilot	missing	
	Obfw Hans Jähn	observer	missing	
	Ogefr Hans Mehler	wireless op	missing	
	Uffz Rudolf Schricker	gunner	+	

Aircraft:	Dornier 217E-4	U5+DN	w/nr 5489	5./KG2
Crew:	Uffz Kurt Keifert[5]	pilot	missing	
	Ogefr Heinz Borcherding	observer	missing	
	Uffz Robert Welz	wireless op	missing	
	Uffz Rudolf Schulte	gunner	+	

Between 22.40-23.15 hours on 24 July 1943, fifty-one Do217s of I./KG2 and II./KG2 took off from their bases in Holland to lay mines off the Humber. Forty-seven aircraft claimed to have reached the target zone between 00.15-00.36 hours and placed a total of eighty-nine mines in the designated area. Two aircraft failed to reach the target area for reasons currently unknown; while the two aircraft shown above failed to return from the operation. It is not known what happened to U5+HK, but it is thought that U5+DN was shot down by anti-aircraft fire northwards of Hull at 01.51 hours and crashed into the sea. Ulf Balke claims that U5+DN crashed at Criften's Farm[6], but he seems to have confused this aircraft with U5+AN, piloted by Uffz Kolwe (see below). A third aircraft, Do217M-1 (U5+KL; w/nr.6046), piloted by Leutnant Manfred Lieddert was shot down by a nightfighter intruder as it prepared to land at Soesterberg on its return from operations. The Dornier's observer took to his parachute and survived; the other three members of the crew did not.[7]

Uffz Robert Welz, wireless operator of Do 217 (U5+DN) of 5./KG2, shot down off the Humber estuary on the night of 24-25 July 1943.
[via Melvin Brown & Steven Hall]

25-26 July 1943 (off Spurn Head)

Aircraft:	Dornier 217M-1	U5+GK	w/nr 6045	2./KG2
Crew:	Uffz Robert Fuchs	pilot	missing	
	Gefr Wolfgang Grob	observer	missing	
	Gefr Hermann Krönig	wireless op	missing	
	Uffz Hubert Toeltsch	gunner	+	

Aircraft:	Dornier 217K-1	U5+BA	w/nr 4412	Stab./KG2
Crew:	Uffz Max Reuthe	pilot	missing	
	Uffz Siegfried Ludwig	observer	pow	
	Uffz Heinrich Böning	wireless op	missing	
	Obgfr Willi Schürleien	gunner	pow	

The port installations of Hull were targeted on the night of 25-26 July 1943 and of the fifty-one Do217s of I./KG2 and II./KG2 that started out forty-seven claimed to have reached their objective, arriving over the designated area between 00.47-00.56 hours on 26 July. Because of poor ground visibility due, seemingly, to mist which was so bad that participating crews could not even see the coast, target marking was not good and bombs were dropped by dead-reckoning or aimed at defenders' searchlights – in the hope that they might be near to intended objectives. The attackers dropped ten 1000kg bombs, eighty-eight 500kg bombs and over 30,000 incendiaries from heights ranging from 4,000 feet – 10,000 feet. However, poor visibility meant that the attack was widely scattered and very little damage was caused. Returning crews reported that British nightfighters had been very active and a number of crews had had to take violent evasive action over the Humber estuary when nightfighters were spotted making approaches from behind and below their intended victims.

Two KG2 crews fell to a night-fighter that night. Do217 (U5+GK), piloted by Unteroffizier Robert Fuchs of 2./KG2, was shot down off Spurn Head at 00.32 hours by Flying Officer B.R. Keele (with Flying Officer G.H. Cowles) in a Beaufighter of 604 Squadron, Scorton. The body of the German gunner, Hubert Toeltsch, was found off

Uffz Heinrich Böning, wireless operator of Do217K-1 (U5+BA), that was shot down off Spurn Point by F/O Keele, 604 Sqdn, on the night of 25-26 July 1943. [via Melvin Brown & Steven Hall]

Spurn Head on 26 July 1943 and he was later buried at Scarthro Road Cemetery, Grimsby. Keele had further success fourteen minutes later when he shot down the Do217 (U5+BA) of Unteroffizier Max Reuthe at 00.46 hours fifteen miles east of Spurn Head. The observer and the gunner of U5+BA managed to bale out before their aircraft struck the sea; their crewmates did not and were never seen again.

Keele (in Beaufighter V8617) had taken off from Scorton at 23.15 hours to carry out a standing patrol over the Humber area with Flight Lieutenant W.N. Wood (in Beaufighter V8552). In the absence of Luftwaffe activity, the fighters were carrying out practice interceptions under Patrington GCI, when the Controller informed Keele that there was a 'bogey' to be investigated. After several vectors and when the fighter was at altitude 9,000 feet, Cowles got an A.I. contact to starboard and below at four and half miles range, the Beaufighter then being on a northerly vector. Keele lost height and followed the evasive action being taken by the 'bogey'. At 00.32 hours, when pursued and pursuer were some fifteen miles east of Spurn Head, Keele closed to range 800 feet, just as his would-be target – now identified as a Do217 – began taking fairly violent evasive action. As Keele eased his aircraft to within 350 feet,

the enemy machine started taking very violent evasive action at about the same time that the night-fighter opened fire with three short bursts from cannon and machine gun. Strikes were seen on the Dornier's starboard engine, wing roots and main plane, from which pieces were seen to break off. The raider then caught fire and slowed: Keele had to break away sharply to avoid collision. When the Beaufighter closed in again and gave another short burst the bomber was already descending rapidly with its starboard engine and mainplane in flames. Owing to the reduced speed of the luckless aircraft, the fighter overshot and the enemy machine was last seen by Cowles as it disappeared into the haze in flames. Fourteen minutes later, Keele replicated almost every detail of this first victory when he despatched his second Do217 of the night.

Immediately following that first success, Keele was informed by the Patrington controller that he had another 'bandit' for him. After being given several vectors, and when the Beaufighter was again at 9,000 feet of altitude, Cowles obtained an A.I. contact ahead and above at four and a half miles range. The hunted aircraft was taking mild evasive action. The night-fighter closed in at approximately 230mph Indicated Air Speed (IAS) and obtained a visual of a silhouette at 1,500 feet range, dead ahead and slightly above. Following mild evasive action by the raider, Keele reduced the range to 800 feet and identified his quarry as a Do217. He eased his aircraft closer to the bomber and, from 300ft dead astern, he opened up with a two-second burst of cannon and machine-gun fire. The bomber immediately burst into flames and began to shed pieces of debris, some of which struck Keele's machine but caused little damage. The flaming Dornier then went down rapidly and was seen by the Beaufighter crew to explode on hitting the sea. Keele had launched his attack at 00.46 hours, when he was in the area of his first success of the night. Squadron Leader Hoy, also of 604 Squadron, confirmed Keele's victory when he subsequently reported seeing an aircraft going down into sea in flames at about 00.50 hours.

Hoy (with Warrant Officer E.F. Le Comte) was destined to have some luck of his own that night. He had taken off from Scorton at 00.30 hours and was subsequently vectored on to a wildly swerving and circling Do217 in the Humber area. He chased it to a point some seventy-five miles east of Filey before his concentrated burst of cannon and machine-gun fire from dead astern resulted in numerous strikes on the enemy's fuselage. The time of attack was 01.18 hours. The German gunners responded with inaccurate tracer from the upper turret before Hoy aimed his second burst at the base of the tracer fire, causing the Dornier's fuselage to explode and the top of the upper turret to blow off. Flames then immediately enveloped the bomber, which disintegrated and fell into the sea. From the particularly violent evasive action taken by the raider during the chase, which lasted over twenty minutes, Hoy considered that the German crew must have detected that they were being followed by a fighter. Later that day (26th), Hoy (with Le Comte) shared the destruction of a Ju88 with another 604 Squadron aircraft 250 miles off Whitby.[8]

25-26 July 1943 (Long Riston, near Beverley)

Aircraft:	Dornier 217E-4	U5+AN	w/nr 4395	5./KG2
Crew:	Uffz Hans-Ulrich Kowle[9]	pilot	+	
	Uffz Fritz Pilger	observer	+	
	Uffz Helmut Gabriel	wireless op	+	
	Uffz Rudolf Trodler	gunner	+	

This aircraft was engaged in an attack on Hull in the early hours of 26 July when it took a direct hit from anti-aircraft fire. It crashed at Criftens Farm, Long Riston (military map ref. 604634) at 01.15 hours and was almost completely buried in the crater it made. The crew of four were killed in the crash and were buried in the churchyard at Brandesburton, near Hornsea. Some days after the crash the *Hull Daily Mail* (29 April 1943) reported:

21 August 1998. Cog wheel recovered from the crash site of Do.217E-4 (U5+AN) of 5./KG2, that crashed at Long Riston, Beverley, after being hit by anti-aircraft fire. [David E. Thompson].

'With an ATS subaltern Doreen A. Gloff of Dover in action for the first

21 August 1998. Propeller boss recovered from the crash site of Do.217E-4 (U5+AN) of 5./KG2, that crashed at Long Riston, Beverley, after being hit by anti-aircraft fire. [David E. Thompson]

time as a plotting officer, a Yorkshire coast mixed AA Battery on Sunday night shot down a German plane. The gun position officer, Lieut. Hubert Lee RA, a Liverpool chartered accountant in peace time, said today:

"After we had fired a dozen rounds or so one of our officers who was some distance from the guns heard the raider's engines cut out. There was a sound of a plane diving and a few seconds later a fire in the direction in which it was travelling. Just after that there was an explosion on the ground."

'This AA Command Battery is composed mainly of Yorkshiremen and ATS girls. Gunners from the site and on a nearby searchlight site confirmed the raider's destruction and when the wreckage was examined by the searchlight battery officer it was found to be a Dornier 217 well-holed by shrapnel.'

Obgrf. Rudolf Trodler, gunner, of Do.217 (U5+AN) of 5./KG2 that was shot down by AA fire and crashed at Criften's Farm, Long Riston, nr Hull, on the night of 25-26 July 1943.
[via Melvin Brown & Steven Hall]

A surface dig by enthusiasts on 21 August 1998 recovered a propeller boss, several small calibre rounds and a couple of cannon shell heads. During the course of the investigation the farmer told the team that an unexploded bomb had been found in one of his hedgerows a few years earlier!

25-26 July 1943 (east of Ravenscar)

On the same night that Flying Officer Keele of 604 Squadron, Scorton, shot down two Do217s and East Yorkshire anti-aircraft guns claimed another (see previous two entries), 604's Commanding Officer, Wing Commander Michael Constable Maxwell (with Flying Officer J.A. Nordberg), in Beaufighter. V8612, chased another Dornier some twenty miles east of Ravenscar and saw strikes on the enemy machine before he lost it.

Constable Maxwell had taken off from Scorton at 23.15 hours to do practice interceptions but after thirty minutes he was taken over by CHL Goldsborough. The fighter was at 15,000 feet altitude when Control ordered Maxwell to reduce height and fly south to investigate an aircraft that turned out to be friendly. Maxwell then went back on a north-easterly course but almost at once he was given a vector of 190 to investigate fifteen 'bogeys' flying on courses between 280° and 360°. After several vectors, and when the Beaufighter was at a height of 4,000 feet, Nordberg got an A.I. contact at range three miles to starboard and at the fighter's altitude. Maxwell gradually closed in on a very slow flying target and at 2,500 feet he obtained a visual of a Do217 some 20° above him. The raider's speed at the time was only 110mph and although Maxwell remained directly under the bomber for ten minutes, the slow speed at which both were flying prevented him from carrying out an attack. When the speed dropped to 100mph, Maxwell decided to do a complete orbit and re-approach, making a rush attack if the Dornier was still going slowly. However, when contact was regained – at two and half miles range – the raider had increased speed to some 270mph IAS and was taking evasive action. It was only with some difficulty that Maxwell was able to close in. Twenty miles east of Ravenscar, Maxwell opened fire with cannon at 900 feet closing to 800 feet. Strikes were seen on the Dornier's starboard wing roots and the machine suddenly reduced speed, forcing the fighter to break away sharply to starboard to avoid collision. Shortly afterwards, the Beaufighter crew caught a momentary glimpse of the Dornier before it disappeared in the haze below.

604s Commanding Officer was awarded 'one Dornier damaged' but at least one witness thought that Maxwell's claim should be raised at least to a 'probable'. Flight Lieutenant Rose, Maxwell's Goldsborough controller, later reported that immediately after the bomber dived away, the plot on the enemy machine completely disappeared from his (Rose's) radar tube. He claimed that on his tube he could see an aircraft right down to sea-level – an assertion he later proved in a test with two 604 Squadron aircraft. However, it seems that Rose's assertions came to nought and that Maxwell had to be satisfied with the initial award.

21-22 September 1943 (Newton, near Withernsea)

Aircraft:	Dornier 217K-1	U5+CM	w/nr 4620	4./KG2
Crew:	Fw Helmut Rumpff	pilot	+	
	Fw Siegfried Vomweg	observer	+	
	Gefr Arno Ehemann	wireless op	+	
	Obgfr Kurt Stiegler	gunner	+	

Shortly after midnight on 21 September, forty-nine Do217s of KG2 took off from their bases in Holland to mine the Humber estuary. One of those, a Do217M-1, U5+IT, (w/nr 56049) of 9./KG2, failed to clear the Dutch coast and crashed north of Walwijk, killing the crew. Three other aircraft subsequently aborted their mission and returned early because of technical problems.

Crews who went on to complete the operation reported that during the attack there were 80-100 searchlights in the area between Hull and Grimsby – but there were also searchlights operating over East Yorkshire and they claimed Do217K-1 ,U5+CM, (w/nr.4620), which crashed near Withernsea at 01.05 hours on 22 September. Its pilot, Unteroffizier Helmut Rumpff, had approached the coast at an estimated height of fifty feet and, after crossing it, was immediately picked up and held by searchlights. He commenced a machine-gun attack on one of these sites, but came too low and struck the ground at a very shallow angle. The bomber crashed one-quarter mile from Southfield Farm (mil. ref. 34/845400), on the Out Newton road four and a half miles east of Patrington, and broke up into fairly large portions before coming to rest 250 yards from the point of impact. There were no survivors.

Two unexploded 1,000kg G ('George')-type parachute mines were found in the vicinity of the wreck. At 10.17 hours on 22 September, three Royal Navy Mine Disposal personnel were attempting to disarm the weapons when one of them exploded. The three men were injured and were taken to the Withernsea Transfer Hospital, where two of them, Lieutenant Commander Peter Tanner and Able Seaman Percy Fouracre, later died. It is believed that the third member, Lieutenant Frank Price, survived. The bodies of the Dornier crew were buried in Hull North Cemetery, where they still lie.

21-22 September 1943 (east of Spurn Head)
Eight minutes after the loss of Unteroffizier Rumpff's Dornier (U5+CM) the raiders suffered another loss when a Beaufighter crew of 604 Squadron, Scorton, sent one crashing into the sea some fifty-five miles off Spurn Head.

Aircraft of No.604 Squadron, Scorton, were practising in pairs with GCI stations at Seaton, Goldsborough and Patrington when they were suddenly detailed for interceptions on mine-laying aircraft in the Humber area. Beaufighters flown by Flight Sergeant E. Moore and Flight

On 22 September 1943 Do217M-1 (U5+AR; w/nr.56042) and its crew failed to return from mining operations off the Humber. L-R: Uffz. Walter Bersieck(gunner); Lt Josef Rohmfeld(pilot); Uffz Johann Cottäus(wireless operator); Uffz Walter Dörr(observer). [via Melvin Brown & Steven Hall]

Do.217M-1 (U5+AR; w/nr. 56042). [via Melvin Brown & Steven Hall]

Sergeant G. Jameson were given various vectors but made no contacts. Flying Officer J. Lomas managed several chases but without any luck but Squadron Leader I.K.S. Joll (with Flight Lieutenant E. Thomas) caught a Do217 flying straight and level and shot it down in flames.

Joll had taken off from Scorton at 22.00hours on Patrington patrol and was nearing the end of his duty when he was informed that there were raiders in the area. He was instructed to reduce height to 4,000 feet and, after a series of vectors, Thomas obtained four simultaneous contacts. Three of these were almost dead ahead at three miles range with a fourth crossing from starboard to port at one and a half miles range. Thomas selected the latter as the most promising prospect and directed Joll into position behind the raider. By then the German was losing altitude in preparation for laying his mines. At altitude 800 feet, and with the enemy machine 2000 feet dead ahead and 10° above, Joll got a visual sighting of a Dornier 217. He eased his machine very gradually upwards until it was positioned 300 yards dead astern of the bomber and then opened fire with cannon and machine-gun. Hits were registered on the Dornier's starboard engine and wing, both of which burst into flames before the raider plummeted into the sea.

Examination of the Luftwaffe Loss Returns for this date reveals no relevant loss. The only possible candidate would seem to be either U5+CR or U5+AR (see box below), although Ulf Balke states that both of these aircraft were lost on the night of 22-23 September. He believes that they may have collided with each other over the North Sea while en route to the Humber[10].

Luftwaffe Losses on operations to Humber on 21-22 and 22-23 September 1943
Locations not always known

I./KG2	Do217M-1	U5+ ?	w/nr.56066 Pilot unknown.Belly-landed at Schipol after being attacked by nightfighter
4./KG2	Do217K-1	U5+CM	w/nr.4620. FTR Uffz Helmut Rumpf(pilot) 4 killed. Crashed near Withernsea at

			01.05 hours on 22 September.
7./KG2	Do217M-1	U5+AR	w/nr.56042. FTR Lt Josef Rohmfeld(pilot). 4 missing
7./KG2	Do217M-1	U5+CR	w/nr.722848. FTR Uffz Herbert Rode(pilot). 4 missing.
III/KG2	Do217M-1	U5+ IT	w/nr.56049. Pilot unknown. Crashed nr Waalwijk shortly after take- off. 4 killed.
II./KG2	Do217E-4	U5+ ?	w/nr.5380. Pilot unknown. Crash-landed at Schipol

Luftwaffe Loss Returns 25-26 September 1943

2-3 October 1943 (off Spurn Head)

Aircraft:	Junkers 188E-1	Z6+GK	w/nr 260175 2./KG66
Crew:	Lt Günther Beubler	pilot	+
	Uffz Heinz Urban	observer	+
	Uffz Albert Fischer	wireless op	+
	Uffz Erwin Pausch	gunner	+

A combined force of fifty-six aircraft drawn from KG2, KG6 and KG66 were detailed for mining operations off the Humber on the night of 2-3 October. Forty-nine aircraft claimed to have carried out their orders, the rest abandoning the mission for reasons currently unknown. Z6+GK is believed to have crashed in the sea half mile off Spurn lighthouse while taking evasive action, but from what is not known at the time of writing. Erwin Pausch and Heinz Urban are buried in Hull North Cemetery

4 March 1945 (Dunnington, near York)

Aircraft:	Junkers 88G-6	D5+AX	w/nr 620028 13./NJG3
Crew:	Hptm Johann Dreher	pilot	+
	Fw Gustav Schmitz	wireless op	+
	Obfw Hugo Böker	radar op	+
	Fw Martin Bechter	mechanic	+

On the night of 3-4 March 1945 German nightfighters launched *Operation Gisela* against RAF heavy bombers returning from a raid on the synthetic oil plants at Kamen, in the Ruhr. At around midnight, approximately one hundred Ju88s crossed the English coast from Essex to Yorkshire and infiltrated the bomber streams. The attacks that followed took their toll and when the last nightfighter left some two hours later, twenty-four bombers had been shot down and a further twenty damaged.

Hptmn Johann Dreher, pilot of Ju.88 (D5+AX) of 13./NJG3 that crashed at Dunnington Lodge, nr Elvington, in the early hours of 4 March 1945.
[via Simon Parry]

Dunnington Lodge, Elvington Lane, Dunnington. Dreher's Ju 88 clipped the left-hand gable. Note the memorial towards bottom left. [Author].

A Ju88 attacked a Halifax bomber that was in the process of landing at RAF Pocklington and then the intruder strafed the airfield. It was subsequently seen to open fire on a taxi travelling with its headlights on along a road which ran parallel to one of the runways at RAF Elvington. It is believed that the German pilot might have mistaken the lights for those of an aircraft which was in the process of landing. As the Ju88 reduced altitude to almost zero height, its starboard wing touched a tree and the aircraft clipped the corner of Dunnington Lodge, a farmhouse in Elvington Lane, Dunnington, before disintegrating along the lane. The crew of four were killed instantly and a man

In June 1993, a memorial to the seven people who lost their lives on 4 March 1945 was unveiled at Dunnington Lodge. Wreaths were laid by members of the RAF Air Gunners' Association and by representatives of the Luftwaffe Nightfighters' Association. The picture shows Arthur Tate, ex-RAF rear gunner, and Herbert Thomas, ex-Luftwaffe nightfighter crew. [Yorkshire Evening Post]

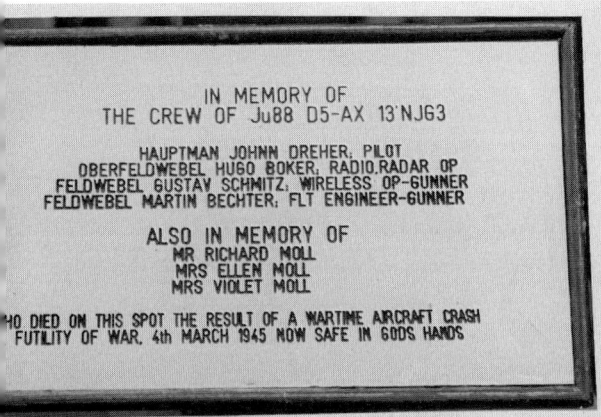

Dunnington memorial plaque. [Author].

IN MEMORY OF
THE CREW OF Ju88 D5-AX 13'NJG3

HAUPTMAN JOHNN DREHER, PILOT
OBERFELDWEBEL HUGO BOKER, RADIO.RADAR OP
FELDWEBEL GUSTAV SCHMITZ, WIRELESS OP-GUNNER
FELDWEBEL MARTIN BECHTER, FLT ENGINEER-GUNNER

ALSO IN MEMORY OF
MR RICHARD MOLL
MRS ELLEN MOLL
MRS VIOLET MOLL

HO DIED ON THIS SPOT THE RESULT OF A WARTIME AIRCRAFT CRASH
FUTILITY OF WAR, 4th MARCH 1945 NOW SAFE IN GODS HANDS

and two women who were in the farmhouse at the time later died of their injuries.

So badly mutilated were the bodies in the aircraft cockpit that only two could be identified. They were Feldwebel Gustav Schmitz, aged 24, and Feldwebel Hugo Böker, aged 28. The bodies of Schmitz and Böker , together with those of two 'unknown' German airman, were buried at Fulford Cemetery, York, on 10 March 1945. Location of death in each case was given as Dunnington. All four corpses were exhumed in 1966 and were re-interred in the German Military Cemetery at Cannock Chase, where Bechter and Dreher were buried under their own names.

Willi Schludecker (ex-KG2)
visits York in search of a gasometer.
18 August 1999

The first time Willi Schludecker visited York he tried to destroy the gas works at Foss Island. In August 1999, curiosity drove him to make a second visit to the city – to seek the remains of his wartime target.

On the night of 28-29 April 1942, York was attacked in a series of Luftwaffe reprisal raids conducted against English historical towns after the RAF had bombed the ancient town of Lübeck a month earlier. At the time, Willi Schludecker was the twenty-two year-old Luftwaffe pilot of a Dornier 217 twin-engine bomber of 6./KG2, based at Soesterberg (Holland). His aircraft was one of seventy-four detailed for the operation. It is believed that of the ninety-five tons of bombs and incendiaries that dropped in the York area that night, fifty-five tons fell on the town, causing numerous fires and extensive damage, particularly in the area of the railway station. Seventy-four civilians were killed and 205 injured.

Willi Schludecker (left) and his friend Richard Flohr-Swann at Yorkshire Air Museum, Elvington, 18 August. [Author].

The Lübeck raid killed 320 and injured 800.

Although Willi cannot remember much about the attack in general, for the last sixty or so years he believed that he had clear recollections of where his bombs fell. In 1999 he explained to the author that:

'The town was already burning when I arrived and I saw the gasworks in the light of the fires. I dived down, released my four 500kg bombs from 3,000ft in a diving attack and then got away as fast as I could.'

He was convinced that at least one of his bombs scored a direct hit on a gasometer and momentarily turned night into day. His claim seemed to be confirmed on 1 May 1942, when the Yorkshire Gazette carried Radio Berlin's report that: 'German pilots observed a large gas holder exploding, with flames several thousands of feet high. A quickly spreading oil fire was also observed'.

Willi Schludecker made good his escape and returned safely to his base in Soesterberg (Holland) but British night-fighters shot down a number of the raiders, including one that crashed near North Lodge at Castle Howard and another which came down near York. The seventy-nine year-old veteran, knows that he was lucky to survive the war.

However, he was not lucky when he travelled from his home near Cologne to visit the gasworks a second time. He was hoping that some trace of 'his' gasometer might still remain – but the steel tank he thought he had hit was demolished a year or so before Willi's visit. Furthermore, enquiries revealed that there is no record of the York gasworks being damaged during the attack of 28-29 April 1942. It is likely that Willi's bombs landed elsewhere – but exactly where remains a mystery.

During his time in the area, Willi and his friend, Richard Flohr-Swann, managed to visit the Yorkshire Air Museum at Elvington, where he showed particular interest in the Mosquito ('It's the first time I have been this close to one and it has not been shooting at me'), the Halifax, and Danny Thornton's home-made Me.109G.

NOTES

1 Ulf Balke: *Der Luftkrieg in Europa: die operativen Einsätze des Kampfgeschwaders 2 im zweiten Weltkrieg vol 2.* Bernard & Graefe Verlag. Koblenz. 1990 p250.
2 Ulf Balke ibid.
3 Hugo Pankuweit was buried in Hull's Northern Cemetery, where he still lies.
4 This from the Luftwaffe Loss Returns. Ulf Balke: op.cit. p460 gives Gürlich.
5 This from the Luftwaffe Loss Returns. Ulf Balke ibid. gives the name Pfeifer.
6 Ulf Balke: ibid.
7 Ulf Balke: ibid. claims that U5+KL was shot down on 26 July 1943 by F/O Knowles, No.605 (Mosquito) Sqdn, Castle Camps. Luftwaffe Loss Returns gives 25 July as date of loss.
8 See Bill Norman: *Broken Eagles vol.2: Norhumberland and Durham* (to be published 2002).
9 Luftwaffe Loss Returns gives Kolwe but buried at Brandesburton under the name Cowle.
10 Ulf Balke op.cit. p266.

'ADVERSARIES BUT NEVER ENEMIES...'

During the funeral service for Heinrich Richter at South Bank, Cleveland, on 14 October 1998, Hans Mondorf, the German Consul-General, said that he had been quite moved and surprised by the sympathy that the case had attracted and he attributed that response to, what he described as, '...the sense of fair play that the British soul enshrines...'. When I began researching material for this book, I found a number of examples to illustrate that Mondorf's 'sense of fair play' was not merely a post-war phenomenon cultivated by the passage of time. Humanity towards an enemy in need also seems to have had its place in wartime, when one might have reasonably expected feelings towards a foreign foe to be running high.

A number of these examples involved non-Service personnel. For example, when Eugen Lange and Bernhard Hochstuhl of 2.(F)/122 came ashore below the cliffs north of Sandsend in October 1939, civilians Jack Barker, George Thomas and Frank Dring retrieved Lange in the most difficult circumstances and ensured his safe removal to hospital. In

George Thomas (left) and Frank Dring at Sandsend c. 1960. [G. Thomas jnr].

Sandsend 1979. Eugen Lange (Left) and Bernhard Hochstuhl visit the site of their rescue forty years earlier. [Courtesy of Whitby Gazette].

February 1940, farmer's wife Ruth Smailes of Bannial Flatt Farm, Whitby, and her friend Miss Sanderson, treated and comforted the wounded Karl Missy and Johann Meyer of KG26 until such time as more qualified help arrived. On 4 April 1940, the Scarborough trawler men of *Silver Line* not only rescued Rudolf Behnisch's KG26 crew from the sea, they also visited the injured observer, Georg Kempe, in hospital some days later. And on 27 October 1940 at Duggleby, the civilian members of the local Home Guard joined with three members of the crew of a Junkers 88 of KG4 to rescue a fourth crew member trapped under the tail of his aircraft.

There were a number of similar examples among Service personnel who had been directly involved in combats with foreign foes. For example, when Peter Townsend learned that Meyer had died and that Missy might lose a leg as a result of the encounter with Townsend's Hurricanes, the fighter pilot felt the need to visit Missy in Whitby hospital – a round trip of some two hundred miles on snow-covered roads. And when Rudolf Leushake and Johann Meyer were buried at Catterick village on 6 February 1940, there was a wreath and a card 'From 43 Squadron, with sympathy'. Roger Hall experienced a similar emotional

202

April 1990. Rudolf Behnisch at the Filey home of Bob Watkinson jnr. Back (L-R): Betty Watkinson, Bob Watkinson. Front (L-R): Rudolf Behnisch, Traundle Behnisch, Susan Watkinson, Emma Watkinson. [Peter Watkinson].

response – 'a feeling of utter horror and loneliness' – when the gunner of his (Hall's) Boulton-Paul Defiant sent a Heinkel 111 to its explosive destruction off the Humber on the night of 10 February 1941. Michael Constable Maxwell, one-time Commanding Officer of 604 Squadron at Scorton and a devout Roman Catholic, used to have a Mass said at the local church for victims of his own encounters, a practice he appears to have shared with Spitfire pilot Tony Lovell.

At Shoreham airport on 9 March 2000. Willi Schludecker (left), Peter McMillan (centre) and Heinrich Buhr (right) [Courtesy of Brighton Evening Argus].

When three Spitfires of the Leconfield-based 616 Squadron intercepted a Do17 off Withernsea on 3 July 1940, one of the fighter pilots, 'Cocky' Dundas, later acknowledged that their opponent had fought back '...gallantly, though it was an unequal exchange which must have been utterly terrifying for him...' but, of course, such reflections cannot be allowed to govern actions in wartime. Perhaps Spitfire pilot Ted Shipman, who had several successes during his time with 41 Squadron at Catterick during 1940 – including a Heinkel 111 off Scarborough on 21 August 1940 – summed up the attitude of defenders, irrespective of their immediate response to combat:

'I didn't jump for joy at it. I was never elated at a success. I knew I had ended four or five men over Scarborough, but I didn't feel guilt. I knew it was them or us.'

The men who fought each other in the skies over England some sixty years ago faced death and destruction on an almost daily basis. They were all brave men, irrespective of their nationality. In the post-war years, the humanity to which Mondorf referred and which manifested itself on occasions in more dangerous days has developed further and one-time foes have extended the hand of friendship towards each other.

Peter Townsend, whose bullets almost severed the leg of Karl Missy, the Heinkel gunner, met his former foe in the years after the war and remained in contact with him until Missy died in 1981. In October 1979, Sandsend survivors Eugen Lange and Bernhard Hochstuhl returned to Sandsend to thank those who had been involved in their rescue forty years earlier, and Spitfire pilot Ted Shipman exchanged Christmas wishes with them until the Germans died in the mid-1990s. Until he himself died in August 1998, Ted was a firm friend of a Messerschmitt 110 pilot he first met 13,000 feet over County Durham in August 1940.[1] Another German who came back was Rudolf Behnisch. In April 1990 he kept a promise he made to himself fifty years earlier when he returned to Scarborough to thank those who had saved his life. Bob Watkinson, who had plucked Behnisch from the sea in 1940, had died some some years before. His son took his place at an emotional meeting on the anniversary of the rescue.

On 9 March 2000, Willi Schludecker, Heinrich Buhr and Peter McMillan , who had first met over the North Sea on a July night in 1942, came face to face for the first time when they met in Hove, near Brighton, at a meeting arranged by the author. Perhaps both Peter McMillan and his guests felt a little trepidation as the Germans' single-engined Cessna settled on to the runway at Shoreham Airport shortly after 2.00pm on 9 March. If that were the case, any doubts were quickly dispelled when Willi Schludecker's old air gunner, Heinrich Buhr, extended his hand towards the former Beaufighter pilot and broke the ice with the words 'Hallo. We are the Hun – and you are a bloody lousy shot!' It was the beginning of a friendly and most enjoyable three days, during which the three found that they had much in common.

Willi Schludecker, whose visit to my home in August 1999 had prompted me to search for Peter McMillan, seems to have had initial reservations about the meeting once it had been arranged. However, his final comment to assembled reporters at Shoreham summed up his appreciation of the welcome he and his friends had received and betrayed his own engaging brand of dry humour. 'I was afraid that the English people would be very angry, but they are very gentle. It is wonderful to be here. No one is shooting at me.'

During the course of the visit, Peter McMillan admitted that at the time of the combat he had not been concerned about the fate of Willi and his crew.

When I think back on it fifty-eight years later, I realize that I felt fairly neutral about it. It was nothing personal at the time; there was never really any personal hatred between us. We were young men doing our duty. I was only doing the job I was paid to do, and so was Willi; we were doing the same job on different sides. But I think he got the short end of the stick. I'm only glad I didn't kill him.

It was a sentiment with which many old fliers would agree. It certainly struck a cord with Heinrich Buhr, who pointed out that men who had challenged each other to deadly duals in the skies over England some sixty years ago had been the pawns of politicians. 'We were adversaries', he said, ' but we were never enemies...'.

NOTES

1 See Bill Norman: *Luftwaffe over the North.*Leo Cooper/Pen & Sword. 1993. pp62-69.

APPENDICES

Appendix 1
Luftwaffe losses in the Yorkshire area, 1939-1945
(by cause and location)

Date	Aircraft	Unit	Code	w/nr	Cause	Location
17.10.39	He11H-1	2.(F)/122	F6+PK	?	Spitfire	off Whitby
21.10.39	He115B	KuFlGr. 1./406	S4+EH	?	Hurricane	off Spurn Head
10.11.39	Do18D	KuFlGr. 3./406	K6+DL	?	Hudson	off Scarborough
3.02.40	He111H-3	4./KG26	1H+FM	2323	Hurricane	Whitby
3.04.40	He111H-3	StabII./KG26	1H+AC	?	Spitfire	off Redcar
25/26.6.40	He11P-2	3./KG4	5J+BL	?	Spitfire	Humber
1.07.40	He111H-4	3./KG4	5J+EL	?	Spitfire	off Humber
1.07.40	He115	KuFlGr.3./106	M2+CL	?	Tech.prob	off Whitby
8.07.40	Ju88A-1	9./KG4	5J+AT	3094	Fighter	Aldborough
9.08.40	He111H-4	2./KG4	5J+?K	?	Flak?	off NE coast?
11.08.40	Ju88-1	1(F)/121	7A+KH	2086	Spitfire	Scaling, nr. Whitby
15.08.40	Ju88C	7./KG30	4D+DR	?	Spitfire	Bridlington
15.08.40	Ju88A-5	3./KG30	4D+KL	?	Huricane	nr. Bridlington
15.08.40	Ju88	4./KG30	4D+?M	?	Hurricane	nr. Bridlington
15.08.40	Ju88C	7./KG30	4D+?R	?	Fighter?	off Bridlington?
20.08.40	Ju88A-1	8./KG30	4D+IS	?	Hurricane	Ottringham
21.08.40	He111H-2	9./KG53	A1+ ?T	?	Spitfire	off Scarborough
27.10.40	Ju88A-5	7./KG4	5J+ER	6129	Flak	Duggleby
27.10.40	Ju88A-1	8./KG4	5J+HS	6048	Flak	off Tees?
1.11.40	Ju88A-1	8./KG30	4D+TS	7089	Weather	Glaisdale Head
9.02.41	Ju88A-5	4./KG30	4D+FM	8102	Fighter?	off Humber?
30.03.41	Ju88A	1(F)/123	4U+GH	0115	Spitfire	Teesside
8.04.41	Ju88A-5	2./KG30	4D+UK	0541	Tech. prob	off Humber?
15/16.04.41	He111H-5	3./KG53	A1+AL	9370	Tech. prob?	Huby
4/5.05.41	Ju88A-5	6./KG77	3Z+FP	7117	Tech prob?	off Bridlington
4/5.05.41	Ju88A-5	KuFlGr.2./106	M2+DK	0656	Nightfighter	Bradford
8.05.41	He111H-5	Stab.I./KG4	5J+ZB	3987	Hurricane	Withernssea
8/9.05.41	He111P-4	6./KG55	G1+FP	3000	Defiant NF	nr. Beverley
8/9.05.41	He111H-5	4./KG53	A1+FM	4006	Defiant NF	nr. Spurn Point
8/9.05.41	He111H-5	6./KG53	A1+CW	4042	Defiant NF	Patrington
15.05.41	Ju88A-5	6./KG1	V4+GP	6263	Naval flak	off Spurn Head
2/3.06.41	Ju88C-4	2./NJG2	R4+LK	0570	Weather	nr. Whitby
9/10.07.41	Ju88A-5	KuFlGr.3./106	M2+AL	4386	Weather?	nr. Filey
9/10.07.41	Ju88A-5	KuFlGr 3./106	M2+CL	3245	Weather?	nr. Filey

Date	Aircraft	Unit	Code	w/nr	Cause	Location
9/10.07.41	Ju88A-5	KuFlGr 2./106	M2+EK	2227	Weather?	Staithes
11.07.41	He111H-4	8./KG4	5J+ES	3956	unknown	off Humber
2.08.41	Ju88	KuFlGr 1./506	S4+LH	723	Spitfire?	off Flamborough?
8.08.41	Bf110C-5	1(F)/123	4U+XH	2306	Spitfire	off Flamborough?
10.11.41	Ju88A-4	KuFlGr 2./506	S4+HK	1409	Naval flak	Ravenscar
15.01.42	Do217E-4	8./KG2	U5+HS	5314	Naval flak	Teesside
19.01.42	Ju88A-5	3(F)/122	F6+PL	440	Spitfire	off Whitby
18.02.42	Do217E-4	7./KG2	U5+KR	5342	Spitfire	off Humber
26/27.02.42	Do217E-4	9./KG2	U5+St	1176	Unknown	Humber area?
27/28.02.42	Do217E	8./KG2	U5+AS	5346	Naval flak	Humber area?
8/9.03.42	Do217E-4	9./KG2	U5+LT	5336	Unknown	Humber area?
28/29. 04.42	Do217E-2	6./KG2	U5+KP	1164	Nightfighter	Coneysthorpe
28/29.04.42	Ju88A-5	11./KG77	3Z+AV	0289	Beau. NF	off Whitby
28/29.04.42	Ju88D-1	KuFlGr.1./106	M2+CH	1334	Nightfighter	Elvington
7/8.07.42	Do217E-4	4./KG2	U5+BM	5465	Nightfighter	off Scarborough or Tyn
21.07.42	Do217E-4	1./KG2	U5+1H	4260	Mosquito	off Spurn Head?
28/29.08.42	Do217E-4	1./KG2	U5+FH	5341	Beau. NF	off Whitby?
6.09.42	Me210A-1	16./KG6	2H+CA	2348	Typhoon	New Marske
6.09.42	Me210A-1	16./KG6	2H+HA	2331	Typhoon	nr. Robin Hoods Bay
23/24.09.42	Do217E-4	1./KG2	U5+FH	4294	Beau. NF	off Flamborough
17.12.42	Do217E-4	2./KG2	U5+AK	4348	Flak?	nr. Goathland
17.12.42	Do217E-4	7./KG2	U5+GR	4342	Low flying?	nr. Helmsley
3.01.43	Do217E-4	9./KG2	U5+KT	4314	Flak?	Skeffling
15/16.01.43	Do217E-4	9./KG2	U5+AT	4272	Mosquito?	Humber area?
3.02.43	Do217E-4	3./KG2	U5+GL	5462	Beau. NF	Muston
11.03.43	Do217E-4	6./KG40	F8+LP	5313	Beau. NF	off Yorks coast.
15/16 .03.43	Ju88A-14	2./KG6	3E+WK	4532	Beau. NF	off Spurn Head?
13/14. 06.43	Do217E-4	5./KG2	U5+BN	4376	Beau. NF?	off Flamborough?
12/13.07.43	Do217K-1	4./KG2	U5+EM	4478	Mosquito?	off Humber?
13/14.07.43	Do217M-1	3./KG2	U5+EL	56153	Beau. NF?	off Scarborough?
24/25. 07.43	Do217M-1	2./KG2	U5+HK	6058	Unknown	off Humber?
24/25.07.43	Do217E-4	5./KG2	U5+DN	5489	Flak?	off Humber
25/26.07.43	Do217M-1	2./KG2	U5+GK	6045	Beau. NF	off Spurn Head
25/26.07.43	Do217K-1	Stab./KG2	U5+BA	4412	Beau. NF	off Spurn Head
25/26. 07.43	Do217E-4	5./KG2	U5+AN	4395	Flak	Long Riston
21/22.09.43	Do217K-1	4./KG2	U5+CM	4620	Low flying	nr. Withernsea
2/3 .10.43	Ju88E-1	2./KG66	Z6+GK	260175	Low flying?	off Spurn Head
4.03.45	Ju8G-6	13./NJG3	D5+AX	620028	Low flying	Dunnington

Luftwaffe losses in the Yorkshire area, 1939 - 1945   Appendix 1a
(by cause and by date)

Cause	1939	1940	1941	1942	1943	1944	1945	TOTAL	
Day fighter	2	12	4	4				22	(30.5%)
Night fighter			4	8	9			21	(29.2%)
AA flak		3		1	3			7	(9.6%)
Weather		1	4					5	(6.9%)
Low flying				1	2		1	4	(5.6%)
Naval flak			2	2				4	(5.6%)
Tech. probs		1	3					4	(5.6%)
Coastal Command	1							1	(1.4%)
Unknown			1	2	1			4	(5.6%)
Total	**3**	**17**	**18**	**18**	**15**		**1**	**72**	**(100.0%)**

Luftwaffe losses in the Yorkshire area, 1939 - 1945   Appendix 1b
(by aircraft type and date)

Type	1939	1940	1941	1942	1943	1944	1945	TOTAL	
Do217				13	13			26	(36.2%)
Ju88		10	11	3	1		1	26	(36.2%)
He111	1	6	6					13	(18.0%)
He115	1	1						2	(3.0%)
Me210				2				2	(3.0%)
Bf110			1					1	(1.5%)
Do18	1							1	(1.5%)
Ju188					1			1	(1.5%)
Total	**3**	**17**	**18**	**18**	**15**		**1**	**72**	**(100.0%)**

Luftwaffe losses in the Yorkshire area, 1939 - 1945   Appendix 1c
(by location and date)

Location	1939	1940	1941	1942	1943	1944	1945	TOTAL
North (Tees-Scarbro')								
on land		4	4	4				12
in sea	2	4		5	1			12
South (Scarbro'-Humber)								
on land		6	7	3	4		1	21
in sea	1	3	6	7	9			26
West (Bradford)								
on land			1					1
Total	**3**	**17**	**18**	**19**	**14**		**1**	**72**

Appendix 2
Luftwaffe Losses in the Yorkshire area , 1939 -1945
(by aircraft and crews)

Date	Aircraft	Unit	Pilot	Observer	Wireless/op	Mech/Gun.	A.N.O
17.10.39	He111H-1	2. (F)/122	Lange, E.	Kretschmer, J.	Hochstuhl, B.	Sauer, H.	
21.10.39	He115B	KuFlGr. 1./406	Schlict, H.	Meyer, F.	Wessels, B.	?	
10.11.39	Do18D	KuFlGr. 3./406	?	Lütyens, W.	?	?	
3.02.40	He111H-3	4./KG26	Wilms, H.	Leuschake, R.	Missy, K.	Meyer, J.	
3.04.40	He111H-3	StabII./KG26	Behnisch, R.	Kempe, G.	Weber, A.	Bächle, A.	Hefele,
25/26.6.40	He111P-2	3./KG4	Furcht, H.	Schröder, H.	Hartel, M.	Seitz, E	
1.07.40	He111H-4	3./KG4	Raisbach, H.	Koch, F-W.	Weber, A.	Ernst, R.	
1.07.40	He115	KuFlGr.3./106	Schröder, G.	Worms, R.	Soest, S.		
8.07.40	Ju88A-1	9./KG4	Rohloff, K.	Abel, G.	Kühnapfel, A.	Oechler, H.	
9.08.40	He111H-4	2./KG4	Schmidt, R.	Ebald, H	Geisdorf, H.	Soffel, W.	
11.08.40	Ju88-1	1(F)/121	Höfft, O.	Marzuch, H.	Hacker, K-H.	Meier, H.	
15.08.40	Ju88 C	7./KG30	Bachmann, W.	Evers, W.	Henneske, G.	Walther, R.	
15.08.40	Ju88A-5	3./KG30	von Lorentz, L.	Kenski, H.	Prumann, H.	Göbel, J.	
15.08.40	Ju88	4./KG30	Bihr, R.	Pohl, R.	Kürsch, S.	Neumeyer, A.	
15.08.40	Ju88C	7./KG30	Riede, W-D.	Hartwich, F.	Ulbrich, R.	Panhuysen, P.	
20.08.40	Ju88A-1	8./KG30	Wolff, F.G.	Keller, H.	Kruczinski, W.H.	Rautenberg, W.	
21.08.40	He111H-2	9./KG53	Henkel, O.	Pfeiffer. G.	Kiauk, H.	Nussbaum, F.	Christ,
27.10.40	Ju88A-5	7./KG4	Podbielski, F.F.	Heier, H.	von Kidrowski, K.	Piontek, O.	
27.10.40	Ju88A-1	8./KG4	Marwitz, D	Mehrbach, W	Herald, K	Schmitz, H	
1.11.40	Ju.88A-1	8./KG30	Wowereit, W.	Schulte-Mäter, H.	Rodermond, A.	Pohling, G.	
9.02.41	Ju88A-5	4./KG30	Weber, H	Rosa-Maier, K.	Latzel, E.	Kruse, W.	
30.03.41	Ju88A	1(F)/123	Schlott, W.	Meingold, O.	Schmigale, W.	Steigerwald, H.	
8.04.41	Ju88A-5	2./KG30	Öwich, H.	Holaseck, H.	Diagele, S.	Lück, W.	
15/16.04.41	He111H-5	3./KG53	Menzel, K.	Lackner, R.	Seltmann, O.	Wächter, A.	Höring
4/5.05.41	Ju88A-5	6./KG77	Baumann, M.	Auernhammer, K.	Hopfer, W.	Schieting, E.	
4/5.05.41	Ju88A-5	KuFlGr.2./106	Jürgens, E.	Metzger, R.	Beek, H.	Jänichen, H.	
8.05.41	He111H-5	Stab.I./KG4	Tholen, P.	Schröder, H-K.	Schreiber, W.	Hoffman, A.	
8/9.05.41	He111P-4	6./KG55	Ender, G.	Müller, H.	Schackat, B.	Schopf, G.	
8/9.05.41	He111H-5	4./KG53	Reinelt, G.	Magie, F.	Kalle, J.	Lorenz, R.	Wülf,
8/9.05.41	He111H-5	6./KG53	Teschke, H.	London, W.	Kaminski, J.	Steiglitz, H-J.	Decker
15.05.41	Ju88A-5	6./KG1	Schröder, K.	Wingenfeld, E.	Friedel, J.	Dietzsch, W.	
2/3.06.41	Ju88C-4	2./NJG2	Feuerbaum, J.		Denzin, G.	Peters, R.	
9/10.07.41	Ju88A-5	KuFlGr.3./106	Moog, H.	Blome, W.	Wiese, A.	Riehme, H.	
9/10.07.41	Ju88A-5	KuFlGr 3./106	Sinz, H.	Beuting, H.	Quodt, W.	Donder, O.	
9/10.07.41	Ju88A-5	KuFlGr 2./106	Peisert, E.	Belloff, R.	Vogel, G.	Kinder, K.	
10.07.41	He111H-4	8./KG4	Weitz, L.	Pätztel, F.	Ruhl, J.	unknown	

Date	Aircraft	Unit	Pilot	Observer	Wireless/op	Mech/Gun.	A.N.O.
2.08.41	Ju88	KuFlGr 1./506	Eckardt, A.	Rupp, E.	Zanussi, A.	Braun, H.	
3.08.41	Bf110C-5	1(F)/123	Mende, F.		Pietras, M.		
10.11.41	Ju88A-4	KuFlGr 2./506	Weber, H.	Schütz, K.	Hanel, W.	Gräber, A.	
15.01.42	Do217E-4	8./KG2	Lehnis, J.	Matern, R.	Maneke, H.	Richter, H.	
19.01.42	Ju88A-5	3(F)/122	Fichtinger, F.	Drassdo, G.	Blunck, H.	Bauer, J.	
18.02.42	Do217E-4	7./KG2	Palm, E.	Mühlbach, R.	Hoffman, A.	Kammerath, R.	
26/27.02.42	Do217E-4	9./KG2	Scharnbacher, J,	Mischalla, S.	Przybilla, B.	Kappenberg, H.	
27/28.02.42	Do217E	8./KG2	Günther, H.	Erber, K.	Pollok, C.	Volz , W.	
8/9.03.42	Do217E-4	9./KG2	Hedler, H.	Stetler, H.	Kowalski, G.	Materne, H.	
28/29. 04.42	Do217E-2	6./KG2	Mühlen, K-H.	Hacker, O.	Kälber, F.	Fussnecker, O.	
28/29.04.42	Ju88A-5	IV./KG77	Körfer, A.	Müller, H.	Fritz, E.	Schleising, H.	
28/29.04.42	Ju88D-1	KuFlGr.1./106	Boy, W.	Kugler, K-H.	Schindler, W.	Müller, H.	
7/8.07.42	Do217E-4	4./KG2	Grandl, J.	Bredtmeyer, J.	Müller, H.	Meindl, F.	
21.07.42	Do217E-4	1./KG2	Wolpers, H.	Frank, W.	Schmidt, K.	Eyrich, A.	
28/29.08.42	Do217E-4	1./KG2	Weigel, J.	Hanisch, H-J.	Reitter, M.	Schlesinger, W.	
5.09.42	Me210A-1	16./KG6	Mösges, H.		Czerny, E.		
5.09.42	Me210A-1	16./KG6	Maurer, W.		Jansen, R.		
23/24.09.42	Do217E-4	1./KG2	Cornelius, A.	Hawran, W.	Hopf, G.	Müxel, O.	
17.12.42	Do217E-4	2./KG2	Stoll, W.	Röschner, H.	Wicht, G.	Armann, F.	
17.12.42	Do.217E-4	7./KG2	Häusner, R.	Erd, S.	Hupe, H.	Wiederer, E.	
8.01.43	Do217E-4	9./KG2	Reis, A.	Küster, H.	Salz, A.	Muschiol, A.	
15/16.01.43	Do217E-4	9./KG2	Unglaube, H.	Holtz, F.	Vögerle, R.	Bongardt, H.	
3.02.43	Do217E-4	3./KG2	Müller, K.	Lewald, H.	Fruth, F.	Wilmsen, H.	
11.03.43	Do217E-4	6./KG40	Schuld, E.	Beihofer, W.	Deihard, W.	Pyttel, W.	
15/16 .03.43	Ju88A-14	2./KG6	Deimer, A.	Kretching, H.	Atzwanger, J.	Schmidt, A.	
13/14. 06.43	Do217E-4	5./KG2	Sünneman, F.	Orchel, H.	Duwe, G.	Oesterle, H.	
12/13.07.43	Do217K-1	4./KG2	Saliger, H.	Dähler, H.	Labinschuhs, W.	Nürnberger, K.	
13/14.07.43	Do217M-1	3./KG2	Spielmann, W.	Richter, H.	Concemius, H.	Wickel. W.	
24/25. 07.43	Do217M-1	2./KG2	Querlich, O.	Jähn, H.	Mehler, H.	Schricker, R.	
24/25.07.43	Do217E-4	5./KG2	Keifert, K.	Borcherding, H.	Welz, R.	Schulte, R.	
25/26.07.43	Do217M-1	2./KG2	Fuchs, R.	Grob, W.	Krönig, H.	Toeltsch, H.	
25/26.07.43	Do217K-1	Stab./KG2	Reuthe, M.	Ludwig, S.	Böning, H.	Schürleiden, W.	
25/26. 07.43	Do217E-4	5./KG2	Kowle, H-U.	Pilger, F.	Gabriel, H.	Trodler, R.	
21/22.09.43	Do217K-1	4./KG2	Rumpff, H.	von Weg, S.	Ehemann, A.	Stiegler, K.	
2/3 .10.43	Ju188E-1	2./KG66	Beubler, G.	Urban, H.	Fischer, A.	Pausch, E.	
4.03.45	Ju88G-6	13./NJG3	Dreher, J.	Schmitz, G.	Böker, H.	Bechter, M.	

Unit	Crew killed	Crew missing	Crew pow	Total
1(F)/121	1		3	4
2(F)/122	2		2	4
3(F)/122		4		4
1(F)/123	1	5		6
6./KG1	2		2	4
Stab./KG2		2	2	4
1./KG2		12		12
2./KG2	6	6		12
3./KG2	1	8		9
4./KG2	5	7		12
5./KG2	5	7		12
6./KG2	1		3	4
7./KG2	4	4		8
8./KG2	4	4		8
9./KG2		12	4	16
Stab./KG4	2		2	4
2./KG4		4		4
3./KG4		4	4	8
7./KG4	1		3	4
8./KG4	1	6	1	8
9./KG4	1		3	4
2./KG6		4		4
16./KG6	2		2	4
StabII./KG26			5	5
4./KG26	2		2	4
2./KG30		4		4
3./KG30			4	4
4./KG30	2	6		8
7./KG30	2	3	3	8
8./KG30	6		2	8
6./KG40		4		4
3./KG53		4	5	5
4./KG53	3	1	1	5
6./KG53	4		1	5
9./KG53	5			5
6./KG55	2		2	4
2./KG66	4			4
6./KG77	3		1	4
11./KG77		4		4
Ku/Fl.Gr.1/106	1		3	4
Ku.Fl.Gr.2/106	4		4	8
Ku.Fl.Gr.3/106	4		7	11
Ku/Fl.Gr.1/406	3			3
Ku.Fl.Gr.3/406		1		1
Ku.Fl.Gr.1/506	3	1		4
Ku.Fl.Gr.2/506	2	2		4
2./NJG2	3			3
13./NJG3	4			4
Total	**96**	**115**	**71**	**282**
	34.00%	**40.80%**	**25.20%**	**100%**

Luftwaffe crew losses in the Yorkshire area, 1939 - 1945 (by name and by fate)

	Number	Name	Rank	Unit	Date of loss	Fate	Burial place
1	53558/9	Abel, George	Uffz.	9./Kg4	8.07.40	pow	Acklam Road Cem. Thornaby-on-Tees
2	57358/169	Armann, Franz	Obgfr	2./KG2	17.12.42	killed	
3		Atzwanger, Jochen	Uffz.	2./KG6	15/16.03.43	missing	
4		Auernhammer, Karl	Obfw.	6./KG77	4/5.05.41	killed	
5		Bächle, Alfred	Uffz.	Stabl /KG26	3.04.40	pow	
6		Bachmann, Werner	Obit.	7/LG30	15.08.40	pow	
7		Bauer, Johann	Gefr	3(F)/122	19.01.42	missing	
8		Baumann, Martin	Obit.	6./KG77	4/5.05.41	killed	
9		Bechter, Martin	Fw.	13/NJG3	4.03.45	killed	German Military Cem. Cannock Chase
10		Beek, Hans	Obfw.	KuFlG.2/106	4/5.05.41	pow	
11		Behnisch, Rudolf	Lt.	StabII/JKG26	3.04.40	pow	
12		Beihofer, Werner	Uffz.	6./KG40	11.03.43	missing	Acklam Road Cem. Thornaby-on-Tees
13	73045/70	Bellof, R.	Lt.	KuFlGr2/106	9/10.07.41	killed	
14		Beubler, Günther	Lt.	2./KG66	2/3.10.43	killed	
15	73175/8	Beuting, Harald	Fw.	KuFlGr3/106	9/10.07.41	killed	German Military Cem. Cannock Chase
16		Bihr, Rudolf	Fw.	4./KG30	15.08.40	killed	German Military Cem. Cannock Chase
17	9/62747	Blome, Werner	Lt.	KuFlGr.3/106	9/10.07.41	pow	
18		Blunck, Hans	Gefr	3(F)/122	19.01.42	missing	
19		Böker, Hugo	Obfw.	13/NJG3	4.03.45	killed	German Military Cem. Cannock Chase
20		Bongardt, Heinz	Obgfr.	9./KG2	15/16.01.43	missing	
21		Böning, Heinrich	Uffz.	Stab/KG2	25/26.07.43	missing	
22		Borcherding,Heingz	Obgfr.	5./KG2	23/25.07.43	missing	
23	73172/90	Boy, Werner	Lt.	KuFlG.1/106	28/29.04.42	killed	German Military Cem. Cannock Chase
24		Braun, Hans	Fw.	KuFlGr 1/506	2.08.41	killed	
25		Bredmeyer, Johannes	Lt.	4./KG2	7/8.07.42	missing	
26	69044/48	Christ, Kurt	Gefr.	9./KG53	21.08.40	killed	
27		Concemius, Hans	Uffz.	3./KG2	13/14.07.43	missing	
28		Cornelius, Alfred	Obit.	1./KG2	23/24.09.42	missing	
29	64476/21	Czerny, Eduard	Obgfr.	16./KG6	6.09.42	killed	Acklam Road Cem. Thornaby-on-Tees
30		Dähler, Hans	Gerf.	4./KG2	12/13.07.43	missing	
31		Decker, Hermann	Gefr.	6./KG53	8/9.05.41	killed	The Churchyard, Brandesburton, nr Hornsea
32		Deihard, Walter	Uffr.	6./KG540	11.03.43	missing	
33		Deimer, Arno	Uffr.	2./KG6	15/16.03.43	missing	
34	53578/716	Denzin, G.	Gefr.	2./NJG2	2/3.06.41	killed	Acklam Road Cem. Thornaby-on-Tees
35		Diagele, Sebastion	Gefr.	2./KG30	8.04.41	missing	
36	535445/23	Dietzsch, Willi	Obfw.	6./KG1	15.05.41	killed	German Military Cem. Cannock Chase
37	53557/81	Donder, Otto	Fw.	KuFlGr3/106	9/10.07.41	killed	German Military Cem. Cannock Chase

Number	Name	Rank	Unit	Date of loss	Fate	Burial place
38	Drassdo, Gerhard	Fw.	3(F)/122	19.01.42	missing	
39	Dreher, Johann	Hptm.	13/NJG3	4.03.45	killed	German Military Cem. Cannock Chase
40	Duwe, Gerhard	Fw.	5/KG2	13/14.06.43	missing	
41	Ebald, Herbert	Gefr.	2/KG4	9.08.40	missing	
42	Eckardt, Alfons	Fw.	KuFlGr 1/506	2.08.41	killed	Northern Cem. Hull
43	69645/186	Ehemann, Arno	Gefr.	4/KG2	21/22.09.43	killed	German Military Cem. Cannock Chase
44	67021/140	Ender, Gerhard	Fw.	6/KG55	8/9.05.41	killed	
45	Erber, Karl	Ofw.	8/KG2	27/28.02.42	missing	
46	53577/693	Erd, Sirius	Uffz.	7/KG2	17.12.42	killed	
47	Ernst, Rudolf	Obfw.	3/KG4	1.07.40	pow	
48	Evers, Werner	Uffz.	7/KG30	15.08.40	pow	
49	Eyrich, Arnim	Ofw.	1/KG2	21.07.42	missing	
50	53578/704	Feuerbaum, Johann	Lt.	2/NJG2	2/3.06.41	killed	Acklam Road Cem. Thornaby-on-Tees
51	Fichtinger, Franz	Uffz.	3(F)122	19.01.42	missing	
52	Fischer, Albert	Uffz.	2/KG66	2/3.10.43	killed	
53	Frank, Walter	Hptm.	1/KG2	21.07.42	missing	
54	Friedel, Josef	Uffz.	6/KG1	15.05.41	pow	
55	Fritz, Ernst	Uffz.	11/KG77	28/29.04.42	missing	
56	Fruth, Friedrich	Uffz.	3/KG2	3.02.43	missing	
57	Fuchs, Robert	Uffz.	2/KG2	25/26.07.43	missing	
58	Furcht, Helmut	Lt.	3/KG4	25/26.6.40	missing	
59	Fussnecker, Oskar	Fw.	6/KG2	28/29.04.42	pow	
60	Gabriel, Helmut	Uffz.	5/KG2	25/26.07.43	killed	The Churchyard, Brandesburton, nr Hornsea
61	Geisdorf, Hans	Fw.	2/KG4	9.08.40	missing	
62	Göbel, Johann	Gefr.	3/KG30	15.08.40	pow	
63	Gräber, Artur	Uffz.	KuFlGr 2/506	10.11.41	missing	Acklam Road Cem. Thornaby as 'unknown'?
64	Grandi, Johann	Fw.	4/KG2	7/8.07.42	killed	
65	Grob, Wolfgang	Gefr.	2/KG2	25/26.07.43	missing	Buried at sea
66	Günther, Helmut	Uffz.	8/KG2	27/28.02.42	missing	
67	Hacker, Karl-Heinz	Fw.	1(F)/121	11.08.40	pow	
68	Hacker, Otto	Uffz.	6/KG2	28/29.04.42	pow	
69	73563/197	Hanel, Werner	Obfw.	KuFlG 2/506	10.11.41	killed	Acklam Road Cem. Thornaby-on-Tees
70	Hanisch, Hans Joachim	Uffz.	1/KG2	28/29.08.42	missing	
71	Hartel, Martin	Obfw.	3/KG4	25/26.6.40	missing	
72	Hartwich, Fritz	Uffz.	7/KG30	15.08.40	killed	
73	69645/96	Häusner, Rolf	Obit.	7/KG2	17.12.42	killed	
74	Hawran, Werner	Uffz.	1/KG2	23/24.09.42	missing	

Number	Name	Rank	Unit	Date of loss	Fate	Burial place
75	Hedler Helmut	Obit.	9/KG2	8/9.03.42	missing	
76	Hefele, Hans	Oberstlt.	StabII/KG26	3.04.40	pow	
77	55542/38	Heier, Hans	Uffz.	7/KG4	27.10.40	pow	
78	69044/17	Henkel, Otto	Fw.	9/KG53	21.08.40	killed	German Military, Cannock Chase
79	62756/60	Henneske, Georg	Fw.	7/KG30	15.08.40	killed	
80	55543/73	Herold, Karl	Gefr.	8/KG4	28.10.40	missing	
81	Hochstuhl, B.	Uffz.	2(F)/122	17.10.39	pow	
82	Hoffman, Alfred	Obfw.	Stab.I/KG4	8.05.41	killed	The Churchyard, Brandesburton, nr Hornsea
83	Hoffman, Arthur	Uffz.	7/KG2	18.02.42	missing	
84	535001/13	Höfft, Otto	Fw.	1(F)/121	11.08.40	pow	
85	Holaseck, Hans	Gefr.	2/KG30	8.04.41	missing	
86	Holtz, Franz	Oblt.	9/KG2	15/16.01.43	missing	
87	Hopf, Gerhard	Fw.	1/KG2	23/24.09.42	missing	
88	Hopfer, Wilhelm	Fw.	6/KG77	4/5.05.41	killed	
89	Höring, Werner	Hptm.	3/KG53	15/16.04.41	missing	
90	53582/13	Hupe, Hartwig	Obfw.	7/KG2	17.12.42	killed	German Military Cem. Cannock Chase
91	Jähn, Hans	Obfw.	2/KG2	24/25.07.43	missing	
92	Jänichen, Heinrich	Fw.	KuFlGr2/106	4/5.05.41	pow	
93	65201/1	Jansen, Rudolf	Fw.	16/KG6	6.09.42	pow	
94	Jürgens, Ernst	Obit.	KuFlGr.2/106	4/5.05.41	pow	
95	53576/571	Kälber, Fritz	Uffz.	6/KG2	28/29.04.42	killed	German Military Cem. Cannock Chase
96	Kalle, Jakob	Uffz.	4/KG53	8/9.05.41	killed	The Churchyard, Brandesburton, nr Horsea
97	Kaminski, Johannes	Gefr.	6/KG53	8/9.05.41	killed	The Churchyard, Brandesburton, nr Hornsea
98	Kammerath, Reinhard	Obgfr.	7/KG2	18.02.42	missing	
99	Kappenberg, Hans	Uffz.	9/KG2	26/27.02.42	missing	
100	Keifert, Kurt	Uffz.	5/KG2	24/25.07.43	missing	
101	Keller, Hugo	Fw.	8/KG30	20.08.40	missing	
102	4/KG26Nr.28	Kempe, Georg	Lt.	StabII/KG26	3.04.40	pow	
103	Kenski, Heinrich	Uffz.	3/KG30	15.08.40	pow	
104	69044/34	Kiauk, Hans	Uffz.	9/KG53	21.08.40	killed	
105	73175/9	Kinder, K	Fw.	KuFlG2/106	9/10.07.41	killed	Acklam Road Cem. Thornaby-on-Tees
106	Koch, Fried-Wilhelm	Obitz See	3/KG4	1.07.40	pow	
107	Kolwe, Hans-Ulrich	Uffz.	5/KG2	25/26.07.43	killed	The Churchyard, Brandesburton, nr Hornsea
108	Körfer, Armin	Ltn.	11/KG77	28/29.04.42	missing	
109	Kowalski, Günther	Fw.	9/KG2	8/9.03.42	missing	
110	Kretching, Heinz	Obgfr.	2/KG6	15/16.03.43	missing	
111	2(F)122Nr7	Kretschmer, Joachim	Lt.	2(F)/122	17.10.39	killed	

Number	Name	Rank	Unit	Date of loss	Fate	Burial place
112	Krönig, Herrman	Gefr.	2/KG2	25/26.07.43	missing	
113 NP64L30733	Kruczinski, Werner Hans	Uffz.	8/KG30	20.08.40	killed	German Military Cem. Cannock Chase
114	Kruse, W.	Uffz.	4/KG30	9.02.41	missing	
115	Kugler, Karl-H.	Uffz.	KuFlGr.1/106	28/29.04.42	pow	
116	Kühnapfel, Artur	Uffz.	9/KG4	8.07.40	pow	German Military Cem. Cannock Chase
117 62748/23	Kürsch, Severin	Uffz.	4/KG30	15.08.40	killed	
118	Küster, Horst	Obgfr.	9/KG2	3.01.43	pow	
119	Labinschuhs, Walter	Uffz.	4/KG2	12/13.07.43	missing	
120	Lackner, Rudolf	Obfw.	3/KG53	15/16.04.41	pow	
121 2(F)122Nr 72	Lange, Eugen	Obfw.	2(F)/122	17.10.39	pow	
122	Latzel, E.	Uffz.	4/KG30	9.02.41	missing	
123 69642/32	Lehnis, Joachim	Fw.	8/KG2	15.01.42	killed	Acklam Road Cem. Thornaby-on-Tees
124 4/KG26Nr33	Leushake, Rudolf	Uffz.	4/KG26	3.02.40	killed	German Military Cem. Cannock Chase
125	Lewald, Heinz	Fw.	3/KG2	3.02.43	missing	
126	London, Willi	Gefr.	6/KG53	8/9.05.41	killed	The Churchyard, Brandesburton, nr. Hornsea
127	Lorenz, Rudolf	Obgfr.	4/KG53	8/9.5.41	killed	The Churchyard, Brandesburton, nr. Hornsea
128	Lück, Werner	Gefr.	2/KG30	8.04.41	missing	
129	Ludwig, Siefried	Uffz.	Stab/KG2	25/26.07.43	pow	
130	Lütyens, Wilhelm	Oblt.z.See	KuFlGr.3/406	10.11.39	missing	
131	Magie, Franz	Uffz.	4/KG53	8/9.05.41	pow	
132 57359/75	Maneke, Hans	Uffz.	8/KG2	15.01.42	killed	Acklam Road Cem. Thornaby-on-Tees
133 55543/3	Marwitz, Dietrich	Obit.	8/KG4	28.20.40	missing	
134 53501/5	Marzuch, Hans	Obit.	1(F)/121	11.08.40	pow	
135 5209/15	Matern, Rudolf	Ltn.	8/KG2	15.01.42	killed	Acklam Road Cem. Thornaby-on-Tees
136	Materne, Hermann	Uffz.	9/KG2	8/9.03.42	missing	
137 55566/5	Maurer, Walther	Obit.	16/KG6	6.09.42	pow	
138	Mehler, Hans	Obgfr.	2/KG2	24/25.07.43	missing	
139 55543/18	Mehrbach, Werner	Obfw.	8/KG4	28.20.40	missing	
140	Meier, Heinrich	Lt.	1(F)/121	11.08.40	killed	Removed to Germany in 1954
141	Meindl, Franz	Uffz.	4/KG2	7/8.07.42	missing	
142 69004/201	Meingold, Otto	Ltn.	1(F)/123	30.03.41	missing	
143	Mende, Friedrich	Obit.	1(F)/123	8.08.41	missing	
144	Menzel, Karl	Fw.	3/KG53	15/16.04.41	pow	
145	Metzger, Reinhold	Obit.	KuFlGr.2/106	4/5.05.41	pow	
146	Meyer, Johann	Uffz.	4/KG26	3.02.40	killed	German Military Cem. Cannock Chase
147	Meyer, Fritz	Lt.	KuFlGr. 1/406	21.10.39	killed	German Military Cem. Cannock Chase
148	Mischalla, Sylvester	Uffz.	9/KG2	26/27.02.42	missing	

Number	Name	Rank	Unit	Date of loss	Fate	Burial place
149	4/KG26 Nr37	Missy, Karl	Uffz.	4/KG26	3.02.40	pow	
150		Möller, Heinz	Gefr.	KuFlGr 1/106	28/29.04.42	pow	
151	64476/20	Moog, Heinrich	Hptm.	KuFlGr 3/106	9/10.07.41	pow	
152		Mösges, Heinrich	Fw.	16/KG6	6.09.42	killed	Acklam Road Cem. Thornaby-on-Tees
153		Mühlbach, Rudolf	Fw.	7/KG2	18.02.42	missing	
154		Mühlen, Karl-Heinz	Lt.	6/KG2	28/29.04.42	pow	
155		Müller, Heinrich	Fw.	6/KG55	8/9.05.41	pow	
156		Müller, Heinrich	Uffz.	11/KG77	28/29.04.42	missing	
157		Müller, Horst	Uffz.	4/KG2	7/8.02.42	missing	
158		Müller, Karl	Obfw.	3/KG2	3.02.43	missing	
159		Muschiol, Alfred	Uffz.	9/KG2	3.01.43	pow	
160		Muxel, Otto	Uffz.	1/KG2	23/24.09.42	missing	
161		Neumeyer, A.rnalf	Uffz.	4/KG30	15.08.40	missing	Bridlington Cem. as 'Unknown?'
162		Nürnberger, Kurt	Uffz.	4/KG2	12/13.07.43	missing	
163	69044/52	Nussbaum, Fritz	Gerf.	9/KG53	21.08.40	killed	
164	53558/23	Oechler, Heinz	Uffz.	9/KG4	8.07.40	pow	
165		Oesterle, Heinz	Uffz.	5/KG2	13/14.06.43	missing	
166		Orchel, Heinz	Uffz.	5/KG2	13/14.06.43	missing	
167		Öwich, H.elmut	Uffz.	2/KG30	8.04.41	missing	
168		Palm, Erich	Lt.	7/KG2	18.02.42	missing	
169		Panhuysen, Peter	Uffz.	7/KG30	15.08.40	missing	
170	337/53758	Pankuwweitz, Hugo	Uffz.	3/KG2	13/14.07.43	killed	Northern Cem. Hull
171		Pätztel, Friedrich	Uffz.	8/KG4	10.07.41	missing	
172	214651/259	Pausch, Erwin	Uffz.	2/KG66	2/3.10.43	killed	Northern Cem. Hull
173	53415/6	Peisert, Edgar	Obit.	KuFlG 2/106	9/10.07.41	killed	Acklam Road Cem. Thornaby-on-Tees
174	61/1157	Peters, Rudolf	Gerf.	2/NJG2	2/3.06.41	killed	Acklam Road Cem. Thornaby-on-Tees
175	69044/1	Pfeiffer, Georg	Hptm.	9/KG53	21.08.40	killed	
176		Pietras, Martin	Fw.	1(F)/123	8.08.41	missing	
177		Pilger, Fitz	Uffz.	5/KG2	25/26.07.43	killed	The Churchyard, Brendesburton, nr Hornsea
178	55542/28	Piontek, Oskar	Uffz.	7/KG4	27.10.40	killed	German Military Cem. Cannock Chase
179	55542/4	Podbielski, Friedrick-Franz	Obit.	7/KG4	27.10.40	pow	
180		Pohl, Robert	Fw.	4/KG30	15.08.40	missing	Bridlington Cem. as 'unknown'?
181	55543/41	Pohling, Gerhard	Uffz.	8/KG30	1.11.40	killed	Acklam Road Cem. Thornaby-on-Tees
182		Pollock, Christian	Uffz.	8/KG2	27/28.02.42	missing	
183		Prumann, Heinrich	Obgfr.	3/KG30	15.08.40	pow	
184		Przybilla, Bruno	Uffz.	9/KG2	26/27.02.42	missing	
185		Pytrel, Wilhelm	Obgfr.	6/KG40	11.03.43	missing	

Number	Name	Rank	Unit	Date of loss	Fate	Burial place
186	Querlich, Otto	Uffz.	2/KG2	24/25.07.43	missing	German Military Cem. Cannock Chase
187	Quodt, Wilhelm	Uffz.	KuFlGr 3/106	9/10.07.41	killed	German Military Cem. Cannock Chase
188	Raisbach, Hermann	Obfw.	3/KG4	1.07.40	pow	
189	Rautenberg, Wilhelm		SCHKPB10/JR	20 08..40	killed	German Military Cem. Cannock Chase
190	Reinelt Günter	Uffz.	8/KG30	4/KG53	8/9.05.41	killed	The Churchyard, Brandesburton, nr Hornsea
191	Reis, Anton	Uffz.	9/KG2	3.01.43	pow	
192	Reisinger, Leopold	Obgfr.	8/KG4	10.07.41	killed	
193	Reitter, Maximilian	Obgfr.	1/KG2	28/29.08.42	missing	
194	Reuthe, Max	Uffz.	Stab/KG2	25/26.07.43	missing	
195	Richter, Heinrich	Obfw.	8/KG2	15.01.42	killed	Acklam Road Cem. Thornaby-on-Tees
196	Richter, Hermann	Fw.	3/KG2	13/14.07.43	missing	German Military Cem. Cannock Chase (19.7.43)?
197	Riede, Wolf-Dietrich	Lt.	7/KG30	15.08.40	missing	
198	Riehme, Heinz	Fw.	KuFlGr 3/106	9/10.07.41	pow	Acklam Road Cem. Thornaby-on-Tees
199	Rodermond, Alfred	Uffz.	8/KG30	1.11.40	killed	German Military Cem. Cannock Chase
200	Rohloff, Kurt	Hpt.	9/KG4	8.07.40	killed	Acklam Road Cem. Thornably-on-Tees
201	Röschner, Hans	Obgfr.	2/KG2	17.12.42	killed	
202	Rosa-Maier, K.	Uffz.	4/KG30	9.02.41	killed	
203	Ruhl, Josef	Obgfr.	8/KG4	10.07.41	missing	Northern Cem. Hull
204	Rumpff, Helmut	Fw.	4/KG2	21/22.09.43	killed	
205	Rupp, Ernst	Lt.z.See	KuFlG 1/506	2.08.41	missing	
206	Saliger, Hans	Lt.	4/KG2	12/13.07.43	missing	
207	Salz, Arno	Uffz.	9/KG2	3.01.43	pow	
208	Sauer, Hugo	Uffz.	2/(F)/122	17.10.39	killed	German Military Cem. Cannock Chase
209	Schackat, Bruno	Uffz.	6/KG55	8/9.05.41	killed	German Military Cem. Cannock Chase
210	Scharnbacher, Josef	Lt.	9/KG2	26/27.02.42	missing	
211	Schieting, Emmerich	Obfw.	6/KG77	4/5.05.41	pow	
212	Schindler, Willi	Geffr.	KuFlG	28/29.04.42	pow	
213	Schleising Herman	Obgfr.	11/KG77	26/29.04.42	missing	
214	Schleising, Wilhelm	Obgfr.	1/KG2	28/29.08.42	missing	
215	Schlict, Heinz	Obit z.See	KuFlGr 1/406	21.10.39	killed	German Military Cem. Cannock Chase
216	Schlott, Wolfgang	Lt.	1(F)/123	30.03.41	missing	
217	Schmidt, Albert	Geffr.	2/KG6	15/16.03.43	missing	
218	Schmidt, Karl	Fw.	1/KG2	21.07.42	missing	
219	Schmidt, Richard	Fw.	2/KG4	9.03.40	missing	German Military Cem. Cannock Chase (18.8.40)?
220	Schmigale, Willi	Fw.	1(F)/123	30.03.41	missing	
221	Schmitz, Gustav	Fw.	13/NJG3	4.03.45	missing	German Military Cem. Cannock Chase
222	Schmitz, Hubert	Uffz.	8/KG4	28.10.40	killed	German Military Cem. Cannock Chase

Number	Name	Rank	Unit	Date of loss	Fate	Burial place
223	Schopf, George	Fw	6/KG55	8/9.05.41	pow	
224	Schreiber, Willi	Fw	Stab.I./KG	8.05.41	killed	
225	Schricker, Rudolf	Uffz	2/KG2	24/25.07.43	killed	
226	Schröder, Gottfried	Lt.z.See	KuFlGr.3/106	1.07.40	pow	
227	Schröder, Hans-Karl	Obfw	Stab.I./KG4	8.05.41	pow	
228	Schröder, Heinz	Hptm	3/KG4	25/25.6.40	missing	
229	Schröder, Karl	Obit	6/KG1	15.05.41	killed	
230	Schuld, Erich	Uffz	6/KG40	11.03.43	missing	
231	Schulte, Rudolf	Uffz	5/KG2	24/25.07.43	killed	
232	Schulte-Mäter, Hans	Obfw	8/KG30	1.11.40	killed	Acklam Road Cem. Thornaby-on-Tees
233	Schürleiden, Willi	Obgfr	Stab/KG2	25/26.07.43	pow	
234	Schütz, Karl	Obrfhr	KuFlG2/506	10.11.41	killed	Acklam Road Cem. Thornaby-on-Tees
235	Seitz, Eugen	Fw	3/KG4	25/26.06.40	missing	
236	Seltmann, Oscar	Uffz	3/KG53	15/16.04.41	pow	German Military Cem. Cannock Chase
237	Sinz, Helmut	Lt	KuFlGr 3/106	9/10.07.41	killed	
238	Soest, Siegfried	Uffz	KuFlG 3/106	1.07.40	pow	
239	Soffel, Wilhelm	Uffz	2/KG4	9.08.40	missing	
240	Spielmann, Willi	Uffz	3/KG2	13/14.07.43	missing	
241	Steigerwald, Hans	Uffz	1(F)/123	30.03.41	killed	Acklam Road Cem. Thornaby-on-Tees
242	Steiglitz, Hans-J	Gefr	6/KG53	8/9.05.41	killed	The Churchyard, Brandesburton, nr Hornsea
243	Stetler, Heinz	Uffz	9/KG2	8/9.03.42	missing	
244	Stiegler, Kurt	Obgfr	4/KG2	21/22.09.43	killed	Northern Cem. Hull
245	Stoll, Wilhelm	Fw	2/KG2	17.12.42	killed	Acklam Road Cem. Thornaby-on-Tees
246	Sünneman, Friedrich	Fw	5/KG2	13/14.06.43	missing	
247	Teschke, Helmut	Uffz	6/KG53	8/9.05.41	pow	
248	Tholen, Paul	Oblt.z.See	Stab.1./KG4	8.05.41	pow	
249	Toeltsch, Hubert	Uffz	2/KG2	25/26.07.43	killed	Scarthro Road Cem. Grimsby
250	Trodler, Rudolf	Obgfr	5/KG2	25/26.07.43	killed	The Churchyard, Brandesburton, nr Hornsea
251	Ulbrich, Richard	Flgr	7/KG30	15.08.40	missing	
252	Unglaube, Hans	Uffz	9/KG2	15/16.01.43	missing	
253	Urban, Heinz	Uffz	2/KG66	2/3.10.43	killed	Northern Cem. Hull
254	Vogel, Gerhard	Gefr	KuFlGr 2/106	9/10.07.41	killed	Acklam Road Cem. Thornaby-on-Tees
255	Vögerle, Rudi	Uffz	9/KG2	15/16.01.43	missing	
256	Volz, Wolfgang	Uffz	8/KG2	27/28.02.42	missing	
257	von Kidrowski, Karl	Uffz	7/KG4	27.10.40	pow	
258	von Lorentz, Ludwig	Uffz	3/KG30	15.08.40	pow	
259	von Weg, Siegfried	Fw	21/22.09.43	21/22.09.43	killed	Northern Cem. Hull

Number	Name	Rank	Unit	Date of loss	Fate	Burial place
260	Wächter, Alfons	Fw.	3/KG53	15/16.04.41	pow	
261	Walther, Robert	Flgr.	7/KG30	15.08.40	pow	
262	II./KG26 Nr31	Weber, Albert	Uffz.	Stabll./KG26	3.04.40	pow	
263	Weber, Alfred	Fw.	3/KG4	1.07.40	pow	
264	Weber, Hans	Uffz.	4/KG30	9.02.41	missing	Acklam Road Cem. Thornaby-on-Tees 'unkown'?
265	73778/2	Weber, Heinz	Oblt.	KuFlGr 2/506	10.11.41	missing	German Military Cem. Cannock Chase
266	69645/145	Weiderer, Ernst	Obfw.	7/KG2	17.12.42	killed	
267	Weigel, Josef	Lt.	1/KG2	28/29.08.42	missing	
268	Welz, Robert	Uffz.	5/KG2	24/25.07.43	missing	German Military Cem. Cannock Chase
269	Wessels, Bernhard	Uffz.	KuFlG.1/406	22.10.39	killed	Acklam Road Cem. Thornaby-on-Tees
270	57358/168	Wicht, Gerhard	Obgfr.	2/KG2	17.12.42	killed	
271	Wickel, Walter	Uffz.	3/KG2	13/14.07.43	missing	
272	10/62747	Wiese, Alfons	Obfw.	KuFlGr 3/106	9/10.07.41	pow	
273	Wietz, Lothar	Fw.	8/KG4	10.07.41	pow	
274	4/KG26 Nr63	Wilms, Hermann	Fw.	4/KG26	3.02.40	pow	
275	Wilmsen, Heinrich	Uffz.	3/KG2	3.02.43	missing	
276	Wingenfeld, Ernst	Stfw.	6/KG1	15.05.41	pow	
277	Wolff, Franz Georg	Uffz.	8/KG30	20.08.40	pow	
278	Wolpers, Heinrich	Obfw.	1/KG2	21.07.42	missing	
279	Worms, Rudolf	Obfw.	KuFlGr.3/106	1.07.40	pow	
280	55543/27	Wowereit, Wilhelm	Fw.	8/KG30	1.11.40	killed	Acklam Road Cem. Thornaby-on-Tees
281	Wülf, Heinrich	Gefr.	4/KG53	8/9.05.41	missing	
282	Zanussi, Andreas	Obgfr.	KuFlG 1/506	2..38..41	killed	

BIBLIOGRAPHY

Bundesarchiv-Militärarchiv, Freiburg
Luftwaffe Quartermeistergeneral's Flugzeugverluste (Luftwaffe aircraft losses)

Commonwealth War Graves Commission
German Foreign Nationals in the Care of CWGC (WW2) Commemorated in the United
Kingdom. (from the data base of the CWGC)

County Record Office, Beverley.
East Yorkshire Civil Defence Incident Reports, 1939-1945.
Register of Burials in War Graves. File CM6/30.

Deutsche-Dienststelle, Berlin
Luftwaffe Angehörigeverluste, (Losses of personnel)

Imperial War Museum
Air warfare against England, August 1940 - December 1941. (Luftwaffe 8th Abteilung)
    Document 2402 (Tin 38)
Hauptmann Otto Bechtle: Luftwaffe Operation against England; their tactics and
    deductions, 1940-43. Document 2390 (Tin 38)

National Archives of Canada
406 Squadron RCAF Operations Record Book 1939-45
409 Squadron RCAF. Operations Record Book 1939-45
410 Squadron RCAF. Operations Record Book 1939-45

Northumberland County Council Records Centre, Morpeth
Northumberland Constabulary War Dept Records. NC/6/10.

Public Records Office, Kew
25 Squadron AIR27/305;AIR50/13
41 Squadron AIR27/425; AIR50/18
43 Squadron AIR27/441; AIR50/19
72 Squadron AIR27/624; AIR50/30
111 Squadron AIR27/865; AIR50/43
129 (Mysore) Squadron AIR27/934; AIR50/51
141 Squadron AIR27/969; AIR50/61
145 Squadron AIR50/62
151 Squadron AIR27/1019
152 Squadron AIR27/1025; AIR50/64
249 Squadron AIR50/96
255 Squadron AIR27/1518; AIR50/98.

302(Polish) Squadron AIR27/1661; AIR50/97
406 Squadron AIR27/1791; AIR50/139
604 Squadron AIR27/2084; AIR50/168.
607 Squadron AIR50/170.
609 Squadron AIR27/2102; AIR50/171
611 Squadron AIR27/2109; AIR50/173.
616 Squadron AIR27/2126; AIR50/176.
936 Barrage Balloon(Tyne)Squadron AIR27/
938 Balloon Barrage Squadron AIR27/2281
RAF Usworth Operations Record Book, AIR28/870
63rd Heavy Anti-Aircraft Regiment, Royal Artillery War Diary. WO166/2465
Crashed Enemy Aircraft Reports 7/62, 7/64, 7/68. AIR22/267.
Enemy Attacks on Coastal Convoys, 1941. ADM199/102, ADM199/1181
Interrogation of Prisoners of War AIR40/2394, 2395, 2397, 2398, 2406, 2407
Locations of Enemy Aircraft Brought Down. AIR22/266-267

Tyne & Wear Archives, Newcastle
Deaths due to War Operations. File T15/1475.
Map of county borough of Tynemouth File T383/345.
Reports on Wartime Air Raids. Files 209/110-113.

Journals and Newspapers
Amateur Radio April 1987. Article *The Secret War* by Bryan Johnson
Bradford Telegraph & Argus, 4 May 1991
Bridlington Chronicle, 9 Feb. 1940
Consett Chronicle, 12 Sept. 1940
East Riding Advertiser, 31 December 1998
Grimsby Evening Telegraph, 5 Feb. 1940; 9 Feb. 1940
Hull Daily Mail, 5 Feb. 1940
Northern Daily Mail, 3 Oct. 1941; 8 July 1942; 23 March 1943
North Eastern Evening Gazette, 2 Nov. 1940; 3 Oct.1941; 23 March 1943; 15 Dec. 1994;
   29 April 1995
*QRV: Journal of the RAF Amateur Radio Sociaty Autumn 1993. Article Radio Counter
   Measures - Meaconing* by Vic Flowers
Scarborough Evening News & *Daily Post*, 5 Feb. 1940; 8 July 1942
Sunderland Echo, 28 Sept. 1971; 26 March 1972
The Times Saturday Review, 14 July 1990
West Yorkshireman (date unknown but c.1984). Article *Bomber Crash* by Malcolm
   Richards
Whitby Gazette, 2 Nov.1940

Books
Balke, Ulf: *Der Luftkrieg in Europa: die operativen Ensätze des Kampgeschwaders 2 im zweiten
Weltkrieg*. vol.2 Bernard & Graefe Verlag. 1990 Koblenz.
Baumbach, Werner: *Broken Swastika: the defeat of the Luftwaffe* 1992ed. Dorset Press, USA.

Beedle, J: *43 Squadron.* Beaumont Aviation. 1966.

Bolitho, Hector: *Combat Report, the story of a fighter pilot.* Batsford. 1942.

Bowyer, Chaz: *Fighter Pilots of the RAF.* Kimber. 1984.

Brandon, Lewis: Night Flyer William Kimber. 1969.

Brettingham, Laurie: *Beam Benders: No. 80 [Signals] Wing, 1940-1945.* Midland Pubs. 1997.
- *British Vessels Lost at Sea, 1914-18 and 1939-45.* Patrick Stephens edition 1988.

Clark, Peter: *Where the Hills meet the Sky (a guide to wartime air crashes in the Cheviot Hills).* Glen Graphics 1997.

Clark, Peter: *A Border too High (a guide to wartime crashes in the Border Hills).* Glen Graphics 1999.

Collings, Peter: *The Divers Guide to the North-East Coast.* Collings & Brodie 1986.

Collinson, Amy: *Wartime in Robin Hood's Bay.* Unpublished diary.

Dundas, Hugh: *Flying Start.* Stanley Paul. 1988.

Flagg, Amy: *History of Bomb Damage (South Shields).* Unpublished MSS. South Shields Library.

Franks, Norman L.R.: *Royal Air Force Fighter Command Losses of the Second World War, Vol. 2 1942-1943.* Midland Publishing Ltd. 1998.

Goss, Chris: *It's Suicide But It's Fun.* Crecy 1995.

Gundelach, Karl: *Kampfgeschwader 'General Wever' 4.* Motorbuch Verlag. Stuttgart. 1978.

Hall, Roger: *Clouds of Fear.* Purnell Book Services. 1975.

Halpenny, Bruce B: *Action Stations 4: military airfields of Yorkshire.* Patrick Stephens 1982.

Hersey, Joan: *Riston Remembers 1939-45.* Commemorative. booklet, St. Margaret's Church, Long Riston, 1995.

Hough, Richard and Richards, Dennis: *The Battle of Britain, a jubilee history.* Hodder & Stoughton. 1989.

Jefford, Wing Commander C.G.: *RAF Squadrons: a comprehensive record of the movement and equipment of all RAF squadrons and their antecedents since 1912.* Airlife 1988.

Jones, R.V: *Most Secret War.* Hamish Hamilton, 1978.

Kiehl, Heinz: *Kampfgeschwader 'Legion Condor' 53.* Motorbuch Verlag. 1996.

Kurowski, Franz: *Seekrieg aus der Luft.* ES Mittler Verlag. Germany 1979.

Lee, Asher: *Goering: Air Leader.* Duckworth 1972.

Lenton, H.T: *British and Empire Warships of the Second World War.* Greenhill Books 1998.

Liskutin, M.A: *Challenge in the Air.* Kimber 1988.

MacMillan, Norman, Captain MC AFC: *The Royal Air Force in the World War Vol. IV 1940-1945.* Harrap 1950.

Mason, Francis K.: *Battle over Britain.* Aston Publications 1990.

McKee, Alexander: *The Coal Scuttle Brigade.* Hamlyn. 1981.

Nelson-Edwards, Wing Commander George, DFC: *Spit and Sawdust.* Newton 1995.

Norman, Bill: *Luftwaffe over the North.* Leo Cooper/Pen & Sword. 1993.

Parry, Simon W: *Intruders over Britain (the Luftwaffe night fighter offensive, 1940-45).* Air Research Pubs 1987.

Peskett, S.J.: *Strange Intelligence, from Dunkirk to Nuremberg.* Robert Hale. 1981.

Price, Alfred: *The Luftwaffe Data Book.* Greenhill Books 1997.

Ramsey, Winston G.ed: *The Bitz, then and now. vols 1-3.* Battle of Britain Prints International. 1987-1990.

Ramsey, Winston G. ed: *The Battle of Britain, then and now.* Battle of Britain Prints International. 1980.

Revell, Alex: *The Vivid Air.* Kimber 1978.

Ripley, Roy and Pears, Bryan: *North East Diary, 1939-1945.* Unpublished MSS *The Rise and Fall of the German Air Force.* Arms & Armour edition. 1983.

Schmidt, Rudi: *Achtung - Torpedos Los!: der stratigische und operative Einsätze des Kampfgeschwader 26.* Bernard & Graefe Verlag. 1991 Koblenz.

Townsend, Peter: *Duel of Eagles.* Weidenfeld & Nicholson. 1970.

Wakefield, Ken: *Pfadfinder: Luftwaffe Pathfinder Operations over Britain, 1940-1944.* Tempus 1999.

Walmesley, Leo: *Fisherman at War.* Collins 1941.

Wynn, Humphrey ed: *Fighter Pilot - a self- portrait by George Barclay.* Kimber. 1976.

Wynn, Kenneth G: *Men of the Battle of Britain.* Gliddon Books. 1989.

Ziegler, H. Frank: *The Story of 609 Squadron (under the White Rose).* Crecy ed. (updated by Chris Goss) 1993.